Part 107 Drone Certificate Study Guide

Paul Aitken
with
Rob Burdick
& Tim Ray

Disclaimer

While Drone U has put forth its best efforts in preparing and arranging this study guide, they make no representations or guarantees with respect to the accuracy or completeness of the contents of this study guide, and specifically disclaim any implied guarantees that the reader would pass any tests associated with the Part 107 Drone Certificate or any others.

Hold Harmless

This study guide for the Part 107 Certification was carefully researched, compiled and produced by Drone U utilizing the documents (and links) listed immediately below. With the 107 test outline released by the FAA as our guide, we poured through the over 2,500 pages of content in an effort to break it down for you into this summarized study guide. Therefore, we believe this guide contains the most important, relevant items you need to know as you study for your 107 test. It helps you understand more clearly what you must know, what you should know and even what you don't need to know.

However, by obtaining this guide, you agree to hold harmless Drone U and its subsidiaries from any items missing or unintentionally left out that may be ultimately included on the FAA Part 107 Drone Certificate Test from the below FAA provided resources.

FAA - H - 8083 -25B Pilot's Handbook of Aeronautical Knowledge:

AC 107 -2 Part 107

Part 107 Summary

FAA - H - 8083- 2 (Risk Management Handbook)

SIDA 1198

14 CFR 107

150/5200-32B

SAFO 09013

SAFO 10017

SAFO 10015

SAFO 15010

FAA AIM

AC 006

TABLE OF CONTENTS

I. Regulations (Section 1)

A. General

1. The applicability of 14 CFR part 107 to small unmanned aircraft operations

    a) Part 107 does not apply to Model aircraft, what is model aircraft?

        (1) Strictly for hobby or recreational use
        (2) Operating in accordance with a community based set of safety guidelines
        (3) Not more than 55 lbs
        (4) Gives way to manned aircraft
        (5) Provides prior notice when flying within 5 miles of an airport
        (6) Aircraft is flown within VLOS

    b) Part 107 does not apply to operations conducted outside of the US
    c) PART 107 does not apply to amateur rockets, moored balloons, unmanned free balloons, kites, public aircraft operations, air carrier operations
    d) No person may manipulate the flight controls of a SUAS unless

        (1) Person has a remote pilot certificate
        (2) That person is under the direct supervision of a remote pilot in command and the RPIC has the ability to immediately take direct control of the flight of the small UA

2. Definitions used in 14 CFR part 107

    a) Control Station: means an interface used by the remote pilot to control the flight path of the small unmanned aircraft
    b) Corrective lenses: means spectacles or contact lenses
    c) Small Unmanned aircraft: means an unmanned aircraft weight less than 55lbs on takeoff, including everything that is on board or otherwise attached to the aircraft
    d) Small Unmanned Aircraft System: means a small unmanned aircraft and its associated elements that are required for the safe and efficient operation of the small unmanned aircraft in the national airspace system
    e) Unmanned aircraft: means an aircraft operated without the possibility of direct human intervention from within or on the aircraft
    f) Visual Observer: means a person who is designated by the remote pilot in command to assist the remote pilot in command and the person manipulating the flight controls of the sUAS to see and avoid other air traffic or objects aloft or on the ground

g) Person Manipulating the controls: a person other than the remote pilot in command who is controlling the flight of an sUAS under the supervision of the remote PIC

h) Remote Pilot in Command (RPIC): a person who holds a remote pilot certificate with an sUAS rating and has the final authority and responsibility for the operation and safety of an sUAS operation conducted under part 107

(1) Remote PIC. A person acting as a remote PIC of an sUAS in the National Airspace System (NAS) under part 107 must obtain a remote pilot certificate with an sUAS rating issued by the FAA prior to sUAS operation. The remote PIC must have this certificate easily accessible during flight operations.

i) Unmanned Aircraft: an aircraft without a human pilot onboard. Instead, the UAS is controlled from an operator on the ground.

3. Ramifications of falsification, reproduction or alteration of a certificate rating or authorization or report

a) The FAA relies on information provided by owners and remote pilots of sUAS when it authorizes operations or when it has to make a compliance determination. Accordingly, the FAA may take appropriate action against an sUAS owner, operator, remote PIC, or anyone else who fraudulently or knowingly provides false records or reports, or otherwise reproduces or alters any records, reports, or other information for fraudulent purposes. Such action could include civil sanctions and the suspension or revocation of a certificate or waiver.

4. Accident reporting

a) The remote PIC of the sUAS is required to report an accident to the FAA within 10 days if it meets any of the following thresholds:

(1) At least serious injury to any person or loss of consciousness.
(2) A serious injury is defined as one that qualifies as Level 3 or higher on the Abbreviated Injury Scale or (AIS).
(3) The AIS is an anatomical scoring system that provides a means of ranking the severity of an injury and is widely used by emergency medical personnel. Within the AIS system, injuries are ranked on a scale of 1 to 6, with Level 1 being a minor injury, Level 2 is moderate, Level 3 is serious, Level 4 is severe, Level 5 is critical, and Level 6 is a nonsurvivable injury.

(4) It would be considered a "serious injury" if a person requires hospitalization, but the injury is fully reversible (including, but not limited to, head trauma, broken bone(s), or laceration(s) to the skin that requires suturing).

(5) Damage to any property other than the UA, if the cost is greater than $500 to repair or replace the property (whichever is lower)

> (a) *Note: For example, a small UA damages a property whose fair market value is $200, and it would cost $600 to repair the damage. Because the fair market value is below $500, this accident is not required to be reported. Similarly, if the aircraft causes $200 worth of damage to property whose fair market value is $600, that accident is also not required to be reported because the repair cost is below $500.*

b) Submitting the report: The accident report must be made within 10 calendar-days of the operation that created the injury or damage. The report may be submitted to the appropriate FAA Regional Operations Center (ROC) electronically or by telephone. Electronic reporting can be completed at www.faa.gov/uas/ Reports may also be made at the nearest FSDO office.

> (1) The report should include the following information:
>
>> (a) *RPIC name and contact info*
>> (b) *RPIC FAA airman certificate number*
>> (c) *UAS registration number*
>> (d) *Location of the accident*
>> (e) *Date of the accident*
>> (f) *Time of the accident*
>> (g) *Persons injured and extent of injury*
>> (h) *Property damaged and extent of damage*
>> (i) *Description of what happened*

c) FAA accident reporting and NTSB

> (1) National Transportation Safety Board (NTSB) Reporting. In addition to the report submitted to the ROC, and in accordance with the criteria established by the NTSB, certain sUAS accidents must also be reported to the NTSB. For more information, visit www.ntsb.gov. (NTSB 830).

5. Inspection, testing and demonstration of compliance

a) A remote pilot in command, owner, or person manipulating the flight controls of a small unmanned aircraft system must, upon request, make available to the Administrator:

> (1) Remote Pilot certificate

    (2) Any other document, record or report required to be kept under the regulations of this chapter

    (3) Must upon request, allow the administrator to make any test or inspection of the SUAS, the RPIC, the person manipulating the flight controls of a small unmanned aircraft system, and the VO to determine compliance with this part

B. Operating rules

1. Registration requirements for sUAS

a) A small UA must be registered, as provided for in 14 CFR part 47 or part 48 prior to operating under part 107. Part 48 is the regulation that establishes the streamlined online registration option for sUAS that will be operated only within the territorial limits of the United States. Alternatively, sUAS can elect to register under Part 47 in the same manner as manned aircraft.

2. The requirement for the sUAS to be in a condition for safe operation

a) An sUAS must be maintained in a condition for safe operation. Prior to flight, the remote PIC is responsible for conducting a check of the sUAS and verifying that it is actually in a condition for safe operation. Guidance regarding how to determine that an sUAS is in a condition for safe operation is found in Chapter 7, sUAS Maintenance and Inspection.

b) How to inspect: Before each flight, the remote PIC must inspect the sUAS to ensure that it is in a condition for safe operation, such as inspecting for equipment damage or malfunction(s). The preflight inspection should be conducted in accordance with the sUAS manufacturer's inspection procedures when available (usually found in the manufacturer's owner or maintenance manual) and/or an inspection procedure developed by the sUAS owner or operator.

c) Even if the sUAS manufacturer has a written preflight inspection procedure, it is recommended that the remote PIC ensure that the following inspection items are incorporated into the preflight inspection procedure required by part 107 to help the remote PIC determine that the sUAS is in a condition for safe operation. The preflight inspection should include a visual or functional check of the following items:

    (1) Visual condition inspection of the UAS components;

    (2) Airframe structure (including undercarriage), all flight control surfaces, and linkages;

    (3) Registration markings, for proper display and legibility;

    (4) Moveable control surface(s), including airframe attachment point(s);

    (5) Servo motor(s), including attachment point(s);

(6) Propulsion system, including powerplant(s), propeller(s), rotor(s), ducted fan(s), etc.;

(7) Verify all systems (e.g., aircraft and control unit) have an adequate energy supply for the intended operation and are functioning properly;

(8) Avionics, including control link transceiver, communication/navigation equipment, and antenna(s);

(9) Calibrate UAS compass prior to any flight;

(10) Control link transceiver, communication/navigation data link transceiver, and antenna(s);

(11) Display panel, if used, is functioning properly;

(12) Check ground support equipment, including takeoff and landing systems, for proper operation;

(13) Check that control link correct functionality is established between the aircraft and the CS;

(14) Check for correct movement of control surfaces using the CS;

(15) Check onboard navigation and communication data links;

(16) Check flight termination system, if installed;

(17) Check fuel for correct type and quantity;

(18) Check battery levels for the aircraft and CS;

(19) Check that any equipment, such as a camera, is securely attached;

(20) Verify communication with UAS and that the UAS has acquired GPS location from at least four satellites;

(21) Start the UAS propellers to inspect for any imbalance or irregular operation;

(22) Verify all controller operation for heading and altitude;

(23) If required by flight path walk through, verify any noted obstructions that may interfere with the UAS; and

(24) At a controlled low altitude, fly within range of any interference and recheck all controls and stability.

3. Medical conditions that would interfere with safe operation of sUAS

a) Being able to safely operate the sUAS relies on, among other things, the physical and mental capabilities of the remote PIC, person manipulating the controls, VO, and any other direct participant in the sUAS operation. Though the person manipulating the controls of an sUAS and VO are not required to obtain an airman medical certificate, they may not participate in the operation of an sUAS if they know or have reason to know that they have a physical or mental condition that could interfere with the safe operation of the sUAS.

b) Physical or Mental Incapacitations:

(1) The temporary or permanent loss of the dexterity necessary to operate the CS to safely control the small UA.

(2) The inability to maintain the required "see and avoid" vigilance due to blurred vision.

(3) The inability to maintain proper situational awareness of the small UA operations due to illness and/or medication(s), such as after taking medications with cautions not to drive or operate heavy machinery.

(4) A debilitating physical condition, such as a migraine headache or moderate or severe body ache(s) or pain(s) that would render the remote PIC, person manipulating the controls, or VO unable to perform sUAS operational duties. A hearing or speaking impairment that would inhibit the remote PIC, person manipulating the controls, and VO from effectively communicating with each other. In a situation such as this, the remote PIC must ensure that an alternative means of effective communication is implemented. For example, a person who is hearing impaired may be able to effectively use sign language to communicate.

4. The responsibility and authority of the remote PIC

a) Just like a manned-aircraft PIC, the remote PIC of an sUAS is directly responsible for, and is the final authority as to, the operation of that UAS. The remote PIC will have final authority over the flight. Additionally, a person manipulating the controls can participate in flight operations under certain conditions. It is important to note that a person may not operate or act as a remote PIC or VO in the operation of more than one UA at the same time.

5. Allowing a person other than the PIC to manipulate the flight controls

a) Part 107 permits transfer of control of an sUAS between certificated remote pilots. Two or more certificated remote pilots transferring operational control (i.e., the remote PIC designation) to each other may do so only if they are both capable of maintaining Visual Line of Sight (VLOS) of the UA and without loss of control (LOC). For example, one remote pilot may be designated the remote PIC at the beginning of the operation, and then at some point in the operation another remote pilot may take over as remote PIC by positively communicating that he or she is doing so. As the person responsible for the safe operation of the UAS, any remote pilot who will assume remote PIC duties should meet all of the requirements of part 107, including awareness of factors that could affect the flight.

b) Autonomous Operations:

(1) An autonomous operation is generally considered an operation in which the remote pilot inputs a flight plan into the CS, which sends it to the autopilot onboard the small UA. During automated flight, flight control inputs are made by components onboard the aircraft, not from a CS. Thus, the remote PIC could lose the control link to the small UA and the aircraft would still continue to fly the programmed mission/return home to land. During automated flight, the remote PIC also must have the ability to change routing/altitude or command the aircraft to land immediately. The ability to direct the small UA may be through manual manipulation of the flight controls or through commands using automation.

    (a) The remote PIC must retain the ability to direct the small UA to ensure compliance with the requirements of part 107

    (b) The use of automation does not allow a person to simultaneously operate more than one small UA

c) Use of a Visual Observer:

(1) The use of a VO is optional. The remote PIC may choose to use a VO to supplement situational awareness and VLOS. Although the remote PIC and person manipulating the controls must maintain the capability to see the UA, using one or more VOs allows the remote PIC and person manipulating the controls to conduct other mission-critical duties, while still ensuring situational awareness of the UA.

6. Regulatory deviation and report requirements for in flight emergencies

a) An in-flight emergency is an unexpected and unforeseen serious occurrence or situation that requires urgent, prompt action. In case of an in-flight emergency, the remote PIC is permitted to deviate from any rule of part 107 to the extent necessary to respond to that emergency. A remote PIC who exercises this emergency power to deviate from the rules of part 107 is required, upon FAA request, to send a written report to the FAA explaining the deviation. Emergency action should be taken in such a way as to minimize injury or damage to property.

7. Hazardous operations

a) No person may operate a small unmanned aircraft system in a careless or reckless manner as to endanger the life or property of another or allow an object to be dropped from a small unmanned aircraft in a manner that creates an undue hazard to persons or property.

b) TFR: Certain temporary flight restrictions (http://tfr.faa.gov/tfr2/list.html) may be imposed by way of a NOTAM (https://pilotweb.nas.faa.gov/PilotWeb/). Therefore, it is necessary for the sUAS remote PIC to check for NOTAMs before each flight to determine if there are any applicable airspace restrictions.

c) Over persons: Part 107 prohibits a person from flying a small UA directly over a person who is not under a safe cover, such as a protective structure or a stationary vehicle. However, a small UA may be flown over a person who is directly participating in the operation of the sUAS, such as the remote PIC, other person manipulating the controls, a VO, or crewmembers necessary for the safety of the sUAS operation, as assigned and briefed by the remote PIC.

8. Careless or reckless

a) Part 107 also prohibits careless or reckless operation of an sUAS. Flying an sUAS while driving a moving vehicle is considered to be careless or reckless because the person's attention would be hazardously divided. Therefore, the remote PIC or person manipulating the flight controls cannot operate an sUAS and drive a moving vehicle in a safe manner and remain in compliance with part 107.

9. Dropping an object

a) You may not allow an object to be dropped from a small unmanned aircraft in a manner that creates an undue hazard to persons or property.

b) Part 107 does not allow the carriage of hazardous materials because the carriage of hazardous materials poses a higher level of risk.

10. Operating from a moving aircraft or moving land or water borne vehicle

a) No person may operate a small unmanned aircraft system from a moving aircraft or from a moving land or water borne vehicle unless the small unmanned aircraft is flown over a sparsely populated area and is not transporting another person's property for compensation or hire.

11. Alcohol or drugs and the provisions on prohibition of use

a) Part 107 does not allow operation of an sUAS if the remote PIC, person manipulating the controls, or VO is unable to safely carry out his or her responsibilities.

b) 14 CFR 107 Prohibits a person from serving as a remote PIC, person manipulating the controls, VO or other crewmember if he or she:

(1) Consumed any alcoholic beverage within the preceding 8 hours
(2) Is under the influence of alcohol
(3) Has a blood alcohol concentration of .04 percent or greater
(4) Is using a drug that affects the person's mental or physical capabilities

12. Daylight operation

a) Part 107 prohibits operation of an sUAS at night, which is defined in part 1 as the time between the end of evening civil twilight and the beginning of morning civil twilight, as published in The Air Almanac, converted to local time.

b) Operations during civil twilight:

(1) When sUAS operations are conducted during civil twilight, the small UA must be equipped with anti-collision lights that are capable of being visible for at least 3 sm. However, the remote PIC may reduce the visible distance of the lighting less than 3 sm during a given flight if he or she has determined that it would be in the interest of safety to do so, for example if it impacts his or her night vision. sUAS not operated during civil twilight are not required to be equipped with anti-collision lighting.

13. Visual line of sight aircraft operations

a) The remote PIC and person manipulating the controls must be able to see the small UA at all times during flight. Therefore, the small UA must be operated closely enough to the CS to ensure visibility requirements are met during small UA operations. This requirement also applies to the VO, if used during the aircraft operation. However, the person maintaining VLOS may have brief moments in which he or she is not looking directly at or cannot see the small UA, but still retains the capability to see the UA or quickly maneuver it back to VLOS.

b) For operational necessity, the remote PIC or person manipulating the controls may intentionally maneuver the UA so that he or she loses sight of it for brief periods of time. Should the remote PIC or person manipulating the controls lose VLOS of the small UA, he or she must regain VLOS as soon as practicable.

c) VLOS must be accomplished and maintained by unaided vision, except vision that is corrected by the use of eyeglasses (spectacles) or contact lenses. Vision aids, such as binoculars, may be used only momentarily to enhance situational awareness.

14. The requirement when a visual observer is used

a) The use of a VO is optional. The remote PIC may choose to use a VO to supplement situational awareness and VLOS. Although the remote PIC and person manipulating the controls must maintain the capability to see the UA, using one or more VOs allows the remote PIC and person manipulating the controls to conduct other mission-critical duties (such as checking displays) while still ensuring situational awareness of the UA. The VO must be able to effectively communicate:

    (1) UA location, attitude, altitude and direction of flight.
    (2) Position of other aircraft or hazards in the airspace
    (3) The determination that the UA does not endanger the life or property of another.

15. The prohibition of carrying hazardous material

a) A small unmanned aircraft may not carry hazardous material. For purposes of this section, the term hazardous material is defined in 49 CFR 171.8

16. Staying safely away from other aircraft and right of way rules

a) Each small unmanned aircraft must yield the right of way to all aircraft, airborne vehicles, and launch and reentry vehicles. Yielding the right of way means that the small unmanned aircraft must give way to the aircraft or vehicle and may not pass over, under, or ahead of it unless well clear.

b) A remote PIC has a responsibility to operate the small UA so it remains clear of and yields to all other aircraft. This is traditionally referred to as "see and avoid." To satisfy this responsibility, the remote PIC must know the location and flight path of his or her small UA at all times. The remote PIC must be aware of other aircraft, persons, and property in the vicinity of the operating area, and maneuver the small UA to avoid a collision, as well as prevent other aircraft from having to take action to avoid the small UA.

c) No person may operate a small unmanned aircraft so close to another aircraft as to create a collision hazard.

17. See and avoid other aircraft and other potential hazard considerations of the remote PIC

a) This is traditionally referred to as "see and avoid." To satisfy this responsibility, the remote PIC must know the location and flight path of his or her small UA at all times.

18. Operations over human beings

a) No person may operate a sUAS over a human being unless that human being is:

> (1) Directly participating in the operation of the small unmanned aircraft or
> (2) Location under a covered structure or inside a stationary vehicle that can provide reasonable protection from a falling small unmanned aircraft.

19. Prior authorization required for operation in certain airspace

a) No person may operate a small unmanned aircraft in Class B, Class C, or Class D airspace or within the lateral boundaries of the surface area of Class E airspace designated for an airport unless that person has prior authorization from Air Traffic Control (ATC).

b) Though many sUAS operations will occur in uncontrolled airspace, there are some that may need to operate in controlled airspace. Operations in Class B, Class C, or Class D airspace, or within the lateral boundaries of the surface area of Class E airspace designated for an airport, are not allowed unless that person has prior authorization from air traffic control (ATC). The link to the current authorization process can be found at www.faa.gov/uas/. The sUAS remote PIC must understand airspace classifications and requirements. Failure to do so would be in violation of the part 107 regulations and may potentially have an adverse safety effect.

20. Operating in the vicinity of airports

a) No person may operate a small unmanned aircraft in prohibited or restricted areas unless that person has permission from the using or controlling agency, as appropriate.

21. Operating in prohibited or restricted areas

a) No person may operate a small unmanned aircraft in prohibited or restricted areas unless that person has permission from the using or controlling agency, as appropriate.

22. Flight restrictions in the proximity of certain areas designated by notice to airmen (NOTAM)

a) A person acting as a remote pilot in command must comply with the provisions of §§ 91.137 through 91.145 and 99.7 of this section.

23. Preflight familiarization inspection and actions for aircraft operations

a) Prior to flight, the remote pilot in command must:

(1) Assess the operating environment, considering risks to persons and property in the immediate vicinity both on the surface and in the air.

    (a) Local weather conditions
    (b) Local airspace and any flight restrictions
    (c) The location of persons and property on the surface
    (d) Other ground hazards

(2) Ensure that all persons directly participating in the small unmanned aircraft operation are informed about the operating conditions, emergency procedures, contingency procedures, roles and responsibilities, and potential hazards;

(3) Ensure that all control links between ground control station and the small unmanned aircraft are working properly.

(4) If the small unmanned aircraft is powered, ensure that there is enough available power for the small unmanned aircraft system to operate for the intended operational time.

(5) Ensure that any object attached or carried by the small unmanned aircraft is secure and does not adversely affect the flight characteristics or controllability of the aircraft.

24. Operating limitations of sUAS

a) A remote pilot in command and the person manipulating the flight controls of the small unmanned aircraft system must comply with all of the following operating limitations when operating a small unmanned aircraft system:

(1) Maximum ground speed - sUAS may not exceed 87 knots or 100 mph.

(2) Altitude limitations - the altitude of the small unmanned aircraft cannot be higher than 400 feet above ground level, unless the small unmanned aircraft:

    (a) Is flown within a 400 foot radius of a structure and
    (b) Does not fly higher than 400 feet above the structure's immediate uppermost limit

(3) Minimum visibility - the minimum flight visibility, as observed from the location of the control station must be no less than 3 statute miles. For purposes of this section, flight visibility means the average slant distance from the control station at which prominent unlighted objects may be seen and identified by day and prominent lighted objects may be seen and identified by night.

(4) Cloud clearance requirements - The minimum distance of the small unmanned aircraft from clouds must be no less than:

    (a) 500 feet below the cloud; and
    (b) 2,000 feet horizontally from the cloud

25. The requirements for a remote pilot certification with an sUAS rating

a) Be at least 16 years of age
b) Be able to read speak and write and understand the English language.
c) Not know or have reason to know that he has a physical or mental condition that would interfere with the safe operation of a small unmanned aircraft system
d) Demonstrate aeronautical knowledge by pass an initial aeronautical knowledge test

26. Remote pilot certification with an sUAS rating

a) Offenses involving alcohol or drugs

   (1) A conviction for the violation of any Federal or State statute relating to the growing, processing, manufacture, sale, disposition, possession, transportation, or importation of narcotic drugs, marijuana, or depressant or stimulant drugs or substances is grounds for:

   (a) *Denial of application for RPIC for a period of up to 1 year after the date of final conviction or*
   (b) *Suspension or revocation of a remote pilot certificate with a small UAS rating*

b) The consequences of refusing to submit to a drug or alcohol test or to furnish test results

   (1) A refusal to submit to a test to indicate the percentage by weight of alcohol in the blood, when requested by a law enforcement officer in accordance with § 91.17(c) of this chapter, or a refusal to furnish or authorize the release of the test results requested by the Administrator in accordance with § 91.17(c) or (d) of this chapter, is grounds for:

   (a) *Denial of an application for a RPIC*
   (b) *Suspension or revocation of a remote pilot certificate*

c) Aeronautical knowledge recency

   (1) A person may not operate a small unmanned aircraft system unless that person has completed one of the following, within the previous 24 calendar months:

   (a) *Passed an initial aeronautical knowledge test covering the areas of knowledge specified in 107.73a*
   (b) *Passed a recurrent aeronautical knowledge test covering the areas of knowledge specified in 107.73b*

(c) If a person holds a pilot certificate (other than a student pilot certificate) issued under part 61 of this chapter and meets the flight review requirements specified in §

(d) § 61.56, passed either an initial or recurrent training course covering the areas of knowledge specified in § 107.74(a) or (b) in a manner acceptable to the Administrator.

27. Waivers

a) The waiver policy and requirements

(1) Part 107 includes the option to apply for a Certificate of Waiver (CoW). This CoW will allow an sUAS operation to deviate from certain provisions of part 107 if the Administrator finds that the proposed operation can be safely conducted under the terms of that CoW. A list of the waivable sections of part 107 can be found in § 107.205 and are listed below:

(a) Section 107.25, Operation from a moving vehicle or aircraft. However, no waiver of this provision will be issued to allow the carriage of property of another by aircraft for compensation or hire

(b) Section 107.29, Daylight operation.

(c) Section 107.31, Visual line of sight aircraft operation. However, no waiver of this provision will be issued to allow the carriage of property of another by aircraft for compensation or hire.

(d) Section 107.33, Visual observer.

(e) Section 107.35, Operation of multiple small unmanned aircraft systems.

(f) Section 107.37(a), Yielding the right of way.

(g) Section 107.39, Operation over people.

(h) Section 107.41, Operation in certain airspace.

(i) Section 107.51, Operating limitations for small unmanned aircraft.

(2) How to apply for a COW, an applicant must go to www.faa.gov/uas and follow the instructions

(3) What needs to be in the COW?

(a) The application must contain a complete description of the proposed operation and a justification, including supporting data and documentation (as necessary), that establishes that the proposed operation can safely be conducted under the terms of a COW.

(b) If a COW is granted, that certificate may include specific special provisions designed to ensure that the sUAS operation may be conducted as safely as one conducted under the provisions of part 107.

QUIZ QUESTIONS - Regulations

1. A professional wildlife photographer operates an sUAS from a moving truck to capture aerial images of migrating birds in remote wetlands. The driver of the truck does not serve any crewmember role in the operation. Is this sUAS operation in compliance with 14 CFR Part 107?
    A. Compliant with Part 107
    B. Not compliant with Part 107
    C. Not compliant with state and local traffic laws

2. Remote Pilots are required to complete the following operational area surveillance prior to sUAS flight:
    A. Make a plan to keep non-participants in viewing distance for the whole operation
    B. Select an operational area that is populated
    C. Keep the operational area free of and at an appropriate distance from all non-participants

3. Personnel at an outdoor concert venue use an sUAS to drop promotional t-shirts and CDs over the audience. Is this sUAS operation in compliance with 14 CFR 107?
    A. No, unless authorized by the venue
    B. Yes, compliant with Part 107
    C. Not compliant with Part 107

4. Which of the following crewmembers must be used during Part 107 sUAS operations?
    A. Remote PIC
    B. Remote PIC, Visual Observer
    C. Remote PIC, Visual Observer, Person manipulating the controls

5. The remote PIC may operate how many sUAS at a time?
    A. 5
    B. 1
    C. No more than 2

6. "Unmanned aircraft" is defined as a device operated
    A. during search and rescue operations other than the public
    B. without the possibility of direct human intervention from within or on the aircraft
    C. for hobby and recreational use when not certified

7. Under what conditions may objects be dropped from the sUAS?
    A. if prior permission is received from the FAA
    B. in an emergency
    C. if precautions are taken to avoid injury or damage to persons or property on the surface

8. Unless otherwise authorized, what is the maximum airspeed at which a person may operate an sUAS below 400 feet?
    A. 80 mph
    B. 100 mph
    C. 200 knots

9. When an ATC clearance has been obtained, no remote PIC may deviate from that clearance, unless that pilot obtains an amended clearance. The one exception to this regulation is
   A. an emergency
   B. when the clearance states "at pilot's discretion"
   C. if the clearance contains a restriction

10. Under what conditions would a small unmanned aircraft not have to be registered before it is operated in the United States?
   A. When the aircraft has a takeoff weight that is more than .55 pounds but less than 55 pounds, not including fuel and necessary attachments
   B. When the aircraft weighs less than .55 pounds on take-off, including everything that is on-board or attached to the aircraft
   C. All small unmanned aircraft need to be registered regardless of the weight of the aircraft before, during, or after the flight

11. According to 14 CFR Part 107, what is required to operate a small unmanned aircraft within 30 minutes after official sunset?
   A. Use of a transponder
   B. Must be operated in a rural area
   C. Use of lighted anti-collision lights

12. Under what circumstances may lithium batteries be carried during sUAS operations?
   A. Lithium batteries may be carried only when installed as the primary power for the operation
   B. Lithium batteries are prohibited from sUAS operations
   C. Lithium batteries may be carried in a sealed storage container away from the sUAS fuel source

13. As a remote pilot with an sUAS rating, under which situation can you deviate from 14 CFR Part 107?
   A. When conducting public operations during a search mission
   B. In response to an in-flight emergency
   C. Flying for enjoyment with family and friends

14. When requesting a waiver, the required documents should be presented to the FAA at least how many days prior to the planned operation?
   A. 90 days
   B. 30 days
   C. 10 days

15. While operating a small unmanned aircraft system (sUAS), you experience a flyaway and several people suffer injuries. Which of the following injuries requires reporting to the FAA?
   A. Scrapes and cuts bandaged on site
   B. Minor bruises
   C. An injury requiring an overnight hospital stay

16. After receiving a Part 107 remote pilot certificate with an sUAS rating, how often must you satisfy recurrent training requirements?
   A. Every 6 months
   B. Every 12 months
   C. Every 24 months

17. A crew conducting surveillance anticipates losing visual line of sight with the sUAS within a small segment of the flight plan. The flight
   A. may be conducted using binoculars
   B. must be rerouted to maintain visual line of sight
   C. may be conducted if the visual line of sight can be maintained for 50% of the route

18. Which of the following individuals may process an application for a Part 107 remote pilot certificate with an sUAS rating?
   A. Commercial Balloon pilot
   B. Designated Pilot examiner
   C. Remote Pilot in command

19. Who holds the responsibility to ensure all crew members who are participating in the operation are not impaired by drugs or alcohol?
   A. The FAA
   B. Site supervisor
   C. Remote Pilot in Command

20. According to 14 CFR Part 48, when must a person register a small UA with the Federal Aviation Administration?
   A. When the small UA is used for any purpose other than as a model aircraft
   B. Only when the operator will be paid for commercial services
   C. All civilian small UAs weighing greater than 0.55 pounds must be registered regardless of its intended use

21. Which preflight action is specifically required of the pilot prior to each flight?
   A. Check the aircraft logbooks for appropriate entries
   B. Visually inspect the pilot certificates of all crew members
   C. Assess the operating environment including local weather conditions, local airspace and any flight restrictions, the location of persons and property on the surface, and other ground hazards

22. Which is true regarding the presence of alcohol within the human body?
   A. A small amount of alcohol increases vision acuity
   B. Judgement and decision making abilities can be adversely affected by even small amounts of alcohol
   C. An increase in altitude decreases the adverse effect of alcohol

23. What actions should the pilots take if collision is anticipated.
   A. The remote pilot should adjust the sUAS course
   B. The manned aircraft pilot should give way to the right
   C. Both pilots should give way to the right

24. Which of the following types of operations are excluded from the requirements in 14 CFR Part 107?
   A. Model aircraft for hobby use
   B. Quadcopter capturing aerial imagery for crop monitoring
   C. UAS used for motion picture filming

25. According to 14 CFR Part 48, when would a small unmanned aircraft owner not be permitted to register it?
   A. All persons must register their small unmanned aircraft
   B. The owner is less than 13 years of age
   C. If the owner does not have a valid US driver's license

26. Each person who holds a pilot certificate, a US driver's license, or a medical certificate shall present it for inspection upon the request for the Administrator, the National Transportation Safety board, or any
   A. authorized representative of the Department of State
   B. federal, state, or local law enforcement officer
   C. authorized Administrator of the Department of Transportation

27. A person without a Part 107 remote pilot certificate may operate an sUAS for commercial operations
   A. under the direct supervision of a remote PIC
   B. only when visual observers participate in the operation
   C. alone, if operating during daylight hours

28. You plan to operate a 33 lb SUAS to capture aerial imagery over real estate for use in sales listings. What FAA regulation is this sUAS operation subject to?
   A. 14 CFR Part 101
   B. 14 CFR Part 107
   C. This operation is not subject to FAA regulations

29. According to 14 CFR Part 107, the responsibility to inspect the small unmanned aircraft system (sUAS) to ensure it is in safe operating condition rests with the
   A. Remote Pilot in Command
   B. Owner of the sUAS
   C. Visual Observer

30. In accordance with 14 CFR Part 107, at what maximum altitude can you operate an sUAS when inspecting a tower with a top at 1,000 AGL at close proximity (within 100 feet)?
   A. 1,400 feet MSL
   B. 1,400 feet AGL
   C. 400 feet AGL

31. You wish to start a local delivery business using an sUAS to drop small packages at the front door of customer. The customer's residence is not always within visual line-of-sight (VLOS) of the Remote PIC located at the delivery facility. under which circumstances would this be authorized?
   A. With a waiver from the FAA
   B. By utilizing a vehicle to follow the sUAS while en-route to maintain VLOS
   C. There is currently no way to do this in compliance with AC 107-2

32. What action, if any, is appropriate if the remote pilot deviates from Part 107 during an emergency?
   A. Take no special action since you are pilot-in-command
   B. File a report to the FAA Administrator, as soon as possible
   C. File a detained report to the FAA Administrator, upon request

33. You are part of a news crew, operating an sUAS to cover a breaking story. You experience a flyaway during landing. The unmanned aircraft strikes a vehicle, causing approximately $800 worth of damage. when must you report the accident to the FAA?
   A. Within 10 days
   B. Anytime
   C. Not to exceed 30 days

34. Under Title 14 of the Code of Federal Regulations what is the maximum penalty for falsification, alteration, or fraudulent reproduction of certificates, logbooks, reports, and records?
   A. Ineligibility to receive a certificate or rating for one year
   B. Suspension or revocation of any certificate held
   C. imprisonment for 1 year and a $5,000.00 fine

35. When must a current remote pilot certificate be in the pilot's personal possession or readily accessible in the aircraft?
   A. Anytime when acting as pilot-in-command or as a required crewmember
   B. When acting as a crew chief during launch and recovery
   C. Only when a payload is carried

36. If sunset is 2021 and the end of evening civil twilight is 2043, when must a remote pilot terminate the flight?
   A. 2021
   B. 2043
   C. 2121

37. To avoid a possible collision with a manned airplane, you estimate that your small unmanned aircraft climbed to an altitude greater than 600 feet AGL. To whom must you report the deviation?
   A. Upon request of the Federal Aviation Administration
   B. The National Transportation Safety Board
   C. Air Traffic Control

38. To satisfy medical requirements, all sUAS crewmembers must
   A. hold a valid third-class medical certificate
   B. complete a physical with an Aviation Medical examiner
   C. be free of any physical or mental condition that would interfere with the safe operation of the small unmanned aircraft system

39. A law enforcement officer witnesses careless or reckless behavior while observing sUAS operations and requests the operator submit to a drug or alcohol test. What are the consequences if this request is denied?
   A. the operator may have their remote pilot certificate with sUAS rating suspended or revoked
   B. The operator may be denied an application for a remote pilot certificate for up to 30 days
   C. the operator may have to pay a fine but their remote pilot certificate will not be affected

40. No person may attempt to act as a crewmember of a sUAS with
   A. 0.004 percent by weight or more alcohol in the blood
   B. .04 percent by weight or more alcohol in the blood
   C. .4 percent by weight or more alcohol in the blood

41. Which crewmember must hold a remote pilot certificate with an sUAS rating?
   A. Person manipulating the controls
   B. Visual Observer
   C. Remote pilot-in-command

42. What speed limit applies to sUAS operations?
   A. 200 knots
   B. 80 mph
   C. 100 mph

43. Whose sole task during an sUAS operation is to watch the sUAS and report potential hazards to the rest of the crew?
   A. Visual Observer
   B. Remote pilot-in-command
   C. Person manipulating the controls

44. According to 14 CFR Part 107, an sUAS is an unmanned aircraft system weighing
   A. Less than 55 lbs
   B. 55 kg or less
   C. 55 lbs or less

45. Which of the following operations is compliant with 14 CFR Part 107?
   A. Remote PIC is driving a moving vehicle while operating an sUAS in a sparsely populated area
   B. Remote PIC is a passenger on an aircraft in flight while operating an sUAS
   C. Remote PIC is a passenger on a moving boat while operating an sUAS in an unpopulated area

46. In accordance with 14 CFR Part 107, you may operate an sUAS from a moving vehicle when no property is carried for compensation or hire
   A. Over a sparsely populated area
   B. Over suburban areas
   C. Over a parade or other social event

47. The FAA may approve your application for a waiver of provisions in Part 107 only when it has been determined that the proposed operation
   A. Involves public aircraft or air carrier operations
   B. Can be safely conducted under the terms of that certificate of waiver
   C. Will be conducted outside of the United States

48. Within how many days must an sUAS accident be reported to the FAA?
   A. 10 days
   B. 90 days
   C. 30 days

49. Which of the following operations would be regulated by 14 CFR Part 107?
   A. Conducting public operations during a search mission
   B. Flying for enjoyment with family and friends
   C. Operating your sUAS for an imagery company

50. Which action is specifically required of the remote pilot prior to each flight?
   - A. Make a plan to keep non-participants clear, indoors, or under cover
   - B. Check the aircraft logbooks to ensure maintenance is current
   - C. Identify a non-participant who will be near the sUAS operation to help with and see and avoid procedures

51. Which of the following would medically disqualify a Remote pilot?
   - A. Taking a prescription medication that does not have any noticeable side effect
   - B. A migraine headache with the side effect of blurred vision
   - C. Occasional muscle soreness following exercise

52. What may be used to assist compliance with sUAS see-and-avoid requirements?
   - A. Binoculars
   - B. remote pilot diligence
   - C. First-person view camera

53. As you are flying your sUAS, valued at $1000, over a home to photograph it for real estate sales purposes, the sUAS has a failure causing it to fall onto an awning, causing some minor damage. The fair market value of the awning is $800 but it can be repaired for $400. What type of report is required?
   - A. No report is required
   - B. An sUAS accident report to the FAA, within 10 days of operation
   - C. An sUAS incident report to the FAA, within 10 days of the operation

54. Who is responsible for ensuring that there are enough crewmembers for a given sUAS operation?
   - A. Person manipulating the controls
   - B. Visual Observer
   - C. Remote Pilot in Command

55. If a certified pilot changes permanent mailing address and fails to notify the FAA airmen Certification Branch of the new address, the pilot is entitled to exercise the privileges of the pilot certificate for a period of only
   - A. 60 days after the move
   - B. 30 days after the date of the move
   - C. 90 days after the move

56. A person may not act as a crewmember of the sUAS if alcoholic beverages have been consumed by that person within the preceding
   - A. 8 hours
   - B. 12 hours
   - C. 24 hours

57. In accordance with 14 CFR Part 107, except when within a 400-foot radius of a structure, at what maximum altitude can you operate sUAS?
   - A. 600 feet AGL
   - B. 400 feet AGL
   - C. 500 feet AGL

58. Which crewmember is required to be under the direct supervision of the remote PIC when operating an sUAS?
- A. Remote pilot-in-command
- B. Person manipulating the controls
- C. Visual Observer

59. Which aircraft has right-of-way over other traffic
- A. An sUAS
- B. A quadcopter
- C. An airplane

60. The basic weather minimums for operating an sUAS up to the 400 AGL limit are
- A. 900 foot ceiling and 3 mile visibility
- B. 2000 foot ceiling and 1 mile visibility
- C. clear of clouds and 2 mile visibility

61. You are operating a 1280 g (2.8 lb) quadcopter for your own enjoyment. What FAA regulation is this sUAS operation subject to?
- A. 14 CFR Part 107
- B. This operation is not subject to FAA regulations
- C. 14 CFR Part 101

62. Who is ultimately responsible for preventing a hazardous situation before an accident occurs?
- A. Person manipulating the controls
- B. Visual Observer
- C. Remote Pilot in Command

63. Except when necessary for takeoff or landing, what is the minimum safe altitude required for a remote pilot to operate an sUAS over people?
- A. An altitude allowing, if a power unit fails, an emergency landing without undue hazard to person or property on the surface
- B. You may not operate an sUAS over people who are not part of the sUAS operation
- C. An altitude of 200 feet above the highest obstacle within a horizontal radius of 1000 feet

64. You have accepted football tickets in exchange for using your sUAS to videotape a future construction zone. What FAA regulation is this sUAS operation subject to?
- A. 14 CFR Part 107
- B. 14 CFR Part 101
- C. This operation is not subject to FAA regulations

65. When using a small unmanned aircraft in a commercial operation, who is responsible for informing the participants about emergency procedure?
- A. the lead visual observer
- B. Remote Pilot in Command
- C. the FAA inspection-in-charge

66. An autonomous operation requires the following crewmembers.
    A. Remote PIC, Visual observer
    B. Remote PIC
    C. Remote Pilot, visual observer, person manipulating the controls

67. Power company employees use an sUAS to inspect a long stretch of high voltage powerlines. due to muddy condition, their vehicle must stay beside the road and the crew must use binoculars to maintain visual line of sight with the aircraft. is this sUAS operation in compliance with 14 CFR Part 107?
    A. No, the operation is not in compliance with Part 107
    B. Yes, the operation is in compliance with Part 107
    C. There is not enough information to make a determination

68. If you are caught smoking marijuana the FAA will
    A. Send you to a drug treatment center
    B. Issue an immediate suspension or revocation of your pilot certificate
    C. Deny all future pilot applications

69. Sunrise is 0645. When can you launch your sUAS operation?
    A. 06:45
    B. 06:15
    C. 07:15

70. Which of these operations must comply with 14 CFR Part 107?
    A. Civil operations
    B. Civil and public operations
    C. Public and military operations

71. If requested, to whom must I present my Remote Pilot Certificate?
    A. A person of authority
    B. FAA Inspector
    C. Authorized representative of the Department of State

72. What FAA resource can pilots reference to learn more about the impact of drugs and alcohol on flight?
    A. The Pilot's Handbook of Aeronautical Knowledge
    B. The Pilot Operating Handbook
    C. NOTAMs

73. When can someone with a marijuana conviction apply for a Remote Pilot certificate?
    A. Never
    B. 18 months
    C. 1 year

II. Airspace (Section 2)

A. Airspace classification

1. General airspace

    a) The two categories of airspace are: regulatory and non-regulatory. Within these two categories, there are four types:

        (1) Controlled
        (2) Uncontrolled
        (3) Special use
        (4) Other airspace

    b) Controlled and uncontrolled airspace boundaries and altitude are showcased on the Section Chart. A section chart is used to figure out which airspace they occupy. Which is printed every six months and is the backbone of flying. It is printed by the National Oceanic and Atmospheric Administration and is extremely accurate. The scale is 1:500,000: that is, 1 inch on the chart equals 500,000 inches on the ground. That is also 1 inch = 7 nautical miles. In the section we can find:

        (1) Aeronautical symbols used on the chart
        (2) A map of the United States showing each section chart's coverage
        (3) Topographical symbols
        (4) Radio aids to navigation and airspace information
        (5) List of frequencies used by control towers in the area of the chart
        (6) A list of prohibited, restricted, warning and alert areas on the chart

    c) Class A - "Altitude," it starts at 18,000 MSL, you'll never fly in it.

    d) Class B - This airspace is generally airspace from the surface to 10,000 feet MSL. (Towered Airport, Controlled)

        (1) Keyword: Boeing
        (2) Sectional color: Blue

    e) Class C - This airspace is generally airspace from the surface to 4,000 feet above the airport elevation (charted in MSL) surrounding those airports that have an operational control tower, are serviced by a radar approach control, and have a certain number of IFR operations or passenger enplanements. (Towered Airport, Controlled)

        (1) Keyword: Corporate
        (2) Sectional Color: Red

f) Class D - This airspace is generally airspace from the surface to 2,500 feet above the airport elevation (charted in MSL) surrounding those airports that have an operational control tower. The configuration of each Class D airspace area is individually tailored and, when instrument procedures are published, the airspace is normally designed to contain the procedures. (Smaller Airports, Towered airport, Controlled)

  (1) Keyword: Dog House
  (2) When the tower closes at D airports, the airspace converts to E airspace.

g) Class E controlled, "Everybody," starts at two different altitudes, 700 ft and 1200 feet AGL. (Difference between E and G is that with E you can talk to ATC) Will you fly in E? Not unless you have ATC clearance.

  (1) Class E airspace is the controlled airspace not classified as Class A, B, C, or D airspace. A large amount of the airspace over the United States is designated as Class E airspace.

h) Class G uncontrolled airspace, "Ground".

i) Special use airspace such as prohibited, restricted, warning areas, military operation areas, alert areas, and controlled firing areas.

  (1) No person may operate a small unmanned aircraft in prohibited or restricted areas unless that person has permission from the using or controlling agency, as appropriate.
  (2) Special use airspace or special area of operation (SAO) is the designation for airspace in which certain activities must be confined, or where limitations may be imposed on aircraft operations that are not part of those activities. Certain special use airspace areas can create limitations on the mixed use of airspace. The special use airspace depicted on instrument charts includes the area name or number, effective altitude, time and weather conditions of operation, the controlling agency, and the chart panel location. On National Aeronautical Charting Group (NACG) en route charts, this information is available on one of the end panels.
  (3) Though many sUAS operations will occur in uncontrolled airspace, there are some that may need to operate in controlled airspace. Operations in Class B, Class C, or Class D airspace, or within the lateral boundaries of the surface area of Class E airspace designated for an airport, are not allowed unless that person has prior authorization from air traffic control (ATC). The link to the current authorization process can be found at www.faa.gov/uas/. The sUAS remote PIC must understand airspace classifications and requirements.

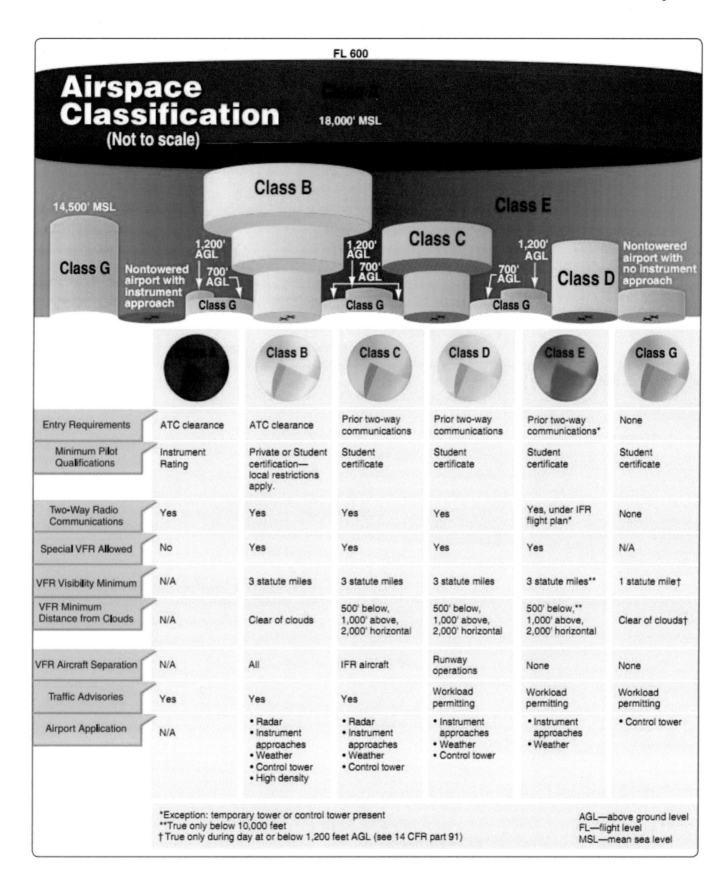

Airspace Classification
(Not to scale)

FL 600

18,000' MSL

14,500' MSL

Class G — Nontowered airport with instrument approach — Class G — 1,200' AGL — 700' AGL — Class B — Class G — 1,200' AGL — 700' AGL — Class C — Class G — 700' AGL — 1,200' AGL — Class D — Class E — Nontowered airport with no instrument approach

		Class B	Class C	Class D	Class E	Class G
Entry Requirements	ATC clearance	ATC clearance	Prior two-way communications	Prior two-way communications	Prior two-way communications*	None
Minimum Pilot Qualifications	Instrument Rating	Private or Student certification— local restrictions apply.	Student certificate	Student certificate	Student certificate	Student certificate
Two-Way Radio Communications	Yes	Yes	Yes	Yes	Yes, under IFR flight plan*	None
Special VFR Allowed	No	Yes	Yes	Yes	Yes	N/A
VFR Visibility Minimum	N/A	3 statute miles	3 statute miles	3 statute miles	3 statute miles**	1 statute mile†
VFR Minimum Distance from Clouds	N/A	Clear of clouds	500' below, 1,000' above, 2,000' horizontal	500' below, 1,000' above, 2,000' horizontal	500' below,** 1,000' above, 2,000' horizontal	Clear of clouds†
VFR Aircraft Separation	N/A	All	IFR aircraft	Runway operations	None	None
Traffic Advisories	Yes	Yes	Yes	Workload permitting	Workload permitting	Workload permitting
Airport Application	N/A	• Radar • Instrument approaches • Weather • Control tower • High density	• Radar • Instrument approaches • Weather • Control tower	• Instrument approaches • Weather • Control tower	• Instrument approaches • Weather	• Control tower

*Exception: temporary tower or control tower present
**True only below 10,000 feet
† True only during day at or below 1,200 feet AGL (see 14 CFR part 91)

AGL—above ground level
FL—flight level
MSL—mean sea level

2. Other airspace areas

    a) No person may operate a small unmanned aircraft in a manner that interferes with operations and traffic patterns at any airport, heliport, or seaplane base.

3. Air traffic control and the NAS

    a) The ATO does not have the authority to deny sUAS operations on the basis of equipage that exceeds the part 107 requirements. Because additional equipage and technologies, such as geo-fencing, have not been certificated by the FAA, they need to be examined on a case-by-case basis in order for the FAA to determine their reliability and functionality. Additionally, requiring equipage would place a burden on ATC and detract from other duties. Instead, a remote pilot who wishes to operate in controlled airspace because he or she can demonstrate mitigations through equipage may do so by applying for a waiver (see paragraph 5.19).

    b) For recurring or long-term operations in a given volume of controlled airspace, prior authorization could perhaps include a letter of agreement (LOA) to identify shortfalls and establish operating procedures for sUAS. This LOA will outline the ability to integrate into the existing air traffic operation and may improve the likelihood of access to the airspace where operations are proposed. This agreement will ensure all parties involved are aware of limitations and conditions and will enable the safe flow of aircraft operations in that airspace. For short-term or short-notice operations proposed in controlled airport airspace, a LOA may not be feasible. Prior authorization is required in all cases.

    c) Though many sUAS operations will occur in uncontrolled airspace, there are some that may need to operate in controlled airspace. Operations in Class B, Class C, or Class D airspace, or within the lateral boundaries of the surface area of Class E airspace designated for an airport, are not allowed unless that person has prior authorization from air traffic control (ATC). The link to the current authorization process can be found at www.faa.gov/uas/. The sUAS remote PIC must understand airspace classifications and requirements.

B. Airspace operational requirements

1. Basic weather minimums

    a) sUAS Minimum weather visibility of 3 miles from the control station, but the FAA has other weather minimums for different airspace designations.

Basic VFR Weather Minimums			Flight Visibility	Distance from Clouds
Airspace			**Flight Visibility**	**Distance from Clouds**
Class			Not applicable	Not applicable
Class **B**			3 statute miles	Clear of clouds
Class **C**			3 statute miles	1,000 feet above 500 feet below 2,000 feet horizontal
Class **D**			3 statute miles	1,000 feet above 500 feet below 2,000 feet horizontal
Class **E**	At or above 10,000 feet MSL		5 statute miles	1,000 feet above 1,000 feet below 1 statute mile horizontal
	Less than 10,000 feet MSL		3 statute miles	1,000 feet above 500 feet below 2,000 feet horizontal
Class **G**	1,200 feet or less above the surface (regardless of MSL altitude).	Day, except as provided in section 91.155(b)	1 statute mile	Clear of clouds
		Night, except as provided in section 91.155(b)	3 statute miles	1,000 feet above 500 feet below 2,000 feet horizontal
	More than 1,200 feet above the surface but less than 10,000 feet MSL.	Day	1 statute mile	1,000 feet above 500 feet below 2,000 feet horizontal
		Night	3 statute miles	1,000 feet above 500 feet below 2,000 feet horizontal
	More than 1,200 feet above the surface and at or above 10,000 feet MSL.		5 statute miles	1,000 feet above 1,000 feet below 1 statute mile horizontal

2. ATC authorizations and related operating limitations

   a) The ATO does not have the authority to deny sUAS operations on the basis of equipage that exceeds the part 107 requirements. Because additional equipage and technologies, such as geo-fencing, have not been certified by the FAA, they need to be examined on a case-by-case basis in order for the FAA to determine their reliability and functionality. Additionally, requiring equipage would place a burden on ATC and detract from other duties. Instead, a remote pilot who wishes to operate in controlled airspace because he or she can demonstrate mitigations through equipage may do so by applying for a waiver (see paragraph 5.19).

   b) For recurring or long-term operations in a given volume of controlled airspace, prior authorization could perhaps include a letter of agreement (LOA) to identify shortfalls and establish operating procedures for sUAS. This LOA will outline the ability to integrate into the existing air traffic operation and may improve the likelihood of access to the airspace where operations are proposed. This agreement will ensure all parties involved are aware of limitations and conditions and will enable the safe flow of aircraft operations in that airspace. For short-term or short-notice operations proposed in controlled airport airspace, a LOA may not be feasible. Prior authorization is required in all cases.

3. Operations near airports

   a) Small UA Operations Near an Airport—Notification and Permissions.

      (1) Unless the flight is conducted within controlled airspace, no notification or authorization is necessary to operate at or near an airport.
      (2) When operating in the vicinity of an airport, the remote PIC must be aware of all traffic patterns and approach corridors to runways and landing areas.
      (3) The remote PIC must avoid operating anywhere that the presence of the sUAS may interfere with operations at the airport, such as approach corridors, taxiways, runways, or helipads. Furthermore, the remote PIC must yield right-of-way to all other aircraft, including aircraft operating on the surface of the airport.

   b) Remote PICs are prohibited from operating their small UA in a manner that interferes with operations and traffic patterns at airports, heliports, and seaplane bases. While a small UA must always yield right-of-way to a manned aircraft, a manned aircraft may alter its flight path, delay its landing, or take off in order to avoid an sUAS that may present a potential conflict or otherwise affect the safe outcome of the flight.

(1) For example, a UA hovering 200 feet above a runway may cause a manned aircraft holding short of the runway to delay takeoff, or a manned aircraft on the downwind leg of the pattern to delay landing. While the UA in this scenario would not pose an immediate traffic conflict to the aircraft on the downwind leg of the traffic pattern or to the aircraft intending to take off, nor would it violate the right-of-way provision of § 107.37(a), the small UA would have interfered with the operations of the traffic pattern at an airport.

c) In order to avoid interfering with operations in a traffic pattern, remote PICs should avoid operating in the traffic pattern or published approach corridors used by manned aircraft. When operational necessity requires the remote PIC to operate at an airport in uncontrolled airspace, the remote PIC should operate the small UA in such a way that the manned aircraft pilot does not need to alter his or her flightpath in the traffic pattern or on a published instrument approach in order to avoid a potential collision. Because remote PICs have an obligation to yield right-of-way to all other aircraft and avoid interfering in traffic pattern operations, the FAA expects that most remote PICs will avoid operating in the vicinity of airports because their aircraft generally do not require airport infrastructure, and the concentration of other aircraft increases in the vicinity of airports.

4. Potential flight hazards

a) Other Risk Assessment Tools for Flight and Operational Risk Management

(1) Other tools can also be used for flight or operational risk assessments and can be developed by the remote PICs themselves. The key thing is to ensure that all potential hazards and risks are identified and appropriate actions are taken to reduce the risk to persons and property not associated with the operations.

b) Reducing Risk

(1) Risk analyses should concentrate not only on assigning levels of severity and likelihood, but on determining why these particular levels were selected. This is referred to as root cause analysis, and is the first step in developing effective controls to reduce risk to lower levels. In many cases, simple brainstorming sessions among crewmembers is the most effective and affordable method of finding ways to reduce risk. This also has the advantage of involving people who will ultimately be required to implement the controls developed.

c) It is also very easy to get quite bogged down in trying to identify all hazards and risks. That is not the purpose of a risk assessment. The focus should be upon those hazards which pose the greatest risks. As stated earlier, by documenting and compiling these processes, a remote PIC can build an arsenal of safety practices that will add to the safety and success of future operations.

d) 107.49 states: Ensure that all persons directly participating in the small unmanned aircraft operation are informed about the operating conditions, emergency procedures, contingency procedures, roles and responsibilities, and potential hazards;

5. Common aircraft accident causal factors

a) The 10 most frequent cause factors for general aviation accidents that involve the pilot-in-command are:

    (1) Inadequate preflight preparation and/or planning
    (2) Failure to obtain and/or maintain flying speed
    (3) Failure to maintain direction control
    (4) Improper level off
    (5) Failure to see and avoid objects or obstructions
    (6) Mismanagement of fuel
    (7) Improper inflight decisions or planning
    (8) Misjudgment of distance and speed
    (9) Selection of unsuitable terrain
    (10) Improper operation of flight controls

b) Alertness. Be alert at all times, especially when the weather is good. Most pilots pay attention to business when they are operating in full IFR weather conditions, but strangely, air collisions almost invariably have occurred under ideal weather conditions. Unlimited visibility appears to encourage a sense of security which is not at all justified. Considerable information of value may be obtained by listening to advisories being issued in the terminal area, even though controller workload may prevent a pilot from obtaining individual service.

c) Giving Way. If you think another aircraft is too close to you, give way instead of waiting for the other pilot to respect the right-of-way to which you may be entitled. It is a lot safer to pursue the right-of-way angle after you have completed your flight.

6. Avoid flight beneath unmanned balloons

a) The majority of unmanned free balloons currently being operated have, extending below them, either a suspension device to which the payload or instrument package is attached, or a trailing wire antenna, or both. In many instances these balloon subsystems may be invisible to the pilot until the aircraft is close to the balloon, thereby creating a potentially dangerous situation. Therefore, good judgment on the part of the pilot dictates that aircraft should remain well clear of all unmanned free balloons and flight below them should be avoided at all times.

b) Pilots are urged to report any unmanned free balloons sighted to the nearest FAA ground facility with which communication is established. Such information will assist FAA ATC facilities to identify and flight follow unmanned free balloons operating in the airspace.

7. Emergency airborne inspection of other aircraft

a) Providing airborne assistance to another aircraft may involve flying in very close proximity to that aircraft. Most pilots receive little, if any, formal training or instruction in this type of flying activity. Close proximity flying without sufficient time to plan (i.e., in an emergency situation), coupled with the stress involved in a perceived emergency can be hazardous.

b) The pilot in the best position to assess the situation should take the responsibility of coordinating the airborne intercept and inspection, and take into account the unique flight characteristics and differences of the category(s) of aircraft involved.

c) Some of the safety considerations are:

    (1) Area, direction and speed of the intercept;
    (2) Aerodynamic effects (i.e., rotorcraft downwash);
    (3) Minimum safe separation distances;
    (4) Communications requirements, lost communications procedures, coordination with ATC;
    (5) Suitability of diverting the distressed aircraft to the nearest safe airport; and
    (6) Emergency actions to terminate the intercept.

d) Close proximity, inflight inspection of another aircraft is uniquely hazardous. The pilot-in-command of the aircraft experiencing the problem/emergency must not relinquish control of the situation and/or jeopardize the safety of their aircraft. The maneuver must be accomplished with minimum risk to both aircraft.

8. Precipitation static

a) Precipitation static is caused by aircraft in flight coming in contact with uncharged particles. These particles can be rain, snow, fog, sleet, hail, volcanic ash, dust; any solid or liquid particles. When the aircraft strikes these neutral particles the positive element of the particle is reflected away from the aircraft and the negative particle adheres to the skin of the aircraft. In a very short period of time a substantial negative charge will develop on the skin of the aircraft. If the aircraft is not equipped with static dischargers, or has an ineffective static discharger system, when a sufficient negative voltage level is reached, the aircraft may go into "CORONA." That is, it will discharge the static electricity from the extremities of the aircraft, such as the wing tips, horizontal stabilizer, vertical stabilizer, antenna, propeller tips, etc. This discharge of static electricity is what you will hear in your headphones and is what we call P-static.

b) A review of pilot reports often shows different symptoms with each problem that is encountered. The following list of problems is a summary of many pilot reports from many different aircraft. Each problem was caused by P-static:

    (1)   Complete loss of VHF communications
    (2)   Erroneous magnetic compass readings (30 percent in error)
    (3)   High pitched squeal on audio
    (4)   Motor boat sound on audio
    (5)   Loss of all avionics in clouds
    (6)   VLF navigation system inoperative most of the time
    (7)   Erratic instrument readouts
    (8)   Weak transmissions and poor receptivity of radios
    (9)   "St. Elmo's Fire" on windshield

9. Light amplification by stimulated emission of radiation (laser) operations and reporting illumination of aircraft

a) Lasers have many applications. Of concern to users of the National Airspace System are those laser events that may affect pilots, e.g., outdoor laser light shows or demonstrations for entertainment and advertisements at special events and theme parks. Generally, the beams from these events appear as bright blue-green in color; however, they may be red, yellow, or white. However, some laser systems produce light which is invisible to the human eye.

b) FAA regulations prohibit the disruption of aviation activity by any person on the ground or in the air. The FAA and the Food and Drug Administration (the Federal agency that has the responsibility to enforce compliance with Federal requirements for laser systems and laser light show products) are working together to ensure that operators of these devices do not pose a hazard to aircraft operators.

c) Pilots should be aware that illumination from these laser operations are able to create temporary vision impairment miles from the actual location. In addition, these operations can produce permanent eye damage. Pilots should make themselves aware of where these activities are being conducted and avoid these areas if possible.

d) Recent and increasing incidents of unauthorized illumination of aircraft by lasers, as well as the proliferation and increasing sophistication of laser devices available to the general public, dictates that the FAA, in coordination with other government agencies, take action to safeguard flights from these unauthorized illuminations.

e) Pilots should report laser illumination activity to the controlling Air Traffic Control facilities, Federal Contract Towers or Flight Service Stations as soon as possible after the event. The following information should be included:

(1) UTC Date and Time of Event
(2) Call Sign or Aircraft Registration Number
(3) Type Aircraft
(4) Nearest Major City
(5) Altitude
(6) Location of Event (Latitude/Longitude and/or Fixed Radial Distance (FRD))
(7) Brief Description of the Event and any other Pertinent Information
(8) Pilots are also encouraged to complete the Laser Beam Exposure Questionnaire (See Appendix 3), and fax or email it, per the directions on the questionnaire, as soon as possible after landing
(9) When a laser event is reported to an air traffic facility, a general caution warning will be broadcasted on all appropriate frequencies every five minutes for 20 minutes and broadcasted on the ATIS for one hour following the report

10. Avoiding flight in the vicinity of thermal plumes, such as smoke stacks and cooling towers

a) Flight Hazards Exist Around Thermal Plumes. Thermal plumes are defined as visible or invisible emissions from power plants, industrial production facilities, or other industrial systems that release large amounts of vertically directed unstable gases. High temperature exhaust plumes may cause significant air disturbances such as turbulence and vertical shear. Other identified potential hazards include, but are not necessarily limited to, reduced visibility, oxygen depletion, engine particulate contamination, exposure to gaseous oxides, and/or icing. Results of encountering a plume may include airframe damage, aircraft upset, and/or engine damage/failure. These hazards are most critical during low altitude flight, especially during takeoff and landing.

11. Flying in the wire environment (Flying near electric infrastructure)

a) Flying below 1,000 feet is the wire environment.

b) The helicopter community in the United States, and world-wide, perform their critical operations typically at 1000 ft or less and often times in a wire/obstruction rich environment. Collisions between aircraft and manmade obstacles have occurred since the beginning of manned flight. A 13 year query of the National Transportation Safety Board (NTSB) database indicates a total of 996 reported aviation accidents/collisions involving wires/power lines in the United States. Of the 996 accidents 301 involved at least one fatality. That averages out to 76.6 accidents annually and with fatalities in 30% of the accidents.

12. The NOTAM system, including how to obtain an established NOTAM through flight service

a) Notices to Airmen, or NOTAMs, are time-critical aeronautical information either temporary in nature or not sufficiently known in advance to permit publication on aeronautical charts or in other operational publications. The information receives immediate dissemination via the National Notice to Airmen (NOTAM) System. NOTAMs contain current notices to airmen that are considered essential to the safety of flight, as well as supplemental data affecting other operational publications. There are many different reasons that NOTAMs are issued. Following are some of those reasons:

   (1) Hazards, such as air shows, parachute jumps, kite flying, and rocket launches
   (2) Flights by important people such as heads of state Closed runways
   (3) Inoperable radio navigational aids
   (4) Military exercises with resulting airspace restrictions Inoperable lights on tall obstructions
   (5) Temporary erection of obstacles near airfields
   (6) Passage of flocks of birds through airspace (a NOTAM in this category is known as a BIRDTAM)
   (7) Notifications of runway/taxiway/apron status with respect to snow, ice, and standing water (a SNOWTAM
   (8) Notification of an operationally significant change in volcanic ash or other dust contamination (an ASHTAM)
   (9) Software code risk announcements with associated patches to reduce specific vulnerabilities

QUIZ QUESTIONS - Airspace

1. You have been asked to inspect the tower just north of Binford. What restrictions should the Remote PIC be concerned to operating the sUAS?

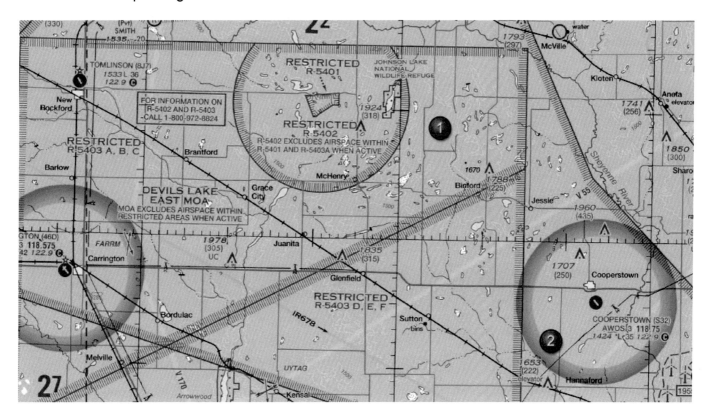

    A. None, the tower is in Class G airspace up to 1200 AGL

    B. Restricted airspace exists around the tower thus permissions is required from the controlling agency

    C. Class E airspace begins at the ground as indicated by the blue hashed lines surrounding the area

2. Which publication contains an explanation of airport signs and markings?

    A. Aeronautical Information Manual (AIM)

    B. Advisory Circulars (AC)

    C. Chart Supplements US

3. In what airspace is Onawa, IA (K36) located?

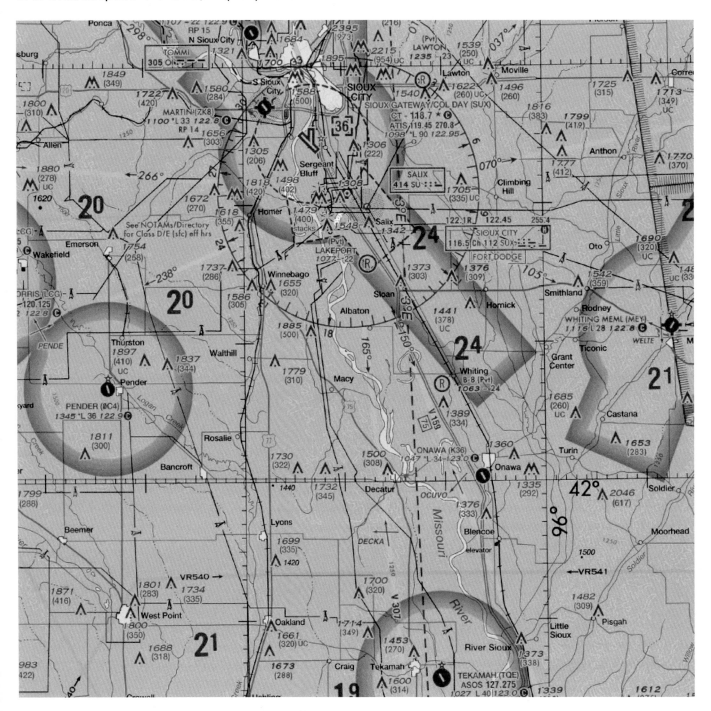

    A. Class G
    B. Class E
    C. Class D

4. Responsibility for collision avoidance in an alert area rests with
    A. the controlling agency
    B. all pilots
    C. Air Traffic Control

5. According to 14 CFR Part 107, how may a Remote Pilot in Command (Remote PIC) operate an unmanned aircraft in Class C airspace?
- A. The remote PIC must contact the ATC facility after launching the unmanned aircraft
- B. The remote PIC must monitor the ATC frequency from launch to recovery
- C. The remote PIC must have prior authorization from the Air Traffic Control (ATC) facility having jurisdiction over that airspace.

6. The chart shows a gray line with "VR 1667, VR1617, VR1638 and VR 1668". Could this area present a hazard to the operations of a small unmanned aircraft?

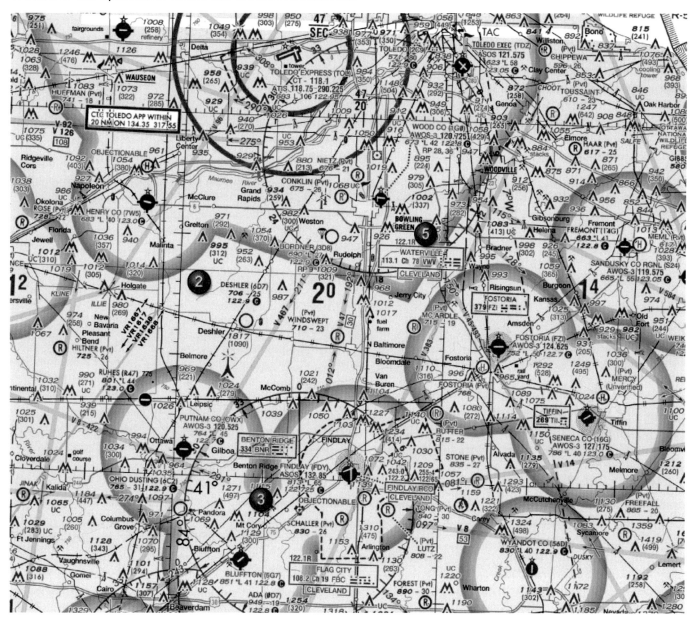

- A. No, all operations will be above 400 feet
- B. Yes, the defined route provides traffic separation to manned aircraft
- C. Yes, this is a Military Training Route from 1500 feet AGL and below

7. What special conditions do remote pilots need to be on the lookout while operating near Lincoln Airport?

LINCOLN (LNK) 4 NW UTC−6(−5DT) N40°51.05′ W96°45.55′ **OMAHA**

1219 B S4 **FUEL** 100LL, JET A TPA—See Remarks ARFF Index—See Remarks H−5C, L−10I

NOTAM FILE LNK IAP, AD

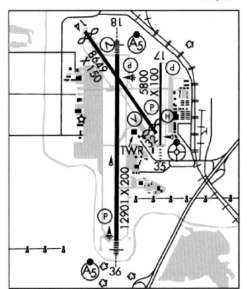

RWY 18−36: H12901X200 (ASPH−CONC−GRVD) S−100, D−200,
2S−175, 2D−400 HIRL
RWY 18: MALSR. PAPI(P4L)—GA 3.0° TCH 55′. Rgt tfc. 0.4%
down.
RWY 36: MALSR. PAPI(P4L)—GA 3.0° TCH 57′.
RWY 14−32: H8649X150 (ASPH−CONC−GRVD) S−80, D−170,
2S−175, 2D−280 MIRL
RWY 14: REIL. VASI(V4L)—GA 3.0° TCH 48′. Thld dsplcd 363′.
RWY 32: VASI(V4L)—GA 3.0° TCH 50′. Thld dsplcd 470′.
Pole. 0.3% up.
RWY 17−35: H5800X100 (ASPH−CONC−AFSC) S−49, D−60
HIRL 0.8% up S
RWY 17: REIL. PAPI(P4L)—GA 3.0° TCH 44′.
RWY 35: ODALS. PAPI(P4L)—GA 3.0° TCH 30′. Rgt tfc.
RUNWAY DECLARED DISTANCE INFORMATION
RWY 14: TORA−8649 TODA−8649 ASDA−8649 LDA−8286
RWY 17: TORA−5800 TODA−5800 ASDA−5400 LDA−5400
RWY 18: TORA−12901 TODA−12901 ASDA−12901 LDA−12901
RWY 32: TORA−8649 TODA−8649 ASDA−8286 LDA−7816
RWY 35: TORA−5800 TODA−5800 ASDA−5800 LDA−5800
RWY 36: TORA−12901 TODA−12901 ASDA−12901 LDA−12901
AIRPORT REMARKS: Attended continuously. Birds invof arpt. Rwy 18 designated calm wind rwy. Rwy 32 apch holdline
on South A twy. TPA−2219 (1000), heavy military jet 3000 (1781). Class I, ARFF Index B. ARFF Index C level
equipment provided. Rwy 18−36 touchdown and rollout rwy visual range avbl. When twr clsd MIRL Rwy 14−32
preset on low ints, HIRL Rwy 18−36 and Rwy 17−35 preset on med ints, ODALS Rwy 35 operate continuously on
med ints, MALSR Rwy 18 and Rwy 36 operate continuously and REIL Rwy 14 and Rwy 17 operate continuously
on low ints. VASI Rwy 14 and Rwy 32, PAPI Rwy 17, Rwy 35, Rwy 18 and Rwy 36 on continuously.
WEATHER DATA SOURCES: ASOS (402) 474−9214. LLWAS
COMMUNICATIONS: CTAF 118.5 ATIS 118.05 UNICOM 122.95
RCO 122.65 (COLUMBUS RADIO)
Ⓡ **APP/DEP CON** 124.0 (180°−359°) 124.8 (360°−179°)
TOWER 118.5 125.7 (1130−0600Z‡) GND CON 121.9 CLNC DEL 120.7
AIRSPACE: CLASS C svc 1130−0600Z‡ ctc **APP CON** other times **CLASS E.**
RADIO AIDS TO NAVIGATION: NOTAM FILE LNK.
(H) VORTACW 116.1 LNK Chan 108 N40°55.43′ W96°44.52′ 181° 4.4 NM to fld. 1370/9E
POTTS NDB (MHW/LOM) 385 LN N40°44.83′ W96°45.75′ 355° 6.2 NM to fld. Unmonitored when twr clsd.
ILS 111.1 I−OCZ Rwy 18. Class IB OM unmonitored.
ILS 109.9 I−LNK Rwy 36 Class IA LOM POTTS NDB. MM unmonitored. LOM unmonitored when twr
clsd.
COMM/NAV/WEATHER REMARKS: Emerg frequency 121.5 not available at twr.

A. Deer near the runway
B. Birds in the vicinity
C. Parachute operations

8. When approaching holding lines from the side with the continuous lines, the pilot
A. should not cross the lines without ATC clearance
B. may continue taxiing
C. should continue taxiing until all parts of the aircraft have crossed the lines

9. The lateral dimensions of class D airspace are based on
   A. the instrument procedures for which the controlled airspace is established
   B. the number of airports that lie within Class D airspace
   C. 5 statute miles from the geographical center of the primary airport

10. Within what airspace is Coeur D' Alene Pappy Boyington Fld located?

IDAHO   31

COEUR D'ALENE–PAPPY BOYINGTON FLD (COE) 9 NW UTC–8(–7DT) · **GREAT FALLS**
  N47°46.46' W116°49.18'
  2320 B S4 **FUEL** 100, JET A   OX 1, 2, 3, 4   Class IV, ARFF Index A   NOTAM FILE COE   H–1C, L–13B
  RWY 05–23: H7400X100 (ASPH–GRVD)   S–57, D–95, 2S–121, 2D–165   HIRL   0.6% up NE   IAP
    RWY 05: MALSR (NSTD). PAPI(P4R)—GA 3.0° TCH 56'.
    RWY 23: REIL. PAPI(P4R)—GA 3.0° TCH 50'.
  RWY 01–19: H5400X75 (ASPH)   S–50, D–83, 2S–105, 2D–150
    MIRL   0.3% up N
    RWY 01: REIL. PAPI(P2L)—GA 3.0° TCH 39'. Rgt tfc.
    RWY 19: PAPI(P2L)—GA 3.0° TCH 41'.
  RUNWAY DECLARED DISTANCE INFORMATION
    RWY 01:   TORA–5400   TODA–5400   ASDA–5400   LDA–5400
    RWY 05:   TORA–7400   TODA–7400   ASDA–7400   LDA–7400
    RWY 19:   TORA–5400   TODA–5400   ASDA–5400   LDA–5400
    RWY 23:   TORA–7400   TODA–7400   ASDA–7400   LDA–7400
  AIRPORT REMARKS: Attended Mon–Fri 1500–0100Z‡. For after hrs
    fuel-self svc avbl or call 208–772–6404, 208–661–4174,
    208–661–7449, 208–699–5433. Self svc fuel avbl with credit
    card. 48 hr PPR for unscheduled ops with more than 30
    passenger seats call arpt manager 208–446–1860. Migratory
    birds on and invof arpt Oct–Nov. Remote cntl airstrip is 2.3 miles
    west AER 05. Arpt conditions avbl on AWOS. Rwy 05 NSTD
    MALSR, thld bar extends 5' byd rwy edge lgts each side. ACTIVATE
    MIRL Rwy 01–19, HIRL Rwy 05–23, REIL Rwy 01 and Rwy 23, MALSR Rwy 05—CTAF. PAPI Rwy 01, Rwy 19, Rwy
    05, and Rwy 23 opr continuously.
  WEATHER DATA SOURCES: AWOS–3 135.075 (208) 772–8215.
    HIWAS 108.8 COE.
  COMMUNICATIONS: CTAF/UNICOM 122.8
    RCO 122.05 (BOISE RADIO)
  ⓡ SPOKANE APP/DEP CON 132.1
  AIRSPACE: CLASS E svc continuous.
  RADIO AIDS TO NAVIGATION: NOTAM FILE COE.
    (T) VORW/DME 108.8   COE   Chan 25   N47°46.42' W116°49.24'   at fld. 2320/19E.   HIWAS.
      DME portion unusable:
      220°–240° byd 15 NM   280°–315° byd 15 NM blo 11,000'.
    POST FALLS NDB (MHW) 347   LEN   N47°44.57' W116°57.66'   053° 6.0 NM to fld.
    ILS 110.7   I–COE   Rwy 05   Class ID.   Localizer unusable 25° left and right of course.

   A. Class B
   B. Class D
   C. Class E

11. You have received authorization to operate an sUAS at an airport. When flying the sUAS, the ATC tower instructs you to stay clear of all runways. Which situation would indicate that you are complying with this request.

    A. You are on the double solid yellow line side of markings near the runway

    B. You are on the double dashed yellow line side of markings near the runway

    C. You are over the dashed white lines in the center of the pavement

12. When a manned aircraft is approaching to land at an airport in Class G airspace without an operating control tower, the pilot will

    A. enter and fly a traffic pattern at 800 feet AGL

    B. make all turns to the left, unless otherwise indicated

    C. fly a left hand traffic pattern at 800 feet AGL

13. What does the line of longitude at area 7 measure?

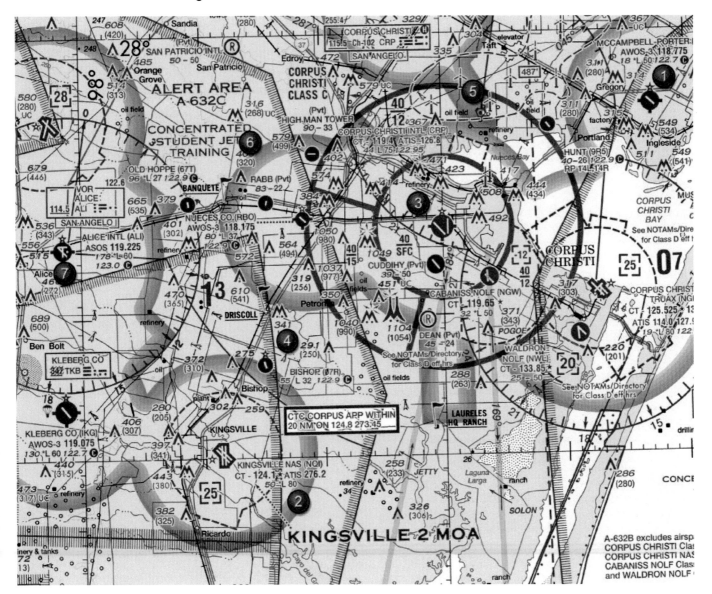

    A. The degrees of longitude east and west of the line that passed through Greenwich, England

    B. The degrees of longitude east and west of the Prime Meridian

    C. The degrees of longitude north and south from the equator

14. Which is true concerning the blue and magenta colors used to depict airports on Sectional Aeronautical Charts?

    A. Airports with control towers underlying Class B, C, D and E airspace are shown in blue

    B. Aircrafts with control towers underlying Class A, B and C airspace are shown in blue, Class D and E airspace are magenta

    C. Airports with control towers underlying Class C, D and E airspace are shown in magenta

15. The airspace surrounding the Gila Bend AF AUX Airport (GXF) (area 6) is classified as

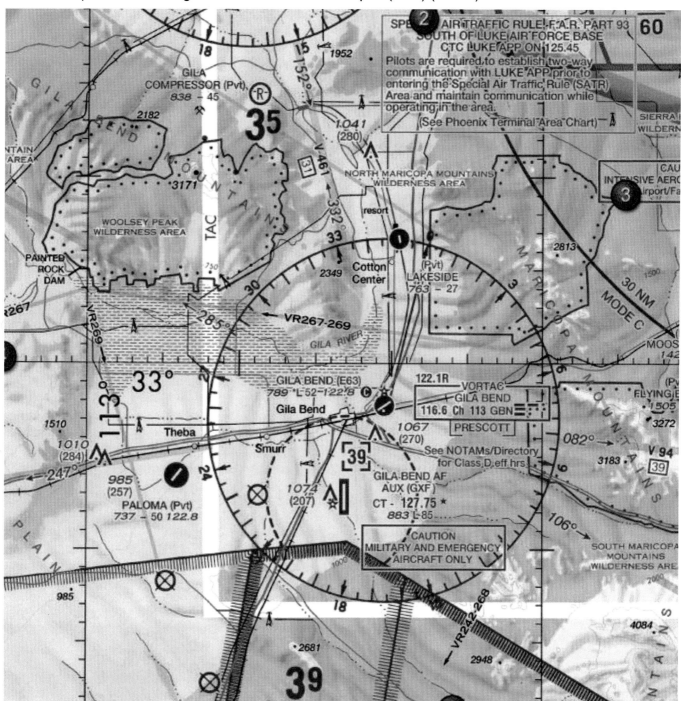

    A. Class B

    B. Class C

    C. Class D

16. Under what condition, if any, may remote pilots fly through a restricted area?
    A. With the controlling agency's authorization
    B. When flying on airways with an ATC clearance
    C. Regulations do not allow this

17. Which technique should a remote pilot use to scan for traffic?
    A. Continuously scan the sky from right to left
    B. Systematically focus on different segments of the sky for short intervals
    C. Concentrate on relative movement detected in the peripheral vision area

18. Flight Data Center (FDC) NOTAMS are issued by the National Flight Data Center and contain regulatory information, such as
    A. temporary flight restrictions
    B. markings and signs used at airports
    C. standard communication procedures at uncontrolled airports

19. An aircraft announces that they are on short final for runway 9. Where will the aircraft be in relation to the airport?
    A. North
    B. East
    C. West

20. You need to operate your sUAS in close proximity of the Elizabeth City CGAS RGL (ECG) airport. What frequency should be used to contact ATC?

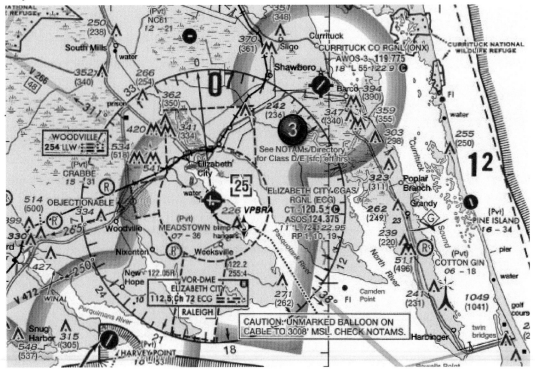

    A. 122.95
    B. 120.5
    C. 124.375

21. What airspace is Hayward Executive in?

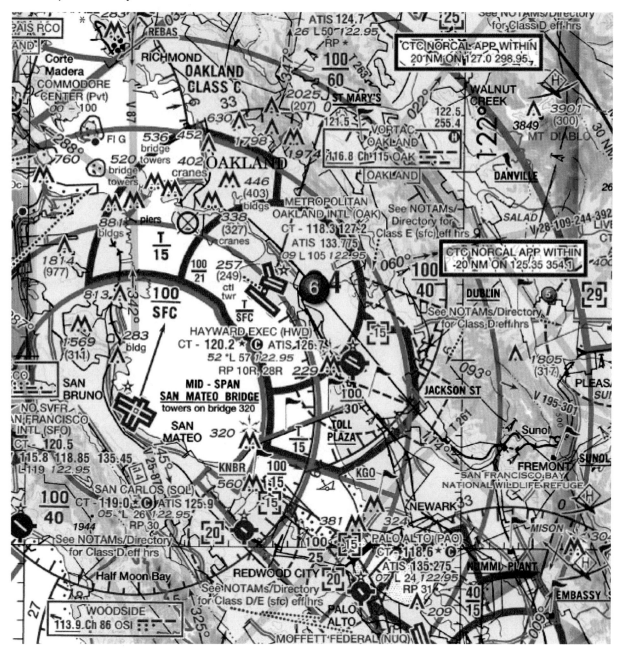

A. Class D
B. Class B
C. Class C

22. Public figures are protected by
    A. special use airspace
    B. temporary flight restrictions
    C. prohibited areas

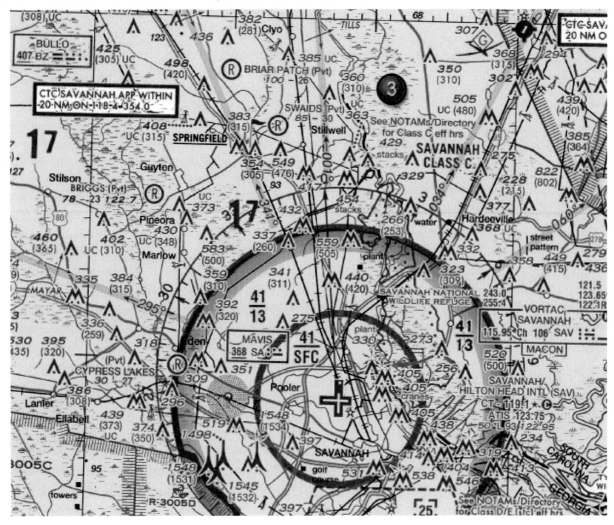

23. What is the height of the lighted obstacle approximately 6 nautical miles southwest of Savannah International?
     A. 1548 feet MSL
     B. 1500 feet MSL
     C. 1531 feet AGL

24. The top of the group obstruction approximately 11 nautical miles from the Savannah VORTAC on the 009-degree radial is
     A. 454 feet MSL
     B. 400 feet AGL
     C. 432 feet MSL

25. What is required to enter an airport SIDA?
     A. You must pass the TSA screening
     B. You must have an airport issued or approved ID
     C. You must have an FAA-issued pilot certificate

26. What airport is located approximately 47 (degrees) 40 (minutes) N latitude and 101 (degrees) 26 (minutes) W longitude?

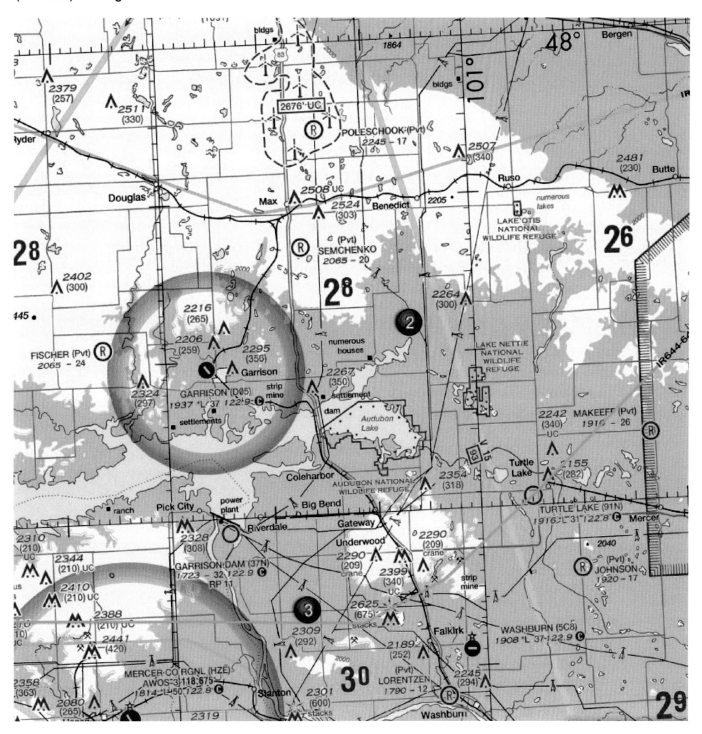

A. Garrison Airport
B. Mercer County Regional Airport
C. Semshenko Airport

27. Time - critical information on airports and changes that affect the national airspace system are provided by

    A. the Chart supplements US (formerly Airport/ Facilities Directory or A/FD)

    B. Advisory Circulars (ACs)

    C. Notice to Airmen (NOTAMS)

28. You have been contracted to photograph Lake Pend Oreille from a vantage point just east of Cocolalla. You notice there is a hill which should provide a good panoramic photographs. What is the maximum altitude (MSL) you are authorized to fly over the hill?

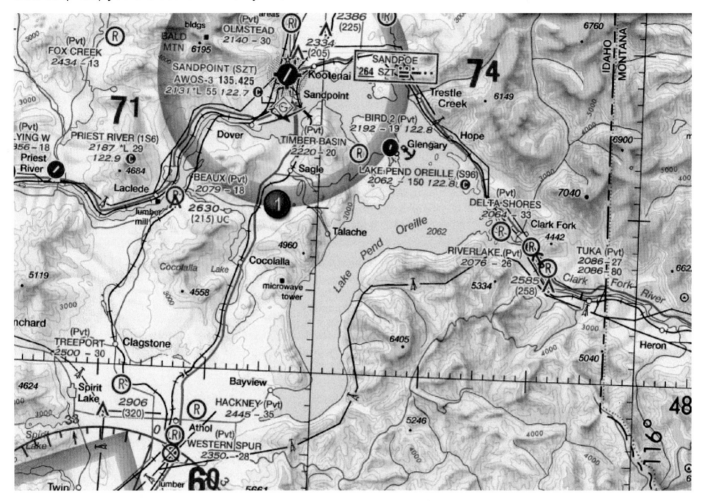

    A. You cannot operate your sUAS above 400 MSL and thus cannot operate anywhere in this part of the country

    B. You cannot operate your sUAS without ATC permission because you will be in class E airspace above 1200 MSL

    C. You may operate up to 5,360 feet MSL in Class G airspace

29. What ATC permissions are required to operate near Anderson Airport?

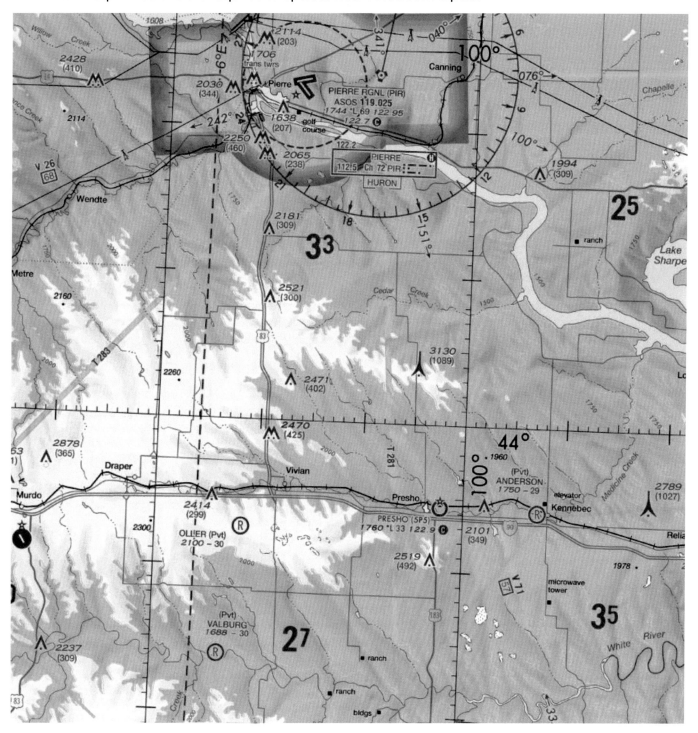

    A. no ATC permission is required

    B. ATC clearance required

    C. Waiver must be requested

30. The most comprehensive information on a given airport is provided by

    A. Notice to Airmen (NOTAMs)

    B. the Chart Supplements US (formerly Airport Facility Directory)

    C. Terminal Area Chart (TAC)

31. What should a remote pilot do if the sUAS they are operating collide with a bird or wildlife?
   A. File an accident report with the NTSB
   B. File an accident report to the FAA
   C. Report the collision to ATC

32. The numbers 9 and 27 on a runway indicate that the runway is oriented approximately
   A. 090 degrees and 270 degrees magnetic
   B. 009 degrees and 027 degrees true
   C. 090 degrees and 270 degrees true

33. Sky Way Airport is

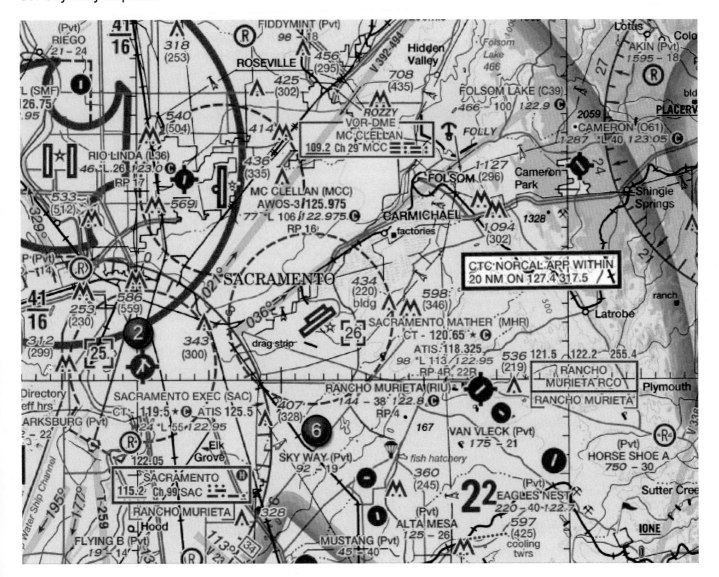

   A. a nonpublic use airport
   B. an airport restricted to use by private and recreational pilots
   C. a restricted military stage field within restricted airspace

34. How would a remote PIC "Check NOTAMs" as noted in the CAUTION box regarding the unmarked balloon?

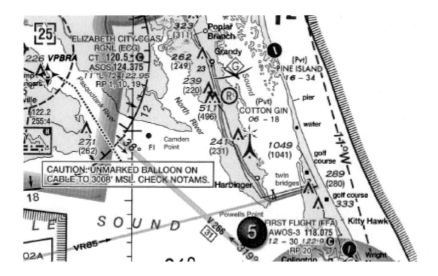

    A. By utilizing the B4UFLY mobile application

    B. by obtaining a briefing via an online source such as 1800WXbrief.com

    C. By contacting the FAA district office

35. What is the purpose of the runway / runway hold position sign?

    A. Denotes intersecting runways

    B. denotes entrance to runway from a taxiway

    C. denotes area protected for an aircraft approaching or departing a runway

36. Entries into traffic patterns by manned aircraft while descending create specific collision hazards and

    A. should be used whenever possible

    B. are illegal

    C. should be avoided

37. The airspace overlying and within 5 miles of Barnes County Airport is

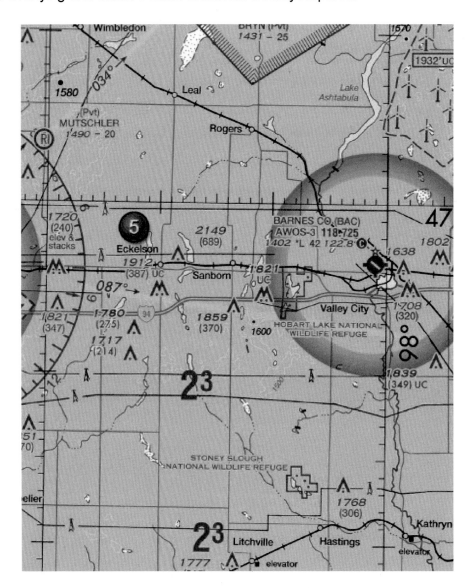

A. Class G airspace from the surface up to but not including 700 feet AGL
B. Class D airspace from the surface to the floor of the overlying Class E airspace
C. Class E airspace from the surface to 1,200 feet MSL

38. What information is contained in the Notices to Airman Publication (NTAP)?
    A. All current NOTAMs
    B. Current NOTAM (D) and FDC NOTAMs
    C. Current FDC NOTAMs

39. Guy wires, which support antenna towers, can extend horizontally; therefore, the towers should be avoided horizontally by at least
    A. 2,000 feet horizontally
    B. 300 feet horizontally
    C. 1,000 feet horizontally

40. What does the line of latitude at area 4 measure?

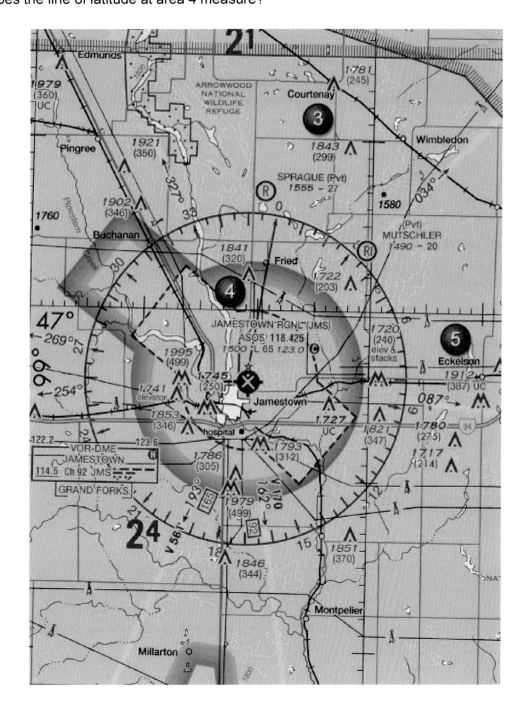

    A. The degrees of latitude east and west of the Prime Meridian

    B. The degrees of latitude east and west of the line that passes through Greenwich, England.

    C. The degrees of latitude north and south from the equator

41. Which statement about longitude and latitude is true?

    A. Lines of longitude cross the Equator at right angles

    B. Lines of longitude are parallel to the Equator

    C. The 0 degree line of latitude passes through Greenwich, England

42. When turning onto a taxiway from another taxiway, what is the purpose of the taxiway directional sign?
   A. Indicates designation and direction of taxiway leading out of an intersection
   B. Indicates direction to take off runway
   C. Indicates designation and direction of exit taxiway from runway

43. How close can the Remote PIC fly their sUAS to the Majors airport (GVT) without having to contact ATC?

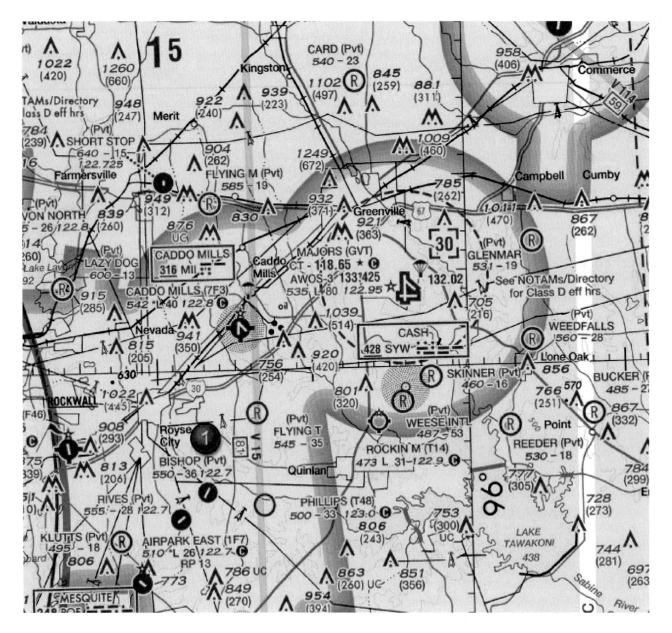

   A. 4 Statute Miles (SM)
   B. Remote PICs must contact ATC whenever operating within the magenta shading on Sectional Charts.
   C. 4 Nautical Miles (NM)

44. According to 14 CFR Part 107, the remote PIC of a small unmanned aircraft planning to operate within in Class C airspace

    A. is required to file a flight plan

    B. is required to receive ATC authorization

    C. must use a visual observer

USE THE FOLLOWING IMAGE FOR QUESTIONS 45 AND 46:

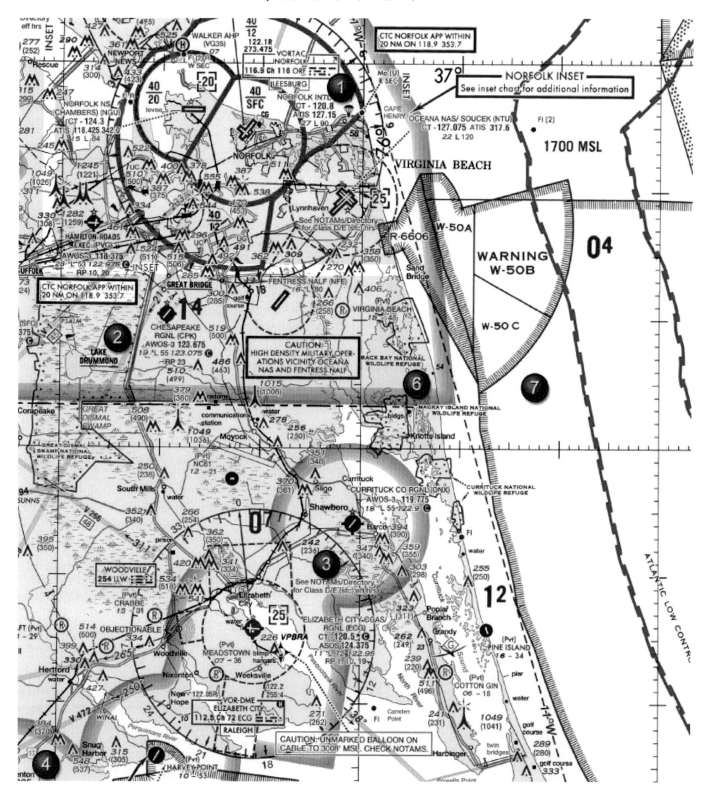

45. What is the latitude and longitude location of the Elizabeth City CGAS RGL (ECG)?
   A. N 36 degrees 16' W 76 degrees 10'
   B. W 36 degrees 16' N 76 degrees 10'
   C. N 37 degrees 0' W 77 degrees 10'

46. With ATC authorization, you are operating your small unmanned aircraft approximately 4 SM southeast of Elizabeth City Regional Airport (ECG). What hazard is indicated to be in that area?
   A. High density military operations in the vicinity
   B. Unmarked balloon on a cable up to 3,008 feet AGL
   C. Unmarked balloon on a cable up to 3,008 feet MSL

47. At Coeur D'Alene, which frequency should be used as a common traffic advisory frequency (CTAF) to monitor airport traffic?

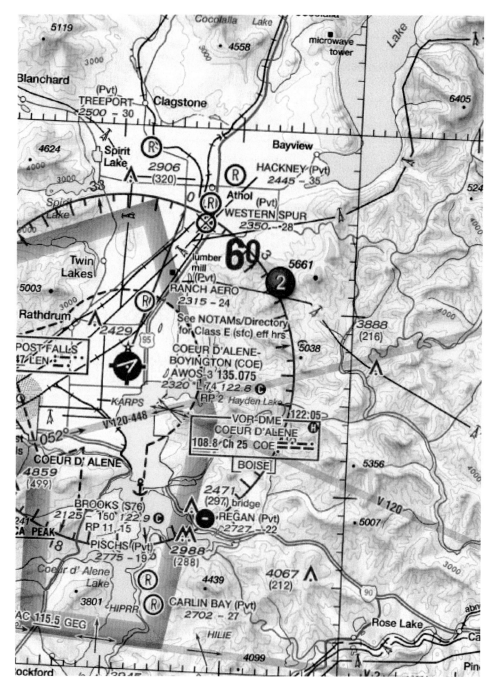

    A. 122.05 MHz
    B. 122.8 MHz
    C. 135.075 MHz

48. While operating a sUAS just south of a controlled airport with authorization, ATC notifies you to stay clear of the runway 6 final approach course. What action should you take to comply with this request?
    A. Stay clear of areas to the east and north of your area of operation
    B. Stay clear of areas to the west and north of your area of operations
    C. stay clear of areas to the west and south of your area of operation

49. What is the purpose for the runway hold position markings on the taxiway?
    A. Holds aircraft short of the runway
    B. Allows an aircraft permission onto the runway
    C. Identifies area where aircraft are prohibited

50. What should remote pilots rely on for wire strike avoidance?
    A. Visual scanning
    B. Sectional chart markings
    C. Chart supplement US airport and airspace details

51. One of the purposes for issuing a Temporary Flight Restriction (TFR) is to
    A. announce Parachute Jump areas
    B. identify Airport Advisory areas
    C. protect public figures

52. You have been hired to inspect the tower under construction at 46.9N and 98.6W, near Jamestown Regional (JMS). What must you receive, prior to flying your unmanned aircraft in this area?

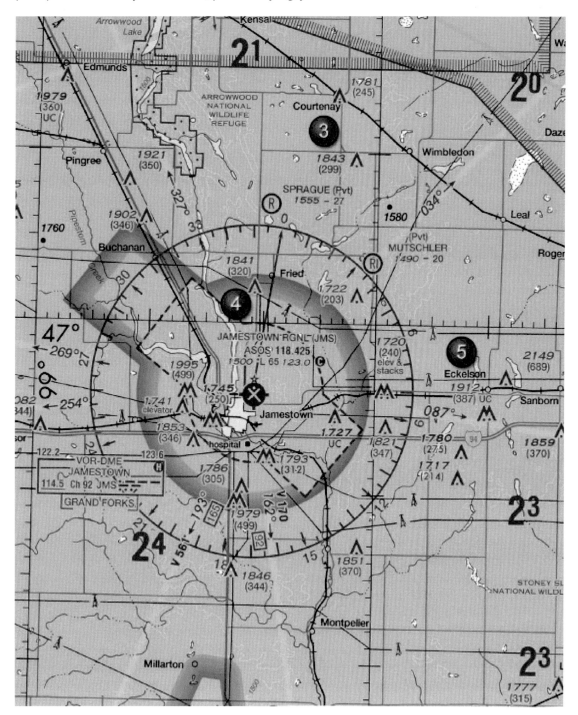

    A. Authorization from ATC
    B. Authorization from the military
    C. Authorization from the National Park Service

53. The "taxiway ending" marker
    A. identifies area where aircraft are prohibited
    B. indicates taxiway does not continue
    C. provides general taxiing direction to named taxiway

54. You are operating an sUAS in the vicinity of Sulphur Springs Airport (SUR) where there is active air traffic. Who has priority and right-of-way within the traffic pattern area?

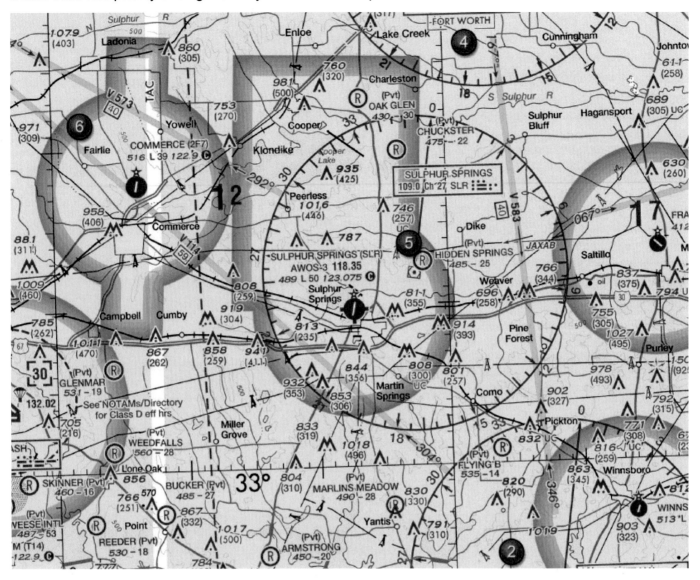

A. The sUAS
B. The existing manned aircraft
C. Priority and right-of-way goes to the aircraft closest to the landing runway

55. You are conducting sUAS operations northeast of a nearby airport. While monitoring the CTAF, an aircraft announces that it is departing runway 36 utilizing a right traffic pattern. Will the aircraft potentially conflict with your operation?
A. Yes, the aircraft may overfly northeast of the airport
B. No, the aircraft will be flying on the west side of the airport
C. No, the aircraft will be flying to the south of the airport

56. The FAA publication that provides the aviation community with basic flight information and Air Traffic control procedures for use in the National airspace system of the United States is the
A. Aeronautical Information Manual (AIM)
B. Chart Supplements US (formerly A/FD)
C. Advisory Circulars Checklist (AC 00-2)

57. The floor of Class B airspace overlying Hicks Airport (T67) north-northwest of Fort Worth Meacham Field is

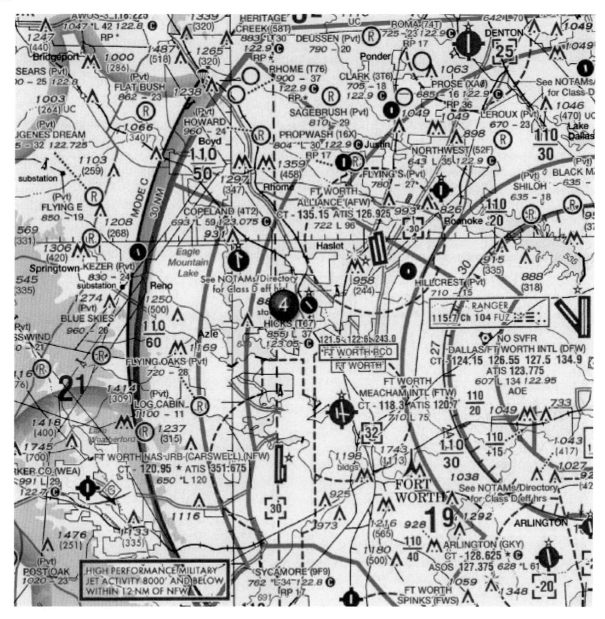

A. at the surface
B. 3,200 feet MSL
C. 4,000 feet MSL

58. What is the floor of Savannah Class C airspace at the shelf area (outer circle)?

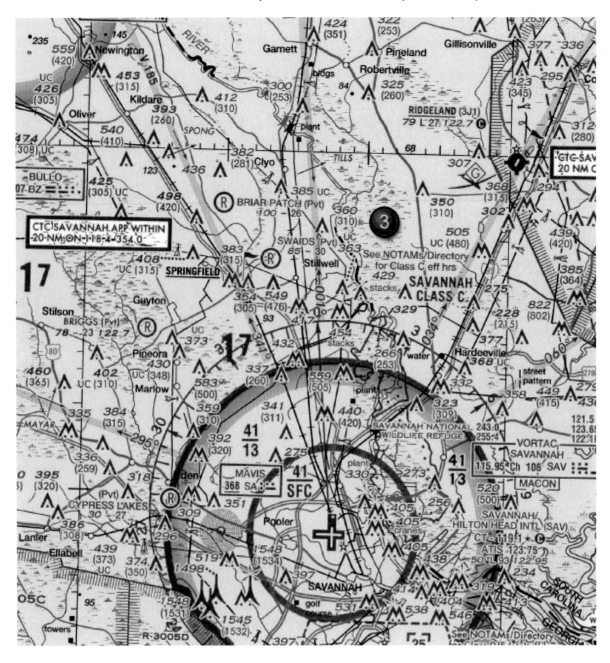

A. 1,300 feet MSL
B. 1,300 feet AGL
C. 1,700 feet MSL

59. The recommended entry position for manned aircraft to enter an airport traffic pattern is
   A. 45 degrees to the base leg just below traffic pattern altitude
   B. to cross directly over the airport at traffic pattern altitude and join the downwind leg
   C. to enter 45 degrees at the midpoint of the downwind left at traffic pattern altitude

60. You have been hired by a farmer to use your small unmanned aircraft to inspect his crops. The area that you are to survey is in the Devil's Lake west MOA, east of area 2. How would you find out if the MOA is active?

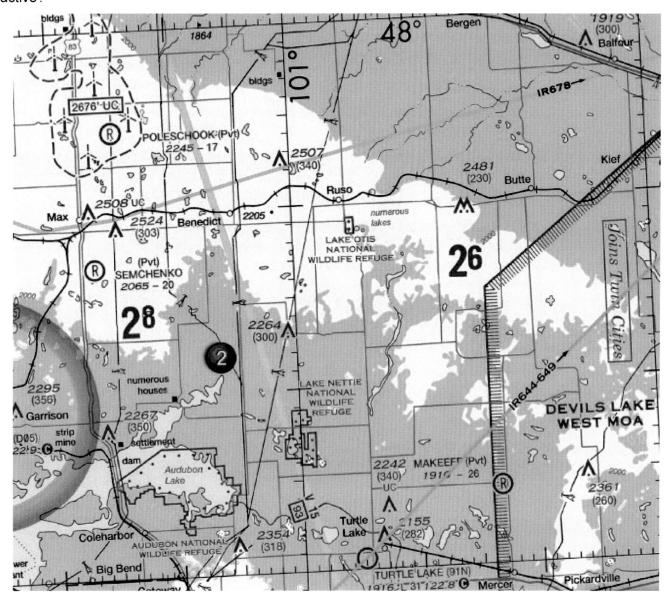

A. Refer to the legend for special use airspace phone number
B. This information is available in the small UAS database
C. Refer to the Military Operations Directory

61. while monitoring the Cooperstown CTAF you hear an aircraft announce that they are midfield left downwind to RWY 13. Where would the aircraft be relative to the runway?

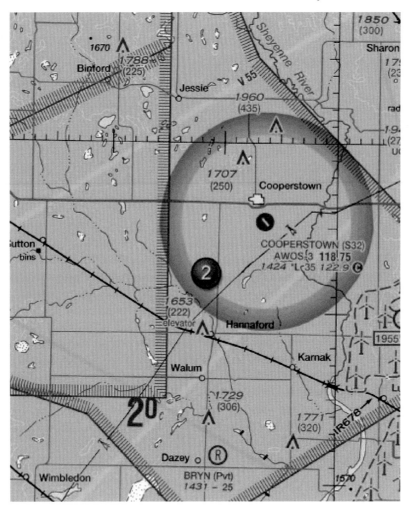

A. The Aircraft is South
B. The aircraft is East
C. The aircraft is south

62. Holding position signs have
   A. white inscriptions on red background
   B. red inscriptions on white background
   C. yellow inscriptions on red background

63. What is the purpose of the No Entry Sign?
   A. Identifies area that doesn't not continue beyond intersection.
   B. Identifies the exit boundary for the runway protected area
   C. Identifies a paved area where aircraft are prohibited from entering

64. Operating an sUAS, can you vertically clear the obstacle on the southeast side of Winnsboro airport

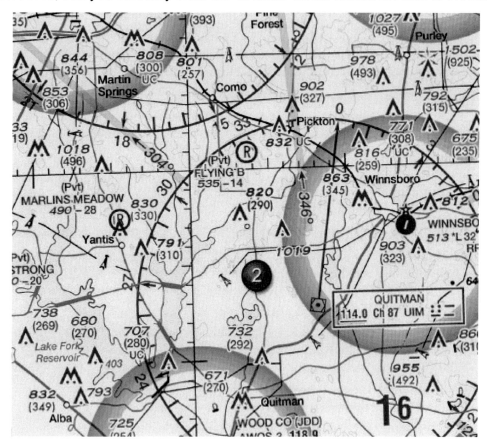

A. No.

B. UAS operations are prohibited in this area

C. Yes.

65. The floor of the Class E airspace above Georgetown Airport (E36) is at

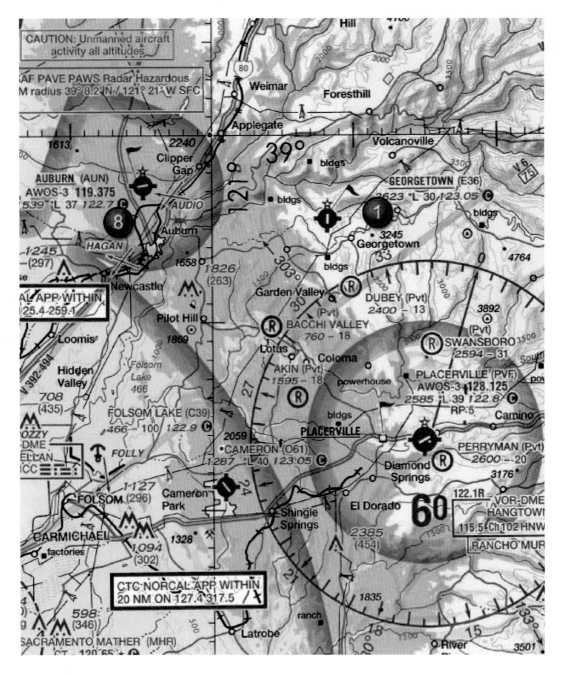

A. 3,823 feet
B. the surface
C. 700 feet AGL

66. Most midair collision accidents occur during
A. hazy days
B. clear days
C. cloudy nights

67. Why would the small flag at lake Drummond be important to a remote pilot?

A. This is a GPS check point that can be used for both manned and remote pilots for orientation

B. This is a VFR check point for manned aircraft, and a higher volume of air traffic should be expected here

C. This indicates that there will be a large obstruction depicted on the next printing of the chart

68. What do the blue shaped lines on the map below indicate throughout this sectional excerpt?

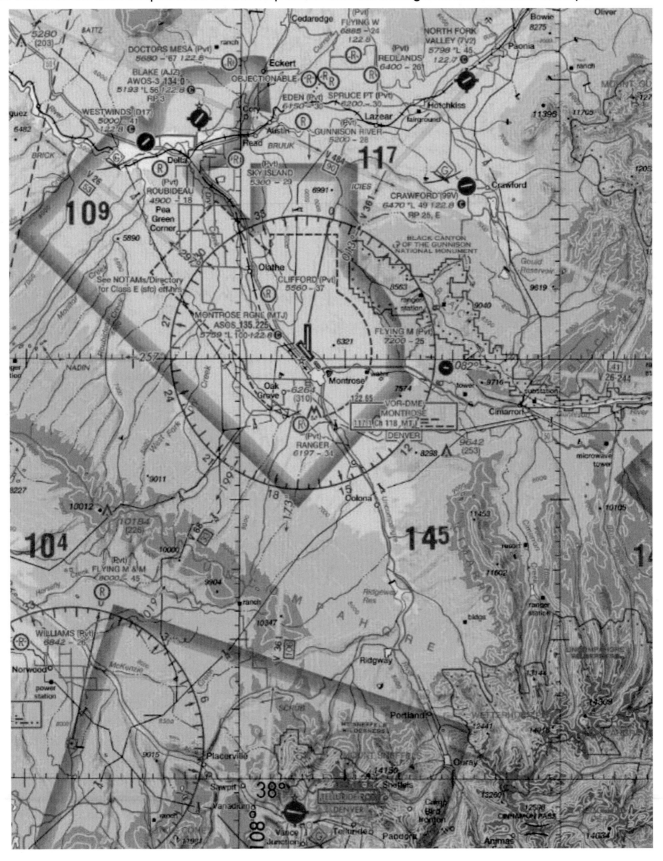

A. Airline corridors
B. Military Training routes
C. Victor Airways

69. What are the requirements for operating an sUAS in Class C airspace?
    A. Two-way radio communications and transponder with altitude reporting capabilities
    B. Two-way radio communications and visual observer
    C. ATC authorization and visual observer

70. An FDC NOTAM will typically contain information
    A. regarding public gatherings of large groups
    B. regarding military operations
    C. regarding available hard surface runways

71. You have been hired to fly your UA to inspect train tracks from the town of Hinton to the town of Winnebago. Will you be able to conduct this flight without contacting ATC?

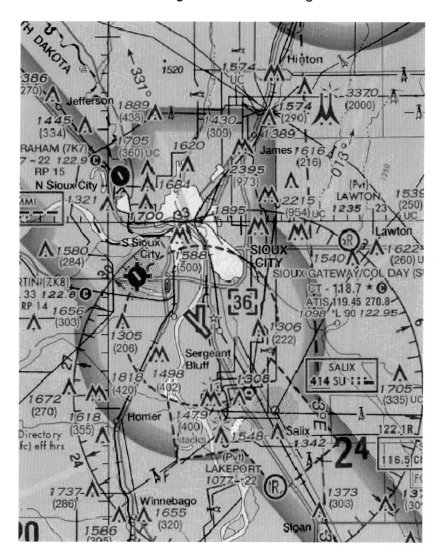

    A. Yes, because you will remain under 400 feet
    B. No, because you will pass through Echo airspace
    C. No, because you will pass through Delta airspace

72. Checking the NOTAMs confirms the Blue Angels are scheduled to perform at the local airport. When can UAS operations resume relative to this NOTAM?

    A. Once the Blue Angels have landed

    B. With ATC authorization

    C. Immediately, so long as a 1 NM distance is maintained

73. Where can you find additional information about "R-2305"?

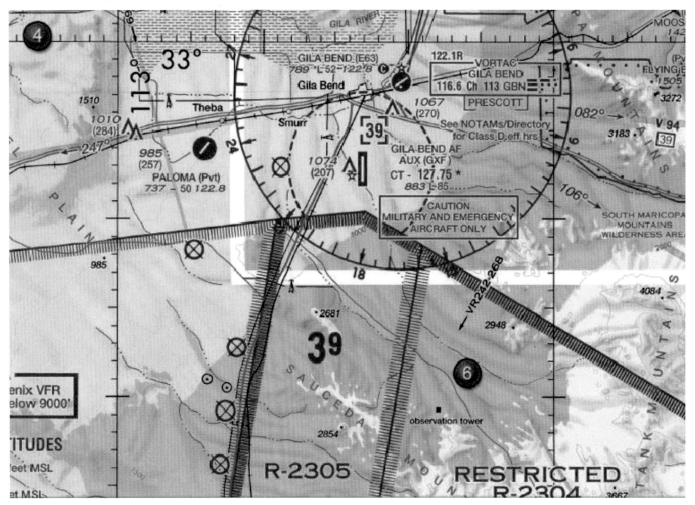

    A. On the Special Use Airspace section of the chart

    B. In the Aeronautical Information Manual

    C. In the Chart Supplements U.S. (Formerly A/FD)

74. A larger UAS is converging head-on; what should you do?

    A. The smaller aircraft should adjust course to the right

    B. The larger aircraft should adjust course to the right

    C. Both aircraft should adjust course to the right

75. Where can you find information about operating in an MOA along your planned route of flight?

    A. Sectional chart

    B. Chart supplement

    C. Aeronautical Information Manual

76. The airspace overlying Tomlinson Airport is

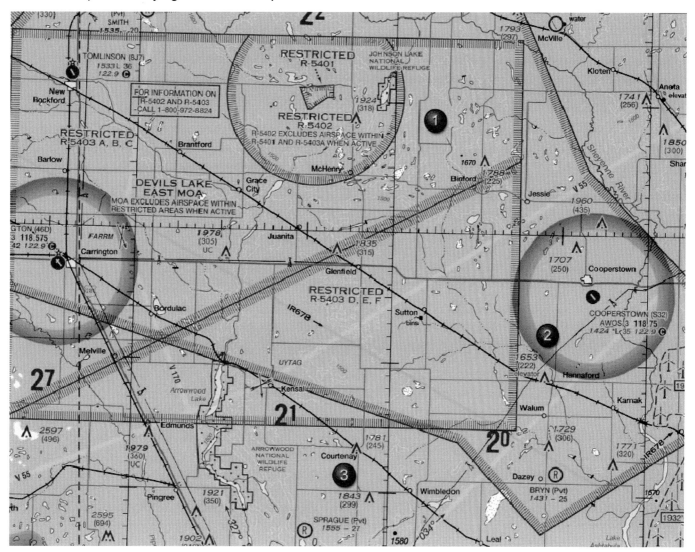

    A. Class G up to 18,000

    B. Class E from 1,200 up to but not including 18,000

    C. Class E from 700 up to but not including 18,000

77. The typical outer radius limits of Class C airspace are

    A. 10 NM

    B. 20 NM

    C. 30 NM

78. The airspace directly overlying Addison Airport (ADS) is

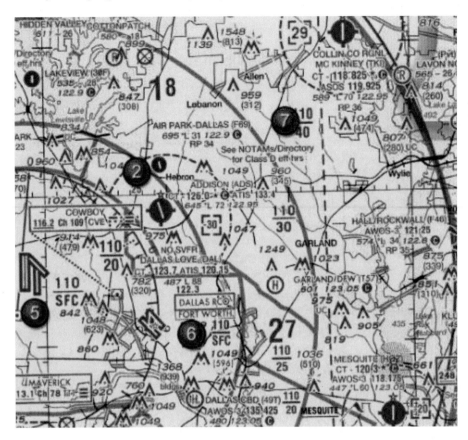

A. Class D up to 3,000 feet MSL
B. Class D up to but not including 3,000 feet MSL
C. Class E from the surface up to 3,000 feet MSL

79. Time-critical information on airports and changes that affect the national airspace system are provided by

A. Notices to Airmen (NOTAMS)
B. the Chart Supplements U.S. (formerly Airport/Facilities Directory or A/FD)
C. Advisory Circulars (ACs)

80. What minimum radio equipment is required for operation within Class C airspace?
A. Two-way radio communications equipment and a 4096-code transponder
B. Two-way radio communications equipment, a 4096-code transponder, and DME
C. Two-way radio communications equipment, a 4096-code transponder, and an encoding altimeter

III. Weather (Section 3)

A. Sources of weather

1. Weather is an important factor that influences aircraft performance and flying safety

    a) It is the state of the atmosphere at a given time and place with respect to variables, such as temperature (heat or cold), moisture (wetness or dryness), wind velocity (calm or storm), visibility (clearness or cloudiness), and barometric pressure (high or low). The term "weather" can also apply to adverse or destructive atmospheric conditions, such as high winds.

    b) This section explains basic weather theory and offers pilots background knowledge of weather principles. It is designed to help them gain a good understanding of how weather affects daily flying activities. Understanding the theories behind weather helps a pilot make sound weather decisions based on the reports and forecasts obtained from a Flight Service Station (FSS) weather specialist and other aviation weather services.

2. Internet weather briefing and sources of weather available for flight planning purposes

    a) Remote PICs are encouraged to obtain weather information prior to flight from Flight Service by using the Web site www.1800wxbrief.com. Remote PICs can create a free account in order to use the briefing service. While Flight Service does offer a telephone-based service, it is intended for manned aircraft pilots only.

    b) Remote PICs are also encouraged to visit the NWS's Aviation Weather Center (AWC) at www.aviationweather.gov. This free, Web-based service does not require registration and offers all of the weather products important to a remote PIC, such as Aviation Routine Weather Reports (METAR) and Terminal Aerodrome Forecast (TAF). While reviewing the weather for your intended operation, it is also critical that the remote PIC review any temporary flight restrictions (TFR) at the FAA's TFR Web site, which can be found at http://tfr.faa.gov.

3. Aviation routine weather reports (METAR)

a) A METAR is an observation of current surface weather reported in a standard international format. While the METAR code has been adopted worldwide, each country is allowed to make modifications to the code. Normally, these differences are minor but necessary to accommodate local procedures or particular units of measure. This discussion of METAR covers elements used in the United States.

    (1) Example: METAR KGGG 161753Z AUTO 14021G26KT 3/4SM +TSRA BR BKN008 OVC012CB 18/17 A2970 RMK PRESFR

b) A typical METAR report contains the following information in sequential order:

    (1) Type of report—there are two types of METAR reports. The first is the routine METAR report that is transmitted on a regular time interval. The second is the aviation selected SPECI. This is a special report that can be given at any time to update the METAR for rapidly changing weather conditions, aircraft mishaps, or other critical information.

    (2) Station identifier—a four-letter code as established by the International Civil Aviation Organization (ICAO). In the 48 contiguous states, a unique three-letter identifier is preceded by the letter "K." For example, Gregg County Airport in Longview, Texas, is identified by the letters "KGGG," K being the country designation and GGG being the airport identifier.

    (3) Date and time of report—depicted in a six-digit group (161753Z). The first two digits are the date. The last four digits are the time of the METAR/SPECI, which is always given in coordinated universal time (UTC). A "Z" is appended to the end of the time to denote the time is given in Zulu time (UTC) as opposed to local time.

    (4) Modifier—denotes that the MET AR/SPECI came from an automated source or that the report was corrected. If the notation "AUTO" is listed in the METAR/SPECI, the report came from an automated source. It also lists "AO1" (for no precipitation discriminator) or "AO2" (with precipitation discriminator) in the "Remarks" section to indicate the type of precipitation sensors employed at the automated station. When the modifier "COR" is used, it identifies a corrected report sent out to replace an earlier report that contained an error (for example: METAR KGGG 161753Z COR).

    (5) Wind—reported with five digits (14021KT) unless the speed is greater than 99 knots, in which case the wind is reported with six digits. The first three digits indicate the direction the true wind is blowing from in tens of degrees. If the wind is variable, it is reported as "VRB." The last two digits indicate the speed of the wind in knots unless the wind is greater than 99 knots, in which case it is indicated by three digits. If the winds are gusting, the letter "G" follows the wind speed (G26KT). After the letter "G," the peak gust recorded is provided. If the wind direction varies more than 60° and the wind speed is greater than six knots, a separate group of numbers, separated by a "V," will indicate the extremes of the wind directions.

(6) Visibility—the prevailing visibility (3/4 SM) is reported in statute miles as denoted by the letters "SM." It is reported in both miles and fractions of miles. At times, runway visual range (RVR) is reported following the prevailing visibility. RVR is the distance a pilot can see down the runway in a moving aircraft. When RVR is reported, it is shown with an R, then the runway number followed by a slant, then the visual range in feet. For example, when the RVR is reported as R17L/1400FT, it translates to a visual range of 1,400 feet on runway 17 left.

(7) Weather—can be broken down into two different categories: qualifiers and weather phenomenon (+TSRA BR). First, the qualifiers of intensity, proximity, and the descriptor of the weather are given. The intensity may be light (–), moderate ( ), or heavy (+). Proximity only depicts weather phenomena that are in the airport vicinity. The notation "VC" indicates a specific weather phenomenon is in the vicinity of five to ten miles from the airport. Descriptors are used to describe certain types of precipitation and obscurations. Weather phenomena may be reported as being precipitation, obscurations, and other phenomena, such as squalls or funnel clouds.

(8) Sky condition—always reported in the sequence of amount, height, and type or indefinite ceiling/height (vertical visibility) (BKN008 OVC012CB, VV003). The heights of the cloud bases are reported with a three-digit number in hundreds of feet AGL. Clouds above 12,000 feet are not detected or reported by an automated station. The types of clouds, specifically towering cumulus (TCU) or cumulonimbus (CB) clouds, are reported with their height. Contractions are used to describe the amount of cloud coverage and obscuring phenomena. The amount of sky coverage is reported in eighths of the sky from horizon to horizon.

(9) Temperature and dew point—the air temperature and dew point are always given in degrees Celsius (C) or (18/17). Temperatures below 0 °C are preceded by the letter "M" to indicate minus.

(10) Altimeter setting—reported as inches of mercury ("Hg) in a four-digit number group (A2970). It is always preceded by the letter "A." Rising or falling pressure may also be denoted in the "Remarks" sections as "PRESRR" or "PRESFR," respectively.

(11) Zulu time—a term used in aviation for UTC, which places the entire world on one time standard.

(12) Remarks—the remarks section always begins with the letters "RMK." Comments may or may not appear in this section of the METAR. The information contained in this section may include wind data, variable visibility, beginning and ending times of particular phenomenon, pressure information, and various other information deemed necessary. An example of a remark regarding weather phenomenon that does not fit in any other category would be: OCNL LTGICCG. This translates as occasional lightning in the clouds and from cloud to ground. Automated stations also use the remarks section to indicate the equipment needs maintenance.

4. Terminal Aerodrome Forecasts (TAF)

a) A TAF is a report established for the five statute mile radius around an airport. TAF reports are usually given for larger airports. Each TAF is valid for a 24 or 30-hour time period and is updated four times a day at 0000Z, 0600Z, 1200Z, and 1800Z. The TAF utilizes the same descriptors and abbreviations as used in the METAR report.

5. Weather charts

a) Weather charts are graphic charts that depict current or forecast weather. They provide an overall picture of the United States and should be used in the beginning stages of flight planning. Typically, weather charts show the movement of major weather systems and fronts. Surface analysis, weather depiction, and significant weather prognostic charts are sources of current weather information. Significant weather prognostic charts provide an overall forecast weather picture.

6. Automated surface observing systems (ASOS) and automated weather observing systems

a) The network is made up of government and privately contracted facilities that provide continuous up-to-date weather information. Automated weather sources, such as the Automated Weather Observing Systems (AWOS), Automated Surface Observing Systems (ASOS), as well as other automated facilities, also play a major role in the gathering of surface observations.

b) Automated Surface Observing System (ASOS)/Automated Weather Observing Station (AWOS) data display, other continuous direct reading instruments, or manual observations available to the specialist.

B. Effects of weather on performance

1. Weather factors and their effects on performance

a) Atmospheric pressure and density, wind, and uneven surface heating are factors that affect sUAS performance and must be considered prior to flight.

b) Wind:

(1) Wind speed and direction are important as they affect takeoff, landing, and cruise of flight operations. Geological features, trees, structures, and other anomalies can affect the wind direction and speed close to the ground. In particular, ground topography, trees, and buildings can break up the flow of the wind and create wind gusts that change rapidly in direction and speed. The remote PIC should be vigilant when operating UAS near large buildings or other man-made structures and natural obstructions, such as mountains, bluffs, or canyons. The intensity of the turbulence associated with ground obstructions depends on the size of the obstacle and the primary velocity of the wind. This same condition is even more noticeable when flying in mountainous regions. While the wind flows smoothly up the windward side of the mountain and the upward currents help to carry an aircraft over the peak of the mountain, the wind on the leeward side does not act in a similar manner. As the air flows down the leeward side of the mountain, the air follows the contour of the terrain and is increasingly turbulent. This tends to push an aircraft into the side of a mountain. The stronger the wind, the greater the downward pressure and turbulence become. Due to the effect terrain has on the wind in valleys or canyons, downdrafts can be severe.

c) Surface heat:

(1) Different surfaces radiate heat in varying amounts. Plowed ground, rocks, sand, and barren land give off a larger amount of heat, whereas water, trees, and other areas of vegetation tend to absorb and retain heat. The resulting uneven heating of the air creates small areas of local circulation called convective currents, which creates bumpy, turbulent air. Convective currents, with their rising and sinking air can adversely affect the controllability of the small UA.

2. Density altitude

a) Density altitude is pressure altitude corrected for nonstandard temperature. As the density of the air increases (lower density altitude), aircraft performance increases; conversely as air density decreases (higher density altitude), aircraft performance decreases. A decrease in air density means a high density altitude; an increase in air density means a lower density altitude. Density altitude is used in calculating aircraft performance because under standard atmospheric conditions, air at each level in the atmosphere not only has a specific density, its pressure altitude and density altitude identify the same level.

b) SDP is a theoretical pressure altitude, but aircraft operate in a nonstandard atmosphere and the term density altitude is used for correlating aerodynamic performance in the nonstandard atmosphere. Density altitude is the vertical distance above sea level in the standard atmosphere at which a given density is to be found. The density of air has significant effects on the aircraft's performance because as air becomes less dense, it reduces:

    (1) Power because the engine takes in less air
    (2) Thrust because a propeller is less efficient in thin air
    (3) Lift because the thin air exerts less force on the airfoils

3.   Wind and currents

a) Air flows from areas of high pressure into areas of low pressure because air always seeks out lower pressure. The combination of atmospheric pressure differences, Coriolis force, friction, and temperature differences of the air near the earth cause two kinds of atmospheric motion: convective currents (upward and downward motion) and wind (horizontal motion). Currents and winds are important as they affect takeoff, landing, and cruise flight operations. Most importantly, currents and winds or atmospheric circulation cause weather changes.

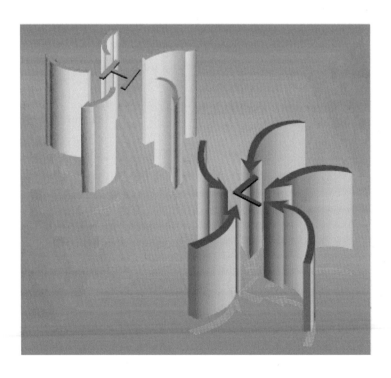

(1) In the Northern Hemisphere, the flow of air from areas of high to low pressure is deflected to the right and produces a clockwise circulation around an area of high pressure. This is known as anticyclonic circulation. The opposite is true of low-pressure areas; the air flows toward a low and is deflected to create a counterclockwise or cyclonic circulation.

(2) While the theory of circulation and wind patterns is accurate for large scale atmospheric circulation, it does not take into account changes to the circulation on a local scale. Local conditions, geological features, and other anomalies can change the wind direction and speed close to the Earth's surface.

    (a) *Convective currents*

        (i) *Plowed ground, rocks, sand, and barren land absorb solar energy quickly and can therefore give off a large amount of heat; whereas, water, trees, and other areas of vegetation tend to more slowly absorb heat and give off heat. The resulting uneven heating of the air creates small areas of local circulation called convective currents.*

(b) Another atmospheric hazard exists that can create problems for pilots. Obstructions on the ground affect the flow of wind and can be an unseen danger. Ground topography and large buildings can break up the flow of the wind and create wind gusts that change rapidly in direction and speed. These obstructions range from man-made structures, like hangars, to large natural obstructions, such as mountains, bluffs, or canyons. It is especially important to be vigilant when flying in or out of airports that have large buildings or natural obstructions located near the runway.

4. Atmospheric stability, pressure, and temperature

   a) The stability of the atmosphere depends on its ability to resist vertical motion. A stable atmosphere makes vertical movement difficult, and small vertical disturbances dampen out and disappear. In an unstable atmosphere, small vertical air movements tend to become larger, resulting in turbulent airflow and convective activity. Instability can lead to significant turbulence, extensive vertical clouds, and severe weather.

   b) Rising air expands and cools due to the decrease in air pressure as altitude increases. The opposite is true of descending air; as atmospheric pressure increases, the temperature of descending air increases as it is compressed. Adiabatic heating and adiabatic cooling are terms used to describe this temperature change.

   c) The rate at which temperature decreases with an increase in altitude is referred to as its lapse rate. As air ascends through the atmosphere, the average rate of temperature change is 2 °C (3.5 °F) per 1,000 feet.

   d) Moisture

      (1) The atmosphere, by nature, contains moisture in the form of water vapor. The amount of moisture present in the atmosphere is dependent upon the temperature of the air. Every 20 °F increase in temperature doubles the amount of moisture the air can hold. Conversely, a decrease of 20 °F cuts the capacity in half.

      (2) Water is present in the atmosphere in three states: liquid, solid, and gaseous. All three forms can readily change to another, and all are present within the temperature ranges of the atmosphere. As water changes from one state to another, an exchange of heat takes place. These changes occur through the processes of evaporation, sublimation, condensation, deposition, melting, or freezing. However, water vapor is added into the atmosphere only by the processes of evaporation and sublimation.

(3) Evaporation is the changing of liquid water to water vapor. As water vapor forms, it absorbs heat from the nearest available source. This heat exchange is known as the latent heat of evaporation. A good example is the evaporation of human perspiration. The net effect is a cooling sensation as heat is extracted from the body. Similarly, sublimation is the changing of ice directly to water vapor, completely bypassing the liquid stage. Though dry ice is not made of water, but rather carbon dioxide, it demonstrates the principle of sublimation when a solid turns directly into vapor.

(4) Humidity refers to the amount of water vapor present in the atmosphere at a given time. Relative humidity is the actual amount of moisture in the air compared to the total amount of moisture the air could hold at that temperature. For example, if the current relative humidity is 65 percent, the air is holding 65 percent of the total amount of moisture that it is capable of holding at that temperature and pressure. While much of the western United States rarely sees days of high humidity, relative humidity readings of 75 to 90 percent are not uncommon in the southern United States during warmer months.

(5) The relationship between dew point and temperature defines the concept of relative humidity. The dew point, given in degrees, is the temperature at which the air can hold no more moisture. When the temperature of the air is reduced to the dew point, the air is completely saturated and moisture begins to condense out of the air in the form of fog, dew, frost, clouds, rain, or snow.

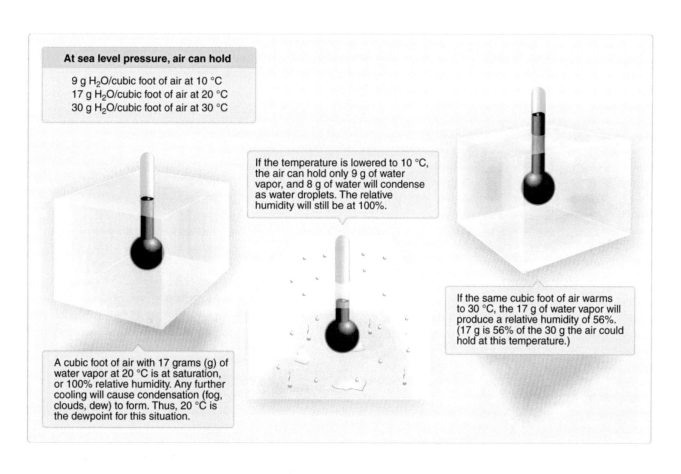

At sea level pressure, air can hold

9 g H_2O/cubic foot of air at 10 °C
17 g H_2O/cubic foot of air at 20 °C
30 g H_2O/cubic foot of air at 30 °C

If the temperature is lowered to 10 °C, the air can hold only 9 g of water vapor, and 8 g of water will condense as water droplets. The relative humidity will still be at 100%.

A cubic foot of air with 17 grams (g) of water vapor at 20 °C is at saturation, or 100% relative humidity. Any further cooling will cause condensation (fog, clouds, dew) to form. Thus, 20 °C is the dewpoint for this situation.

If the same cubic foot of air warms to 30 °C, the 17 g of water vapor will produce a relative humidity of 56%. (17 g is 56% of the 30 g the air could hold at this temperature.)

5. Air masses and fronts

a) Air masses are classified according to the regions where they originate. They are large bodies of air that take on the characteristics of the surrounding area or source region. A source region is typically an area in which the air remains relatively stagnant for a period of days or longer. During this time of stagnation, the air mass takes on the temperature and moisture characteristics of the source region. Areas of stagnation can be found in Polar Regions, tropical oceans, and dry deserts. Air masses are generally identified as polar or tropical based on temperature characteristics and maritime or continental based on moisture content.

b) A continental polar air mass forms over a polar region and brings cool, dry air with it. Maritime tropical air masses form over warm tropical waters like the Caribbean Sea and bring warm, moist air. As the air mass moves from its source region and passes over land or water, the air mass is subjected to the varying conditions of the land or water which modify the nature of the air mass.

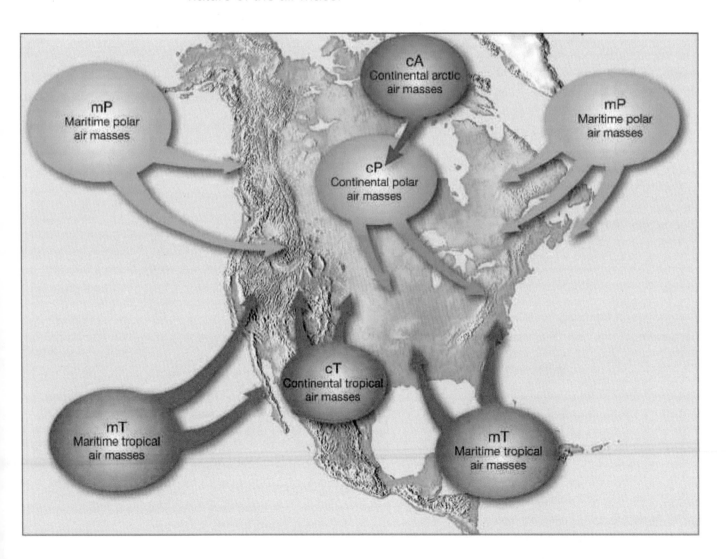

c) An air mass passing over a warmer surface is warmed from below, and convective currents form, causing the air to rise. This creates an unstable air mass with good surface visibility. Moist, unstable air causes cumulus clouds, showers, and turbulence to form.

d) Conversely, an air mass passing over a colder surface does not form convective currents but instead creates a stable air mass with poor surface visibility. The poor surface visibility is due to the fact that smoke, dust, and other particles cannot rise out of the air mass and are instead trapped near the surface. A stable air mass can produce low stratus clouds and fog.

e) Fronts:

(1) As an air mass moves across bodies of water and land, it eventually comes in contact with another air mass with different characteristics. The boundary layer between two types of air masses is known as a front. An approaching front of any type always means changes to the weather are imminent.

f) There are four types of fronts that are named according to the temperature of the advancing air relative to the temperature of the air it is replacing:

(1) Warm
(2) Cold
(3) Stationary
(4) Occluded
(5) Symbols for surface fronts

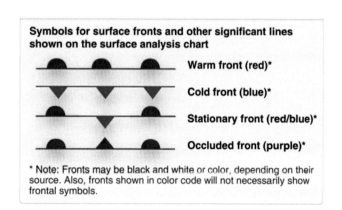

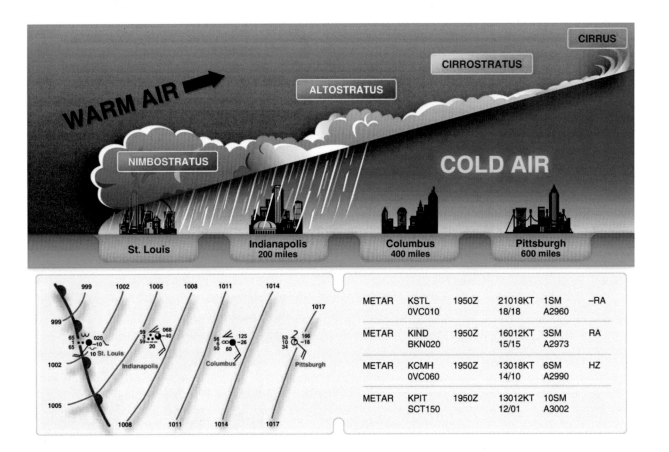

METAR	KSTL	1950Z	21018KT	1SM	−RA
	0VC010		18/18	A2960	
METAR	KIND	1950Z	16012KT	3SM	RA
	BKN020		15/15	A2973	
METAR	KCMH	1950Z	13018KT	6SM	HZ
	0VC060		14/10	A2990	
METAR	KPIT	1950Z	13012KT	10SM	
	SCT150		12/01	A3002	

6. Thunderstorms and microbursts

a) A thunderstorm makes its way through three distinct stages before dissipating. It begins with the cumulus stage, in which lifting action of the air begins. If sufficient moisture and instability are present, the clouds continue to increase in vertical height. Continuous, strong updrafts prohibit moisture from falling. Within approximately 15 minutes, the thunderstorm reaches the mature stage, which is the most violent time period of the thunderstorm's life cycle. At this point, drops of moisture, whether rain or ice, are too heavy for the cloud to support and begin falling in the form of rain or hail. This creates a downward motion of the air. Warm, rising air; cool, precipitation-induced descending air; and violent turbulence all exist within and near the cloud. Below the cloud, the down-rushing air increases surface winds and decreases the temperature. Once the vertical motion near the top of the cloud slows down, the top of the cloud spreads out and takes on an anvil-like shape. At this point, the storm enters the dissipating stage. This is when the downdrafts spread out and replace the updrafts needed to sustain the storm.

The Thunderstorm Life Cycle

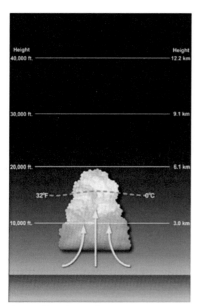

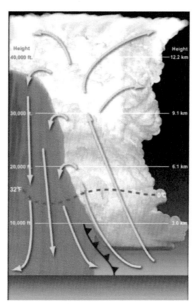

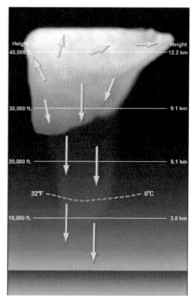

Developing Stage
- Towering cumulus cloud indicates rising air
- Usually little if any rain during this stage
- Lasts about 10 minutes
- Occasional lightning

Mature Stage
- Most likely time for hail, heavy rain, frequent lightning, strong winds, and tornadoes
- Storm occasionally has a black or dark green appearance
- Lasts an average of 10 to 20 minutes but some storms may last much longer

Dissipating Stage
- Downdrafts, downward flowing air, dominate the storm
- Rainfall decreases in intensity
- Can still produce a burst of strong winds
- Lightning remains a danger

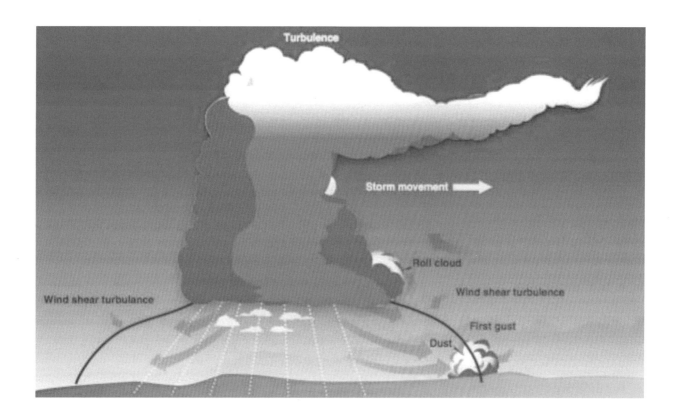

b) For a thunderstorm to form, the air must have sufficient water vapor, an unstable lapse rate, and an initial lifting action to start the storm process. Some storms occur at random in unstable air, last for only an hour or two, and produce only moderate wind gusts and rainfall. These are known as air mass thunderstorms and are generally a result of surface heating. Steady-state thunderstorms are associated with weather systems. Fronts, converging winds, and troughs aloft force upward motion spawning these storms that often form into squall lines. In the mature stage, updrafts become stronger and last much longer than in air mass storms, hence the name steady state.

c) Microbursts: The most severe type of low-level wind shear, a microburst, is associated with convective precipitation into dry air at cloud base. Microburst activity may be indicated by an intense rain shaft at the surface but virga at cloud base and a ring of blowing dust is often the only visible clue. A typical microburst has a horizontal diameter of 1–2 miles and a nominal depth of 1,000 feet. The lifespan of a microburst is about 5–15 minutes during which time it can produce downdrafts of up to 6,000 feet per minute (fpm) and headwind losses of 30–90 knots, seriously degrading performance. It can also produce strong turbulence and hazardous wind direction changes. Consider Figure 12-17: During an inadvertent takeoff into a microburst, the plane may first experience a performance-increasing headwind (1), followed by performance-decreasing downdrafts (2), followed by a rapidly increasing tailwind (3). This can result in terrain impact or flight dangerously close to the ground (4). An encounter during approach involves the same sequence of wind changes and could force the plane to the ground short of the runway.

7. Tornadoes

a) The most violent thunderstorms draw air into their cloud bases with great vigor. If the incoming air has any initial rotating motion, it often forms an extremely concentrated vortex from the surface well into the cloud. Meteorologists have estimated that wind in such a vortex can exceed 200 knots with pressure inside the vortex quite low. The strong winds gather dust and debris and the low pressure generates a funnel-shaped cloud extending downward from the cumulonimbus base. If the cloud does not reach the surface, it is a funnel cloud; if it touches a land surface, it is a tornado; and if it touches water, it is a "waterspout."

8. Icing

a) Thunderstorms are not the only area where pilots could encounter icing conditions. Pilots should be alert for icing anytime the temperature approaches 0 °C and visible moisture is present.

9. Hail

a) Hail competes with turbulence as the greatest thunderstorm hazard to aircraft. Super cooled drops above the freezing level begin to freeze. Once a drop has frozen, other drops latch on and freeze to it, so the hailstone grows—sometimes into a huge ice ball. Large hail occurs with severe thunderstorms with strong updrafts that have built to great heights. Eventually, the hailstones fall, possibly some distance from the storm core. Hail may be encountered in clear air several miles from thunderstorm clouds.

10. Fog

a) Fog is a cloud that is on the surface. It typically occurs when the temperature of air near the ground is cooled to the air's dew point. At this point, water vapor in the air condenses and becomes visible in the form of fog. Fog is classified according to the manner in which it forms and is dependent upon the current temperature and the amount of water vapor in the air.

b) On clear nights, with relatively little to no wind present, radiation fog may develop. [Figure 12-21] Usually, it forms in low-lying areas like mountain valleys. This type of fog occurs when the ground cools rapidly due to terrestrial radiation, and the surrounding air temperature reaches its dew point. As the sun rises and the temperature increases, radiation fog lifts and eventually burns off. Any increase in wind also speeds the dissipation of radiation fog. If radiation fog is less than 20 feet thick, it is known as ground fog.

c) When a layer of warm, moist air moves over a cold surface, advection fog is likely to occur. Unlike radiation fog, wind is required to form advection fog. Winds of up to 15 knots allow the fog to form and intensify; above a speed of 15 knots, the fog usually lifts and forms low stratus clouds. Advection fog is common in coastal areas where sea breezes can blow the air over cooler landmasses.

d) Upslope fog occurs when moist, stable air is forced up sloping land features like a mountain range. This type of fog also requires wind for formation and continued existence. Upslope and advection fog, unlike radiation fog, may not burn off with the morning sun but instead can persist for days. They can also extend to greater heights than radiation fog.

e) Steam fog, or sea smoke, forms when cold, dry air moves over warm water. As the water evaporates, it rises and resembles smoke. This type of fog is common over bodies of water during the coldest times of the year. Low-level turbulence and icing are commonly associated with steam fog.

f) Ice fog occurs in cold weather when the temperature is much below freezing and water vapor forms directly into ice crystals. Conditions favorable for its formation are the same as for radiation fog except for cold temperature, usually −25 °F or colder. It occurs mostly in the arctic regions but is not unknown in middle latitudes during the cold season.

11. Ceiling and visibility

a) Ceiling: For aviation purposes, a ceiling is the lowest layer of clouds reported as being broken or overcast, or the vertical visibility into an obscuration like fog or haze. Clouds are reported as broken when five-eighths to seven-eighths of the sky is covered with clouds. Overcast means the entire sky is covered with clouds. Current ceiling information is reported by the aviation routine weather report (METAR) and automated weather stations of various types.

b) Visibility: Closely related to cloud cover and reported ceilings is visibility information. Visibility refers to the greatest horizontal distance at which prominent objects can be viewed with the naked eye. Current visibility is also reported in METAR and other aviation weather reports, as well as by automated weather systems. Visibility information, as predicted by meteorologists, is available for a pilot during a preflight weather briefing.

12. Lightning

a) A lightning strike can puncture the skin of an aircraft and damage communications and electronic navigational equipment. Although lightning has been suspected of igniting fuel vapors and causing an explosion, serious accidents due to lightning strikes are rare. Nearby lightning can blind the pilot, rendering him or her momentarily unable to navigate either by instrument or by visual reference. Nearby lightning can also induce permanent errors in the magnetic compass. Lightning discharges, even distant ones, can disrupt radio communications on low and medium frequencies. Though lightning intensity and frequency have no simple relationship to other storm parameters, severe storms, as a rule, have a high frequency of lightning.

QUIZ QUESTIONS - Weather

1. The presence of ice pellets at the surface is evidence that there
    A. are thunderstorms in the area
    B. is a temperature inversion with freezing rain at a higher altitude
    C. has been cold frontal passage

2. The minimum distance from clouds required for sUAS part 107 operations is
    A. 500 feet below, 2,000 feet horizontally
    B. clear of clouds
    C. 500 feet above, 1,000 feet horizontally

3. What is the best way for a remote pilot to determine the likelihood of local fog formation?
    A. Monitor the wind conditions to insure the wind speed is not increasing
    B. Monitor the barometric pressure to ensure that it is not decreasing
    C. Monitor the temperature / dew point spread

4. Which weather phenomenon is always associated with a thunderstorm?
    A. Heavy rain
    B. Hail
    C. Lightning

5. What effect does high density altitude have on the efficiency of a UA propeller?
    A. Density altitude does not affect propeller efficiency
    B. Propeller efficiency is increased
    C. Propeller efficiency is decreased

6. What are characteristics of a moist, unstable air mass?
    A. Turbulence and showery precipitation
    B. Poor visibility and smooth air
    C. Haze and smoke

7. In which environment is aircraft structural ice most likely to have the accumulation rate?
    A. Cumulus clouds with below freezing temperatures
    B. Freezing rain
    C. Freezing drizzle

8. One weather phenomenon which will always occur when flying across a front is a change in
    A. wind direction
    B. type of precipitation
    C. stability of the air mass

9. A stable air mass is most likely to have which characteristic?
    A. Showery precipitation
    B. Poor surface visibility
    C. Turbulent air

10. What is the expected duration of an individual microburst?
    A. Two minutes with maximum winds lasting approximately 1 minute
    B. One microburst may continue for as long as 2 to 4 hours
    C. Seldom longer than 15 minutes from the time the burst strikes the ground until dissipation

USE THE FOLLOWING IMAGE FOR QUESTIONS 11, 12, AND 14:

TAF

KMEM 121720Z 1218/1324 20012KT 5SM HZ BKN030 PROB40 2022 1SM TSRA OVC008CB
    FM2200 33015G20KT P6SM BKN015 OVC025 PROB40 2202 3SM SHRA
    FM0200 35012KT OVC008 PROB40 0205 2SM-RASN BECMG 0608 02008KT BKN012
    BECMG 1310/1312 00000KT 3SM BR SKC TEMPO 1212/1214 1/2SM FG
    FM131600 VRB06KT P6SM SKC=

KOKC 051130Z 0512/0618 14008KT 5SM BR BKN030 TEMPO 0513/0516 1 1/2SM BR
    FM051600 18010KT P6SM SKC BECMG 0522/0524 20013G20KT 4SM SHRA OVC020
    PROB40 0600/0606 2SM TSRA OVC008CB BECMG 0606/0608 21015KT P6SM SCT040=

11. Between 1000Z and 1200Z the visibility at KMEM is forecast to be
    A. 3 statute miles
    B. 1/2 statute mile
    C. 6 statute miles

12. In the TAF for KMEM, what does " SHRA" stand for?
    A. A significant change in precipitation is possible
    B. A shift in wind direction is expected
    C. Rain Showers

13. What minimum visibility is required for sUAS operations?
    A. 4 miles
    B. 1 miles
    C. 3 miles

14. What is the forecast wind for KMEM from 1600Z until the end of the forecast?
    A. No significant wind
    B. Variable in direction at 6 knots
    C. Variable in direction at 4 knots

15. What measurement can be used to determine the stability of the atmosphere?
    A. Actual lapse rate
    B. Atmospheric pressure
    C. Surface temperature

16. Which factor would tend to increase the density altitude at a given airport referenced in the weather briefing?
    A. An increase in barometric pressure
    B. An increase in ambient temperature
    C. A decrease in relative humidity

17. Low level turbulence can occur and icing can become hazardous in which type of fog?
    A. Rain induced fog
    B. Steam Fog
    C. Upslope Fog

18. The wind direction and velocity at KJFK is from:

METAR KINK 121845Z 11012G18KT 15SM SKC 25/17 A3000

METAR KBOI 121854Z 13004KT 30SM SCT150 17/6 A3015

METAR KLAX 121852Z 25004KT 6SM BR SCT007 SCT250 16/15 A2991

SPECI KMDW 121856Z 32005KT 1 1/2SM RA OVC007 17/16 A2980 RMK RAB35

SPECI KJFK 121853Z 18004KT 1/2SM FG R04/2200 OVC005 20/18 A3006

    A. 180 degrees true at 4 knots
    B. 180 degrees magnetic at 4 knots
    C. 040 degrees true at 18 knots.

19. During the life cycle of a thunderstorm, which stage is characterized predominately by downdrafts?
    A. Cumulus
    B. Dissipating
    C. Mature

20. A strong steady wind exists out of the north. You need to photograph an area to the south of your location. You are located in an open field with no obstructions. Which of the following is not a concern during this operation?
    A. Turbulent conditions will likely be a significant factor during the operation
    B. Strong wind conditions may consume more battery power at a faster rate than in calm Conditions
    C. Strong wind may exceed the performance of the sUAS making it impossible to recover

21. What situation is most conducive to the formation of radiation fog?
    A. Moist, tropical air moving over cold offshore water
    B. The movement of cold air over much warmer water
    C. Warm, moist air over low, flatland areas on clear, calm nights

22. What causes variations in altimeter settings between weather reporting points?
    A. Unequal heating of the Earth's surface
    B. Variation of terrain elevation
    C. Coriolis force

23. Thunderstorms which generally produce the most intense hazard to aircraft are
    A. steady state thunderstorms
    B. warm front thunderstorms
    C. squall line thunderstorms

24. What conditions are necessary for the formation of thunderstorms?
    A. High humidity, lifting force, and unstable conditions
    B. High humidity, high temperature, and cumulus clouds
    C. Lifting force, moist air, and extensive cloud cover

25. What feature is normally associated with the cumulus stage of a thunderstorm?
    A. Roll cloud
    B. Continuous updraft
    C. Frequent lightning

26. Which of the following considerations is most relevant to a remote PIC when evaluating unmanned aircraft performance?
    A. The number of available ground crew
    B. The type of sUAS operation
    C. Current weather conditions

27. What types of fog depend upon wind in order to exist?
    A. Radiation fog and ice fog
    B. Steam fog and ground fog
    C. Advection fog and upslope fog

28. Thunderstorms reach their greatest intensity during the
    A. mature stage
    B. downdraft stage
    C. cumulus stage

29. A non-frontal, narrow band of active thunderstorms that often develop ahead of a cold front is known as
    A. squall line
    B. prefrontal system
    C. dry line

30. One in-flight condition necessary for structural icing to form is
    A. small temperature dew point spread
    B. visible moisture
    C. stratiform clouds

31. If the outside air temperature (OAT) at a given altitude is warmer than standard, the density altitude is
    A. higher than pressure altitude
    B. equal to pressure altitude
    C. lower than pressure altitude

32. Upon your preflight evaluation of weather, the forecasts you reference state there is an unstable air mass approaching your location. Which would not be a concern for your impending operation?
    A. Thunderstorms
    B. Turbulent conditions
    C. Stratiform clouds

33. Over which area should a remote pilot expect to find the highest amount of thermal currents under normal conditions?

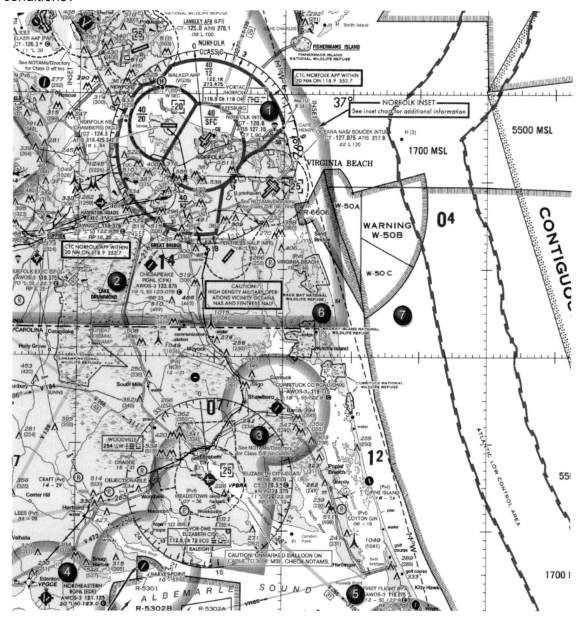

    A. 2
    B. 7
    C. 5

34. According to the KMEM forecast, what is the earliest time on the 12th (today) at which the visibility may be reduced below the 3SM minimum for sUAS operations?

TAF

KMEM 121720Z 1218/1324 20012KT 5SM HZ BKN030 PROB40 2022 1SM TSRA OVC008CB
    FM2200 33015G20KT P6SM BKN015 OVC025 PROB40 2202 3SM SHRA
    FM0200 35012KT OVC008 PROB40 0205 2SM-RASN BECMG 0608 02008KT BKN012
    BECMG 1310/1312 00000KT 3SM BR SKC TEMPO 1212/1214 1/2SM FG
    FM131600 VRB06KT P6SM SKC=

KOKC 051130Z 0512/0618 14008KT 5SM BR BKN030 TEMPO 0513/0516 1 1/2SM BR
    FM051600 18010KT P6SM SKC BECMG 0522/0524 20013G20KT 4SM SHRA OVC020
    PROB40 0600/0606 2SM TSRA OVC008CB BECMG 0606/0608 21015KT P6SM SCT040=

    A. 2000Z
    B. 1720Z
    C. 2200Z

35. The development of thermals depends upon
    A. a counterclockwise circulation of air
    B. temperature inversions
    C. solar heating

36. What are the characteristics of stable air?
    A. Good visibility and steady precipitation
    B. Poor visibility and steady precipitation
    C. Poor visibility and intermittent precipitation

37. While operating around buildings, the remote PIC should be aware of the creation of wind gusts that
    A. enhance stability and imagery
    B. change rapidly in direction and speed causing turbulence
    C. increase performance of the aircraft

38. An air mass moving inland from the coast in winter is likely to result in
    A. fog
    B. rain
    C. frost

39. In which situation is advection fog most likely to form?
    A. A warm, moist air mass on the windward side of mountains
    B. An air mass moving inland from the coast in winter
    C. A light breeze blowing colder air out to sea

40. If there is thunderstorm activity in the vicinity of an airport at which you plan to land, which hazardous atmospheric phenomenon might be expected during recovery/landing of the sUAS?
    A. Wind-shear turbulence
    B. Precipitation static
    C. Steady Rain

41. Which weather phenomenon signals the beginning of the mature stage of a thunderstorm?
    A. the appearance of an anvil top
    B. maximum growth rate of the clouds
    C. Precipitation beginning to fall

42. What are the standard temperatures and pressure values for sea level?
    A. 59 degrees C and 1013.2 millibars
    B. 59 degrees C and 29.92 millibars
    C. 15 degrees C and 29.92 Hg

43. What are the current conditions for Chicago Midway Airport (KMDW)?

METAR KINK 121845Z 11012G18KT 15SM SKC 25/17 A3000

METAR KBOI 121854Z 13004KT 30SM SCT150 17/6 A3015

METAR KLAX 121852Z 25004KT 6SM BR SCT007 SCT250 16/15 A2991

SPECI KMDW 121856Z 32005KT 1 1/2SM RA OVC007 17/16 A2980 RMK RAB35

SPECI KJFK 121853Z 18004KT 1/2SM FG R04/2200 OVC005 20/18 A3006

    A. Sky 700 feet overcast, visibility 1-1/2 SM, rain
    B. Sky 7,000 feet overcast, visibility 1-1/2 SM, heavy rain
    C. Sky 700 feet overcast, visibility 11, occasionally 2 SM, with rain

44. To get a complete weather overview for the planned flight, the remote pilot in command should obtain
    A. An outlook briefing
    B. a standard briefing
    C. An abbreviated briefing

45. What would decrease the stability of an air mass?
    A. Warming from below
    B. Cooling from below
    C. Decrease in water vapor

46. One of the most easily recognized discontinuities across a front is
    A. a change in temperature
    B. an increase in cloud coverage
    C. an increase in relative humidity

47. Which statement is true concerning ASOS/AWOS weather reporting systems?
    A. Each AWOS station is part of a nationwide of weather reporting stations
    B. ASOS locations perform weather observing functions necessary to generate METAR reports
    C. Both ASOS and AWOS have the capability of reporting density altitude, as long as it exceeds the airport elevation by more than 1,000 feet.

48. Which is considered to be the most hazardous condition when flying an sUAS in the vicinity of thunderstorms?
    A. Static electricity
    B. Lightning
    C. Wind shear and turbulence

49. How would high density altitude affect the performance of a small unmanned aircraft?
    A. No change in performance
    B. Increased performance
    C. Decreased performance

50. Which type of weather phenomenon that may concern a remote pilot is common among cold fronts?
    A. Thunderstorms and heavy rain
    B. Long term periods of reduced visibility
    C. Long periods of steady precipitation

51. Every physical process of weather is accompanied by, or is the result of, a
    A. movement of air
    B. pressure differential
    C. Heat exchange

52. In what stage are thunderstorms the strongest?
    A. Raining
    B. Dissipating
    C. Building

53. What is the minimum base of the cloud layer to fly to the top of the towers 4 NM east of Onawa?

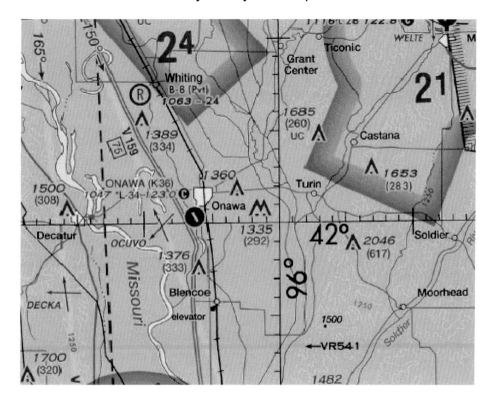

    A. 792 feet AGL
    B. 292 feet AGL
    C. 1,335 feet MSL

54. A non-frontal, narrow band of active thunderstorms that often develop ahead of a cold front is known as a

    A. prefrontal system
    B. squall line
    C. dry line

55. What are the VFR minimum visibility requirements over Plantation Airport?

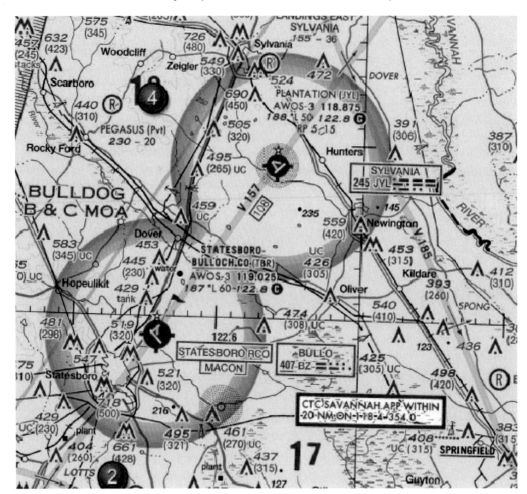

A. 1 SM
B. 5 SM
C. 3 SM

56. Where are squalls most likely to form?
   A. High altitude
   B. Low altitude
   C. At any altitude

57. What will a convective SIGMET be issued for?
   A. Squall line thunderstorms
   B. Visibility less than 3 miles
   C. Surface winds greater than 40 knots

58 What affect does humidity have on performance?
   A. It has no effect on performance
   B. It increases performance
   C. It decreases performance

59. Clouds, fog, or dew will always form when
    A. water vapor condenses
    B. water vapor is present
    C. relative humidity reaches 100 percent

60. What weather provides the best flying conditions?
    A. Warm, moist air
    B. Cool, dry air
    C. Turbulence

61. You are inspecting the lighted towers approximately 8 NM SW of the Corpus Christi Intl airport (CRP). What is the lowest cloud cover that will enable you to inspect the top of the tower?

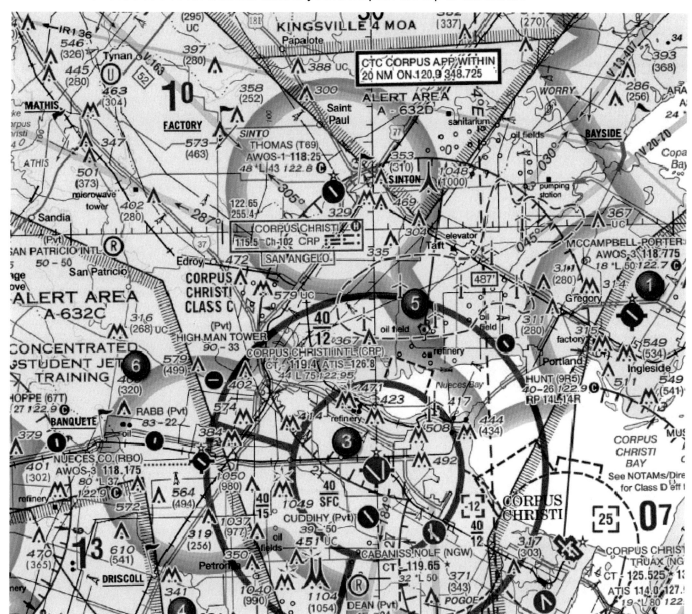

    A. 1,104 feet MSL
    B. 1,604 feet MSL
    C. 1,054 feet MSL

62. You have received an outlook briefing from flight service through 1800wxbrief.com. The briefing indicates you can expect a low-level temperature inversion with high relative humidity. What weather conditions would you expect?
   A. Smooth air, poor visibility, fog, haze, or low clouds
   B. Light wind shear, poor visibility, haze, and light rain
   C. Turbulent air, poor visibility, fog, low stratus type clouds, and showery precipitation

63. The remarks section for KMDW has "RAB35" listed. This entry means

METAR KINK 121845Z 11012G18KT 15SM SKC 25/17 A3000

METAR KBOI 121854Z 13004KT 30SM SCT150 17/6 A3015

METAR KLAX 121852Z 25004KT 6SM BR SCT007 SCT250 16/15 A2991

SPECI KMDW 121856Z 32005KT 1 1/2SM RA OVC007 17/16 A2980 RMK RAB35

SPECI KJFK 121853Z 18004KT 1/2SM FG R04/2200 OVC005 20/18 A3006

   A. blowing mist has reduced the visibility to 1-1/2 SM
   B. rain began at 1835Z
   C. the barometer has risen .35" Hg

64. Wind shear can exist
   A. at all altitudes
   B. at low altitudes
   C. at high altitudes

65. What environment is most conducive to frost formation?
   A. Dewpoint of surface is below freezing, dewpoint is above freezing
   B. Surface temperature is below freezing, air temperature is below freezing
   C. Surface temperature above is freezing, air temperature is below freezing

66. The weather report lists the ceiling at 800 feet. What is the highest you can operate your sUAS?
   A. 200 feet AGL
   B. 800 feet AGL
   C. 300 feet AGL

67. The zone between different temperature, humidity, and wind is called
   A. A front
   B. An air mass
   C. Wind shear

IV. Loading & Performance (Section 4)

A. General loading and performance

1. Load is the force or imposed stress that must be supported by an sUAS structure in flight. Load factor refers to the loads imposed on the wings or rotors in flight. In straight-and-level flight, the sUAS wings/rotors support a load equal to the sum of the weight of the sUAS plus its contents. However, when flying in a non-straight or non-level path, such as turning, climbing or descending, centrifugal force is generated, acting towards the outside of the maneuver.

2. Thus, unmanned aircraft performance can decrease due to an increase in the load factor when flying using non-linear maneuvers. The load factor increases at a significant rate after a bank (turn) has reached 45° or 50°. The load factor for any aircraft in a coordinated level turn at 60° bank is 2 Gs. The load factor in an 80° bank is 5.75 Gs. See the following chart.

Angle of bank ϕ	Load factor n
0°	1.0
10°	1.015
30°	1.154
45°	1.414
60°	2.000
70°	2.923
80°	5.747
85°	11.473
90°	∞

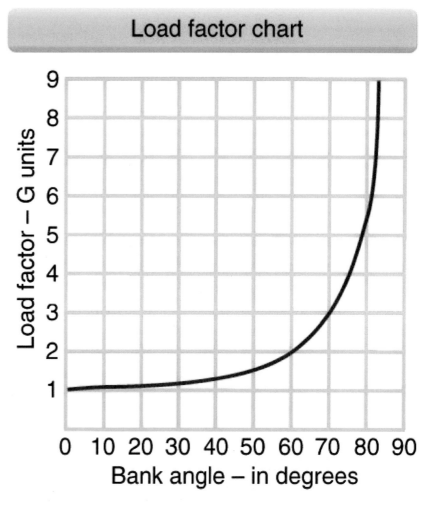

Load factor chart

3. As with manned aircraft, a UAV will stall when the critical angle of attack of the wing or rotors/propeller is exceeded. This can occur when an unmanned aircraft is turned too sharply/tightly or pitched up too steeply or rapidly. Remote pilots of rotor type unmanned aircraft should use caution when descending in a vertical straight line. In some cases, the turbulent downward airflow can disrupt the normal production of lift by the propellers as well as cause problematic air circulation producing vortices. These phenomena are referred to as vortex ring state or settling with power, and when they occur the aircraft can wobble, descend rapidly, or become uncontrollable. Recovery from this state of flight requires forward or rearward motion—counterintuitively, the addition of power to arrest the descent only makes the situation worse. Due to the low-altitude operating environment, consideration should be given to ensure aircraft control is maintained and the aircraft is not operated outside its performance limits. The wing must produce lift equal to these load factors if altitude is to be maintained. The remote PIC should be mindful of the increased load factor and its possible effects on the aircraft's structural integrity and the results of an increase in stall speed. These principles apply to both fixed wing and rotor wing designs, but in the case of rotor wing type unmanned aircraft, the weight/load must be supported by the lift generated by the propellers.

4. As the angle of attack is increased (to increase lift), the air will no longer flow smoothly over the upper airfoil surface but instead will become turbulent or "burble" near the trailing edge. A further increase in the angle of attack will cause the turbulent area to expand forward. At an angle of attack of approximately 18° to 20° (for most airfoils), turbulence over the upper wing surface decreases lift so drastically that flight cannot be sustained and the airfoil "stalls." See the figure below. The angle at which a stall occurs is called the critical angle of attack. An unmanned aircraft can stall at any airspeed or any attitude, but will always stall at the same critical angle of attack. The critical angle of attack of an airfoil is a function of its design therefore does not change based upon weight, maneuvering, or density altitude. However, the airspeed (strength of the relative wind) at which a given aircraft will stall in a particular configuration, however, will remain the same regardless of altitude.

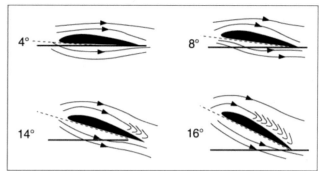

5. Because air density decreases with an increase in altitude, an unmanned aircraft must have greater forward speed to encounter the same strength of relative wind as would be experienced with the thicker air at lower altitudes.

6. Before any flight, the remote PIC should verify the aircraft is correctly loaded by determining the W&B condition of the aircraft. An aircraft's W&B restrictions established by the manufacturer or the builder should be closely followed. Compliance with the manufacturer's W&B limits is critical to flight safety. The remote PIC must consider the consequences of an overweight aircraft if an emergency condition arises.

B. Effects of loading changes

1. Although a maximum gross takeoff weight may be specified, the aircraft may not always safely take off with this load under all conditions. Conditions that affect takeoff and climb performance, such as high elevations, high air temperatures, and high humidity (high density altitudes) may require a reduction in weight before flight is attempted. Other factors to consider prior to takeoff are runway/launch area length, surface, slope, surface wind, and the presence of obstacles. These factors may require a reduction in weight prior to flight.

2. Weight changes during flight also have a direct effect on aircraft performance. Fuel burn is the most common weight change that takes place during flight. As fuel is used, the aircraft becomes lighter and performance is improved, but this could have a negative effect on balance. In UAS operations, weight change during flight may occur when expendable items are used on board (e.g., a jettisonable load).

C. Balance stability and center of gravity

1. Adverse balance conditions (i.e., weight distribution) may affect flight characteristics in much the same manner as those mentioned for an excess weight condition. Limits for the location of the CG may be established by the manufacturer. The CG is not a fixed point marked on the aircraft; its location depends on the distribution of aircraft weight. As variable load items are shifted or expended, there may be a resultant shift in CG location. The remote PIC should determine how the CG will shift and the resultant effects on the aircraft. If the CG is not within the allowable limits after loading or do not remain within the allowable limits for safe flight, it will be necessary to relocate or shed some weight before flight is attempted.

D. The importance and use of performance data to predict the effect on the aircraft's performance of an sUAS

1. The manufacturer may provide operational and performance information that contains the operational performance data for the aircraft such as data pertaining to takeoff, climb, range, endurance, descent, and landing. To be able to make practical use of the aircraft's capabilities and limitations, it is essential to understand the significance of the operational data. The use of this data in flying operations is essential for safe and efficient operation. It should be emphasized that the manufacturers' information regarding performance data is not standardized. If manufacturer-published performance data is unavailable, it is advisable to seek out performance data that may have already been determined and published by other users of the same sUAS manufacturer model and use that data as a starting point.

QUIZ QUESTIONS – Loading & Performance

1. When loading cameras or other equipment on an sUAS, mount the items in a manner that:
   - A. Does not adversely affect the center of gravity
   - B. Is visible to the visual observer or other crewmembers
   - C. Can be easily removed without the use of tools

2. Which of the following is true regarding weight and balance of small unmanned aircraft?
   - A. Operations outside weight and balance limitations may result in loss of control
   - B. CG cannot change during flight
   - C. Lateral CG is not important to small unmanned aircraft operations.

3. A stall occurs when the smooth airflow over the unmanned aircraft's wing/ propeller(s) is disrupted and the lift reduces rapidly. this is caused when the wing/ propeller (s)
   - A. exceeds maximum allowable operating weight
   - B. exceeds critical angle of attack
   - C. exceeds the maximum speed

4. Maximum endurance is obtained at the point of minimum power to maintain the aircraft
   - A. in a long range descent
   - B. in steady, level flight
   - C. at its slowest possible indicated airspeed

5. When range and economy of operation are the principal goals, the remote pilot must ensure that the sUAS will be operated at the recommended
   - A. long range cruise performance
   - B. specific endurance
   - C. equivalent airspeed

6. What is the best source for sUAS performance data and information?
   - A. Pilot report
   - B. Estimates based upon similar systems
   - C. Manufacturer publications

7. If an sUAS weighs 10 pounds, what approximate weight would the sUAS structure be required to support during a 60 degrees banked turn while maintaining altitude?

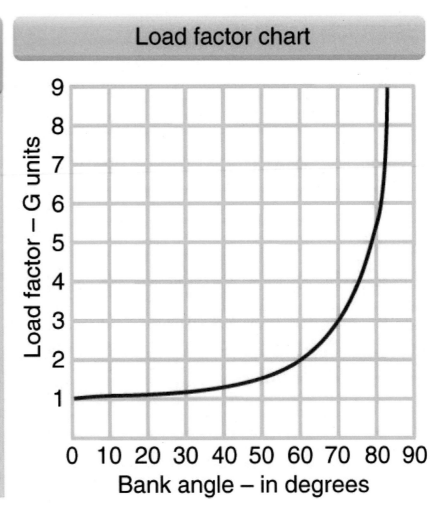

Angle of bank ϕ	Load factor n
0°	1.0
10°	1.015
30°	1.154
45°	1.414
60°	2.000
70°	2.923
80°	5.747
85°	11.473
90°	∞

A. 30 pounds
B. 20 pounds
C. 10.15 pounds

8. What effect does an uphill terrain slope have on launch performance?
    A. Increases launch distance
    B. increase launch speed
    C. decreases launch distances

9. When operating an unmanned aircraft, the remote pilot-in-command should consider that the load factor on the wings or rotors may be increased anytime:
    A. the CG is shifted rearward to the aft CG limit
    B. the gross weight is reduced
    C. the aircraft is subjected to maneuvers other than straight and level flight

10. The most critical conditions of launch performance are the result of some combination of high gross weight, altitude, temperature and
    A. obstacles surrounding the launch site
    B. power plant systems
    C. unfavorable wind

11. Before each flight the remote PIC must ensure that:
    A. objects carried on the sUAS are secure
    B. ATC has granted clearance
    C. the site supervisor has approved the flight

12. An increase in load factor will cause an unmanned aircraft to
    A. have a tendency to spin
    B. stall at a higher airspeed
    C. be more difficult to control

13. You are operating an sUAS that does not have GPS or an installed altimeter. How can you determine the altitude you are operating?
    A. Operating a second sUAS that has an altimeter to gain a visual perspective of 400 feet from the air
    B. Operating the sUAS in close proximity of a tower known to be 400 feet tall
    C. Gaining a visual perspective of what 400 feet looks like on the ground before the flight

14. If an unmanned airplane weighs 33 pounds, what approximate weight would the airplane structure be required to support during a 30 degree banked turn while maintaining altitude?

Angle of bank Φ	Load factor n
0°	1.0
10°	1.015
30°	1.154
45°	1.414
60°	2.000
70°	2.923
80°	5.747
85°	11.473
90°	∞

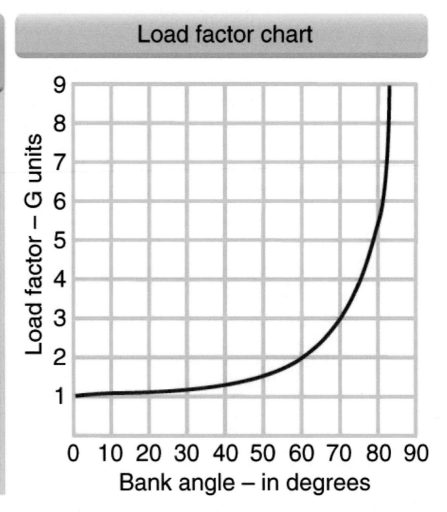

Load factor chart

Load factor – G units vs. Bank angle – in degrees

A. 38 pounds
B. 34 pounds
C. 47 pounds

15. The angle of attack at which an airfoil stalls will
   A. increase if the CG is moved forward
   B. remain the same regardless of gross weight
   C. change with an increase in gross weight

16. You are operating an sUAS that does not have GPS or an installed ground speed limiter. How can you determine the speed you are operating?
   A. Dead reckoning
   B. Pilotage
   C. Wind triangle

17. The amount of excess load that can be imposed on the wing of an airplane depends upon the
   A. position of the CG
   B. speed of the airplane
   C. abruptness at which the load is applied

18. The term "angle of attack" is defined as the angle
    A. between the wing chord line and the relative wind
    B. between the airplane's climb angle and the horizon
    C. formed by the longitudinal axis of the airplane and the chord line of the wing

19. What could be a consequence of operating a small unmanned aircraft above its maximum allowable weight?
    A. increased maneuverability
    B. faster speed
    C. shorter endurance

20. How can a remote pilot determine the altitude of the terrain and structure where the flight will be conducted?
    A. Manufacturer data
    B. Road trips
    C. Sectional chart

21. If an sUAS weighs 50 pounds, what approximate weight would the sUAS structure be required to support during a 30 degree banked turn while maintaining altitude?

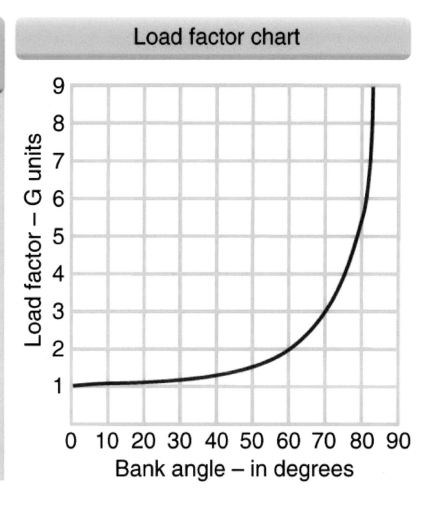

Angle of bank ϕ	Load factor n
0°	1.0
10°	1.015
30°	1.154
45°	1.414
60°	2.000
70°	2.923
80°	5.747
85°	11.473
90°	∞

    A. 60 pounds
    B. 45 pounds
    C. 30 pounds

22. Which basic flight maneuver increases the load factor on an sUAS as compared to straight-level flight?
   A. Climbs
   B. Turns
   C. Stalls

23. To ensure that the unmanned aircraft center of gravity (CG) limits are not exceeded, follow the aircraft loading instructions specified in the
   A. Pilot's Operating Handbook or UAS Flight Manual
   B. Aircraft Weight and Balance Handbook
   C. Aeronautical information Manual (AIM)

24. When operating an aircraft, the Remote PIC is responsible for using
   A. weight and balance data from the factory
   B. recent weight and balance data
   C. the most current weight and balance data

25. According to 14 CFR Part 107, who is responsible for determining the performance of a small unmanned aircraft?
   A. Manufacturer
   B. Remote pilot-in-command
   C. Owner or operator

26. What purpose does a rudder perform on an sUAS airplane?
   A. The rudder controls yaw
   B. The rudder controls bank
   C. The rudder controls pitch

27. How can a remote pilot determine the altitude of the terrain and structures where the flight will be conducted
   A. Sectional chart
   B. Manufacturers data
   C. Road maps

28. In a 45 degree banking turn, a UAV will
   A. be more susceptible to spinning
   B. stall at a higher speed
   C. Stall at a lower airspeed

V. Operations (Section 5)

A. Radio communications procedures

1. Radio requirements and procedures

a) Operating in and out of a towered airport, as well as in a good portion of the airspace system, requires that an aircraft have two- way radio communication capability. For this reason, a pilot should be knowledgeable of radio station license requirements and radio communications equipment and procedures.

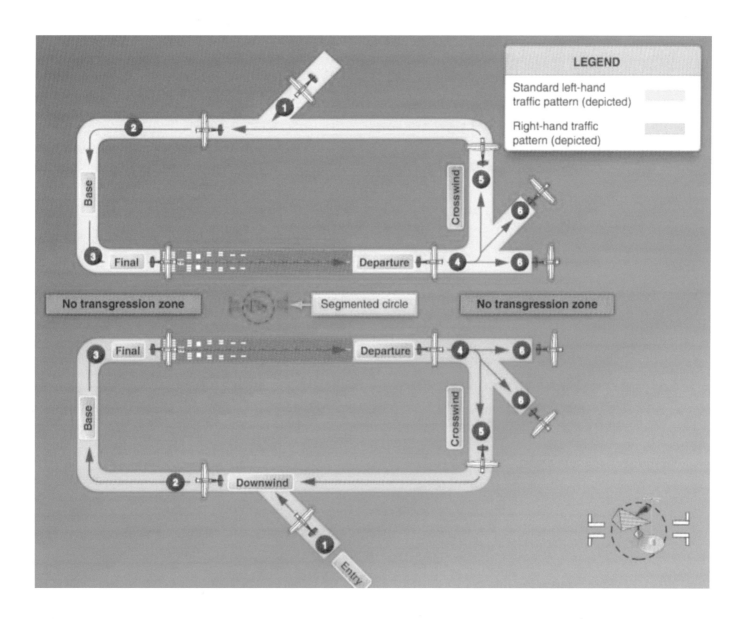

b) There is no license requirement for a pilot operating in the United States; however, a pilot who operates internationally is required to hold a restricted radiotelephone permit issued by the Federal Communications Commission (FCC). There is also no station license requirement for most general aviation aircraft operating in the United States. A station license is required, however, for an aircraft that is operating internationally, that uses other than a VHF radio, and that meets other criteria.

c) AC 1072

2. Airport operations with and without an operating control tower

a) Towered airport: A towered airport has an operating control tower. Air traffic control (ATC) is responsible for providing the safe, orderly, and expeditious flow of air traffic at airports where the type of operations and/or volume of traffic requires such a service. Pilots operating from a towered airport are required to maintain two-way radio communication with ATC and to acknowledge and comply with their instructions. Pilots must advise ATC if they cannot comply with the instructions issued and request amended instructions. A pilot may deviate from an air traffic instruction in an emergency, but must advise ATC of the deviation as soon as possible.

b) Uncontrolled or un-towered airport: A non-towered airport does not have an operating control tower. Two-way radio communications are not required, although it is a good operating practice for pilots to transmit their intentions on the specified frequency for the benefit of other traffic in the area. The key to communicating at an airport without an operating control tower is selection of the correct common frequency. The acronym CTAF, which stands for Common Traffic Advisory Frequency, is synonymous with this program.

3. The description and use of Common Traffic Advisory Frequency (CTAF) to monitor manned aircraft communications

a) A CTAF is a frequency designated for the purpose of carrying out airport advisory practices while operating to or from an airport without an operating control tower. The CTAF may be a Universal Integrated Community (UNICOM), MULTICOM, Flight Service Station (FSS), or tower frequency and is identified in appropriate aeronautical publications. UNICOM is a nongovernment air/ground radio communication station that may provide airport information at public use airports where there is no tower or FSS. On pilot request, UNICOM stations may provide pilots with weather information, wind direction, the recommended runway, or other necessary information. If the UNICOM frequency is designated as the CTAF, it is identified in appropriate aeronautical publications.

4. Recommended traffic advisory procedures used by manned aircraft pilots, such as self-announcing of position and intentions

    a) Non-towered airport traffic patterns are always entered at pattern altitude. How you enter the pattern depends upon the direction of arrival. The preferred method for entering from the downwind side of the pattern is to approach the pattern on a course 45 degrees to the downwind leg and join the pattern at midfield.

    b) There are several ways to enter the pattern if you're coming from the upwind leg side of the airport.

    c) In either case, it is vital to announce your intentions, and remember to scan outside. Before joining the downwind leg, adjust your course or speed to blend into the traffic. Adjust power on the downwind leg, or sooner, to fit into the flow of traffic. Avoid flying too fast or too slow. Speeds recommended by the airplane manufacturer should be used. They will generally fall between 70 to 80 knots for fixed-gear singles and 80 to 90 knots for high-performance retractable.

5. Aeronautical advisory communications station (UNICOM) and associated communication procedures used by manned aircraft pilots

    a) UNICOM is a nongovernment air/ground radio communication station that may provide airport information at public use airports where there is no tower or FSS

Radar Beacon Phraseology	
SQUAWK (number)	Operate radar beacon transponder on designated code in MODE A/3.
IDENT	Engage the "IDENT" feature (military I/P) of the transponder.
SQUAWK (number) and IDENT	Operate transponder on specified code in MODE A/3 and engage the "IDENT" (military I/P) feature.
SQUAWK Standby	Switch transponder to standby position.
SQUAWK Low/Normal	Operate transponder on low or normal sensitivity as specified. Transponder is operated in "NORMAL" position unless ATC specifies "LOW" ("ON" is used instead of "NORMAL" as a master control label on some types of transponders).
SQUAWK Altitude	Activate MODE C with automatic altitude reporting.
STOP Altitude SQUAWK	Turn off altitude reporting switch and continue transmitting MODE C framing pulses. If your equipment does not have this capability, turn off MODE C.
STOP SQUAWK (mode in use)	Switch off specified mode. (Used for military aircraft when the controller is unaware of military service requirements for the aircraft to continue operation on another MODE.)
STOP SQUAWK	Switch off transponder.
SQUAWK Mayday	Operate transponder in the emergency position (MODE A Code 7700 for civil transponder, MODE 3 Code 7700 and emergency feature for military transponder).
SQUAWK VFR	Operate radar beacon transponder on Code 1200 in MODE A/3, or other appropriate VFR code.

6. Automatic Terminal Information Service (ATIS)

a) The Automated Terminal Information Service (ATIS) is a recording of the local weather conditions and other pertinent non-control information broadcast on a local frequency in a looped format. It is normally updated once per hour but is updated more often when changing local conditions warrant. Important information is broadcast on ATIS including weather, runways in use, specific ATC procedures, and any airport construction activity that could affect taxi planning.

b) When the ATIS is recorded, it is given a code. This code is changed with every ATIS update. For example, ATIS Alpha is replaced by ATIS Bravo. The next hour, ATIS Charlie is recorded, followed by ATIS Delta and progresses down the alphabet.

c) Prior to calling ATC, tune to the A TIS frequency and listen to the recorded broadcast. The broadcast ends with a statement containing the ATIS code. For example, "Advise on initial contact, you have information Bravo." Upon contacting the tower controller, state information Bravo was received. This allows the tower controller to verify the pilot has the current local weather and airport information without having to state it all to each pilot who calls. This also clears the tower frequency from being overtaken by the constant relay of the same information, which would result without an ATIS broadcast. The use of A TIS broadcasts at departure and arrival airports is not only a sound practice but a wise decision.

7. Aircraft call signs and registration numbers

a) Before an aircraft can be flown legally, it must be registered with the FAA Aircraft Registry. The Certificate of Aircraft Registration, which is issued to the owner as evidence of the registration, must be carried in the aircraft at all times.

b) A small UA must be registered, as provided for in 14 CFR part 47 or part 48 prior to operating under part 107. Part 48 is the regulation that establishes the streamlined online registration option for sUAS that will be operated only within the 5-26/21/16 AC 107-2 territorial limits of the United States. The online registration Web address is http://www.faa.gov/uas/registration/. Guidance regarding sUAS registration and marking may be found at http://www.faa.gov/licenses_certificates/aircraft_certification/ aircraft_registry/. Alternatively, sUAS can elect to register under part 47 in the same manner as manned aircraft.

8. The phonetic alphabet

Character	Morse Code	Telephony	Phonic (Pronunciation)
A	•—	Alfa	(AL-FAH)
B	—•••	Bravo	(BRAH-VOH)
C	—•—•	Charlie	(CHAR-LEE) or (SHAR-LEE)
D	—••	Delta	(DELL-TAH)
E	•	Echo	(ECK-OH)
F	••—•	Foxtrot	(FOKS-TROT)
G	——•	Golf	(GOLF)
H	••••	Hotel	(HOH-TEL)
I	••	India	(IN-DEE-AH)
J	•———	Juliett	(JEW-LEE-ETT)
K	—•—	Kilo	(KEY-LOH)
L	•—••	Lima	(LEE-MAH)
M	——	Mike	(MIKE)
N	—•	November	(NO-VEM-BER)
O	———	Oscar	(OSS-CAH)
P	•——•	Papa	(PAH-PAH)
Q	——•—	Quebec	(KEH-BECK)
R	•—•	Romeo	(ROW-ME-OH)
S	•••	Sierra	(SEE-AIR-RAH)
T	—	Tango	(TANG-GO)
U	••—	Uniform	(YOU-NEE-FORM) or (OO-NEE-FORM)
V	•••—	Victor	(VIK-TAH)
W	•——	Whiskey	(WISS-KEY)
X	—••—	Xray	(ECKS-RAY)
Y	—•——	Yankee	(YANG-KEY)
Z	——••	Zulu	(ZOO-LOO)
1	•————	One	(WUN)
2	••———	Two	(TOO)
3	•••——	Three	(TREE)
4	••••—	Four	(FOW-ER)
5	•••••	Five	(FIFE)
6	—••••	Six	(SIX)
7	——•••	Seven	(SEV-EN)
8	———••	Eight	(AIT)
9	————•	Nine	(NI-NER)
0	—————	Zero	(ZEE-RO)

9. Phraseology: altitudes, directions speed and time

Radar Beacon Phraseology	
SQUAWK (number)	Operate radar beacon transponder on designated code in MODE A/3.
IDENT	Engage the "IDENT" feature (military I/P) of the transponder.
SQUAWK (number) and IDENT	Operate transponder on specified code in MODE A/3 and engage the "IDENT" (military I/P) feature.
SQUAWK Standby	Switch transponder to standby position.
SQUAWK Low/Normal	Operate transponder on low or normal sensitivity as specified. Transponder is operated in "NORMAL" position unless ATC specifies "LOW" ("ON" is used instead of "NORMAL" as a master control label on some types of transponders).
SQUAWK Altitude	Activate MODE C with automatic altitude reporting.
STOP Altitude SQUAWK	Turn off altitude reporting switch and continue transmitting MODE C framing pulses. If your equipment does not have this capability, turn off MODE C.
STOP SQUAWK (mode in use)	Switch off specified mode. (Used for military aircraft when the controller is unaware of military service requirements for the aircraft to continue operation on another MODE.)
STOP SQUAWK	Switch off transponder.
SQUAWK Mayday	Operate transponder in the emergency position (MODE A Code 7700 for civil transponder, MODE 3 Code 7700 and emergency feature for military transponder).
SQUAWK VFR	Operate radar beacon transponder on Code 1200 in MODE A/3, or other appropriate VFR code.

B. Airport operations

1. Airports defined

a) The definition for airports refers to any area of land or water used or intended for landing or takeoff of aircraft. This includes, within the five categories of airports listed below, special types of facilities including seaplane bases, heliports, and facilities to accommodate tilt rotor aircraft. An airport includes an area used or intended for airport buildings, facilities, as well as rights of way together with the buildings and facilities.

2. Types of airports, such as towered and uncontrolled towered, heliport and seaplane bases

a) Types: There are two types of airports—towered and non-towered. These types can be further subdivided to:

   (1) Civil Airports—airports that are open to the general public
   (2) Military/Federal Government airports—airports operated by the military, National Aeronautics and Space Administration (NASA), or other agencies of the Federal Government
   (3) Private Airports—airports designated for private or restricted use only, not open to the general public

     b)   Heliport/Seaplane Base

         (1)   107.43: No person may operate a small unmanned aircraft in a manner that interferes with operations and traffic patterns at any airport, heliport, or seaplane base.

     c)   Remote PICs are prohibited from operating their small UA in a manner that interferes with operations and traffic patterns at airports, heliports, and seaplane bases. While a small UA must always yield right-of-way to a manned aircraft, a manned aircraft may alter its flightpath, delay its landing, or take off in order to avoid an sUAS that may present a potential conflict or otherwise affect the safe outcome of the flight. For example, a UA hovering 200 feet above a runway may cause a manned aircraft holding short of the runway to delay takeoff, or a manned aircraft on the downwind leg of the pattern to delay landing. While the UA in this scenario would not pose an immediate traffic conflict to the aircraft on the downwind leg of the traffic pattern or to the aircraft intending to take off, nor would it violate the right-of-way provision of § 107.37(a), the small UA would have interfered with the operations of the traffic pattern at an airport.

     d)   Where to find out where there are seaplane bases and heliports?

         (1)   Sectional
         (2)   Chart Supplement US (Formerly Airport/Facility Directory)
         (3)   http://www.faa.gov/air_traffic/flight_info/aeronav/

3.   ATC towers such as ensuring the remote pilot can monitor and interpret ATC communications to improve situational awareness

     a)   107: the operator of a small UAS flying in controlled airspace should be required to monitor ATC frequency in the area in order to maintain situational awareness.

     b)   A towered airport has an operating control tower. Air traffic control (ATC) is responsible for providing the safe, orderly, and expeditious flow of air traffic at airports where the type of operations and/or volume of traffic requires such a service. Pilots operating from a towered airport are required to maintain two-way radio communication with ATC and to acknowledge and comply with their instructions. Pilots must advise A TC if they cannot comply with the instructions issued and request amended instructions. A pilot may deviate from an air traffic instruction in an emergency, but must advise ATC of the deviation as soon as possible.

c) A non-towered airport does not have an operating control tower. Two-way radio communications are not required, although it is a good operating practice for pilots to transmit their intentions on the specified frequency for the benefit of other traffic in the area. The key to communicating at an airport without an operating control tower is selection of the correct common frequency. The acronym CTAF, which stands for Common Traffic Advisory Frequency, is synonymous with this program. A CTAF is a frequency designated for the purpose of carrying out airport advisory practices while operating to or from an airport without an operating control tower. The CTAF may be a Universal Integrated Community (UNICOM), MULTICOM, Flight Service Station (FSS), or tower frequency and is identified in appropriate aeronautical publications.

4. Runway markings and signage

a) Runway markings vary depending on the type of operations conducted at the airport. A basic VFR runway may only have centerline markings and runway numbers. Refer to Appendix C of this publication for an example of the most common runway markings that are found at airports.

AIRPORT SIGN SYSTEMS

TYPE OF SIGN AND ACTION OR PURPOSE		TYPE OF SIGN AND ACTION OR PURPOSE	
4-22	**Taxiway/Runway Hold Position:** Hold short of runway on taxiway		**Runway Safety Area/Obstacle Free Zone Boundary:** Exit boundary of runway protected areas
26-8	**Runway/Runway Hold Position:** Hold short of intersecting runway		**ILS Critical Area Boundary:** Exit boundary of ILS critical area
8-APCH	**Runway Approach Hold Position:** Hold short of aircraft on approach	J→	**Taxiway Direction:** Defines direction & designation of intersecting taxiway(s)
ILS	**ILS Critical Area Hold Position:** Hold short of ILS approach critical area	↙L	**Runway Exit:.** Defines direction & designation of exit taxiway from runway
⊖	**No Entry:** Identifies paved areas where aircraft entry is prohibited	22↑	**Outbound Destination:** Defines directions to takeoff runways
B	**Taxiway Location:** Identifies taxiway on which aircraft is located	↖MIL	**Inbound Destination:** Defines directions for arriving aircraft
22	**Runway Location:** Identifies runway on which aircraft is located	/////	**Taxiway Ending Marker** Indicates taxiway does not continue
4	**Runway Distance Remaining** Provides remaining runway length in 1,000 feet increments	↙A G L→	**Direction Sign Array:** Identifies location in conjunction with multiple intersecting taxiways

b) Since aircraft are affected by the wind during takeoffs and landings, runways are laid out according to the local prevailing winds. Runway numbers are in reference to magnetic north. Certain airports have two or even three runways laid out in the same direction. These are referred to as parallel runways and are distinguished by a letter added to the runway number (e.g., runway 36L (left), 36C (center), and 36R (right)).

5. Traffic patterns used by manned aircraft pilots

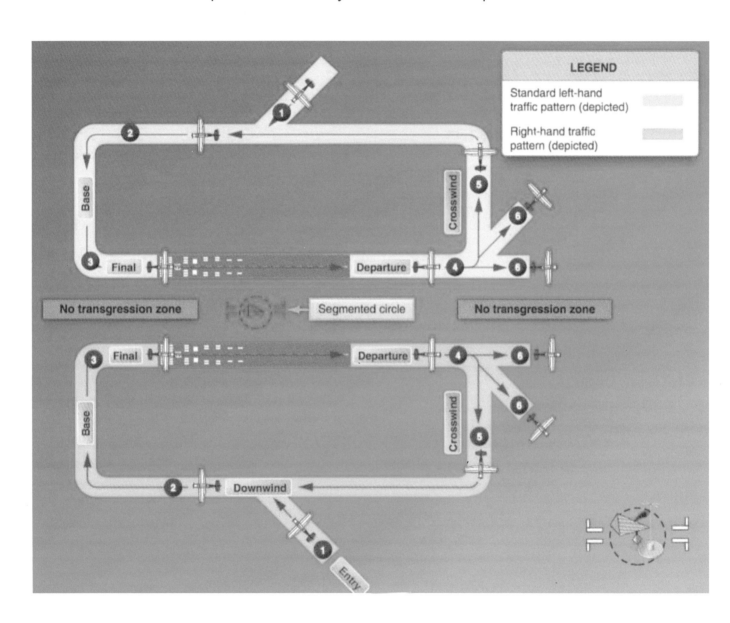

6. Security identification display areas(SIDA)

    a) Federal Aviation Regulation (FAR) Part 107: Airport Security stipulates various requirements for protecting airports from crimes against civil aviation. Part 107 requires employment history, verification and criminal history records checks (if applicable) of individuals applying for airport identification badges that permit unescorted access authority to the Security Identification Display Area (SIDA).

7. Sources for airport data

    a) Aeronautical charts: Aeronautical charts provide specific information on airports. Chapter 16, "Navigation," contains an excerpt from an aeronautical chart and an aeronautical chart legend, which provides guidance on interpreting the information on the chart.

    b) Chart supplements: The Chart Supplement U.S. (formerly Airport/Facility Directory) provides the most comprehensive information on a given airport. It contains information on airports, heliports, and seaplane bases that are open to the public. The Chart Supplement U.S. is published in seven books, which are organized by regions and are revised every 56 days.

8. Avoiding bird and wildlife hazards and reporting collisions between aircraft and wildlife

    a) Types of animals to report if involved in a strike with aircraft

        (1) All birds.
        (2) All bats.
        (3) All terrestrial mammals larger than 1 kg (2.2 lbs) (e.g., report rabbits, muskrats, armadillos, foxes, coyotes, domestic dogs, deer, feral livestock, etc., but not rats, mice, voles, chipmunks, shrews, etc.). If in doubt, report the incident with a note in the comment section and the Database Manager will determine whether to include the report into the NWSD based on body mass.
        (4) Reptiles larger than 1 kg (2.2 lbs).

    b) When to report a wildlife aircraft strike

        (1) A strike between wildlife and aircraft has been witnessed
        (2) Evidence or damage from a strike has been identified on an aircraft
        (3) Bird or other wildlife remains, whether in whole or in part, are found:

            (a) *Within 250 feet of a runway centerline or within 1,000 feet of a runway end unless another reason for the animal's death is identified or suspected*

    c)   How to report a bird/wildlife strike

        (1)   The FAA strongly encourages pilots, airport operations, aircraft maintenance personnel, Air Traffic Control personnel, engine manufacturers, or anyone else who has knowledge of a strike to report it to the NWSD. The FAA makes available an online reporting system at the Airport Wildlife Hazard Mitigation web site (http://www.faa.gov/go/wildlife) or via mobile devices at http://www.faa.gov/mobile. Anyone reporting a strike can also print the FAA's Bird/Other Wildlife Strike Report Form (Form 5200-7) at the end of this AC or download it from the web site to report strikes. Paper copies of Form 5200-7 may also be obtained from the appropriate Airports District Offices (ADO), Flight Standards District Offices (FSDO), and Flight Service Stations (FSS) or from the Airman's Information Manual (AIM). Paper forms are pre-addressed to the FAA. No postage is needed if the form is mailed in the United States. It is important to include as much information as possible on the strike report.

C. Emergency procedures

1. When to deviate from emergency procedures

    a)   107.21: (a) In an in-flight emergency requiring immediate action, the remote pilot in command may deviate from any rule of this part to the extent necessary to meet that emergency.

    b)   (b) Each remote pilot in command who deviates from a rule under paragraph (a) of this section must, upon request of the Administrator, send a written report of that deviation to the Administrator.

2. Emergency planning and communication

    a)   Checklists describing the recommended procedures and airspeeds for coping with various types of emergencies or critical situations are located in the Emergency Procedures section. Some of the emergencies covered include: engine failure, fire, and system failure. The procedures for inflight engine restarting and ditching may also be included. Manufacturers may first show an emergency checklist in an abbreviated form with the order of items reflecting the sequence of action. Amplified checklists that provide additional information on the procedures follow the abbreviated checklist. To be prepared for emergency situations, memorize the immediate action items and, after completion, refer to the appropriate checklist.

3. Characteristics and potential hazards of lithium batteries

a) Lithium-based batteries are highly flammable and capable of ignition.

b) A battery fire could cause an in-flight emergency by causing a LOC of the small UA. Lithium battery fires can be caused when a battery short circuits, is improperly charged, is heated to extreme temperatures, is damaged as a result of a crash, is mishandled, or is simply defective. The remote PIC should consider following the manufacturer's recommendations, when available, to help ensure safe battery handling and usage.

4. Safe transportation, such as proper inspection and handling of lithium batteries

a) From SAFO 15010: Ensure all crewmembers and ground personnel handling passengers and baggage understand that they must report incidents where fire, violent rupture, explosion, or heat sufficient to be dangerous to packaging or personal safety to include charring of packaging, melting of packaging, scorching of packaging, or other evidence, occurs as a result of a battery or battery-powered device.

b) Battery terminals (usually the ends) must be protected from short circuit (i.e., the terminals must not come in contact with other metal). Methods include: leaving the batteries in their retail packaging, covering battery terminals with tape, using a battery case, using a battery sleeve in a camera bag, or putting them snugly in a plastic bag or protective pouch.

c) Batteries must be protected from damage.

d) Inspection of batteries from AC107-2: Further inspect to determine integrity of the battery as a reliable power source. Distorted battery casings may indicate impending failure resulting in abrupt power loss and/or explosion. An electrical hazard may be present, posing a risk of fire or extreme heat negatively impacting aircraft structures, aircraft performance characteristics, and flight duration. Assess the need and extent of repairs that may be needed for continued safe flight operations.

5. Safe charging
6. Safe usage
7. Risk of fires involving lithium batteries
8. Loss of aircraft control link and flyaways

a) Loss link: Discontinue flight and/or avoid further flight operations until further inspection and testing of the control link between the ground control unit and the aircraft. Ensure accurate control communications are established and reliable prior to further flight to circumvent possible loss of control resulting in the risk of a collision or flyaway. Assess the need and extent of repairs that may be needed for continued safe flight operations.

b) The 2.4 GHz and 5.8 GHz systems are the unlicensed band RFs that most sUAS use for the connection between the CS and the small UA. Note the frequencies are also used for computer wireless networks and the interference can cause problems when operating a UA in an area (e.g., dense housing and office buildings) that has many wireless signals. LOC and flyaways are some of the reported problems with sUAS frequency implications.

c) It should be noted that both RF bands (2.4 GHz and 5.8 GHz) are considered line of sight and the command and control link between the CS and the small UA will not work properly when barriers are between the CS and the UA. Part 107 requires the remote PIC or person manipulating the controls to be able to see the UA at all times, which should also help prevent obstructions from interfering with the line of sight frequency spectrum.

9. Loss of GPS signal during flight and potential consequences

a) AIM: In summary, be careful not to rely on GPS to solve all VFR navigational problems. Unless an IFR receiver is installed in accordance with IFR requirements, no standard of accuracy or integrity can be assured. While the practicality of GPS is compelling, the fact remains that only the pilot can navigate the aircraft, and GPS is just one of the pilot's tools to do the job.

b) Since the FAA is really behind on this issue, if you ever lose GPS or believe you're experiencing a flyaway simply turn off GPS by engaging the attitude or manual mode on your vehicle.

10. Frequency spectrums and associated limitations

a) Frequency spectrum (RF) Basics.

(1) The 2.4 GHz and 5.8 GHz systems are the unlicensed band RFs that most sUAS use for the connection between the CS and the small UA. Note the frequencies are also used for computer wireless networks and the interference can cause problems when operating a UA in an area (e.g., dense housing and office buildings) that has many wireless signals. LOC and flyaways are some of the reported problems with sUAS frequency implications.

b) To avoid frequency interference, many modern sUAS operate using a 5.8 GHz system to control the small UA and a 2.4 GHz system to transmit video and photos to the ground. Consult the sUAS operating manual and manufacturer's recommended procedures before conducting sUAS operations.

c) It should be noted that both RF bands (2.4 GHz and 5.8 GHz) are considered line of sight and the command and control link between the CS and the small UA will not work properly when barriers are between the CS and the UA. Part 107 requires the remote PIC or person manipulating the controls to be able to see the UA at all times, which should also help prevent obstructions from interfering with the line of sight frequency spectrum.

d) Spectrum Authorization.

(1) Frequency spectrum used for small UA operations are regulated by the Federal Communications Commission (FCC). Radio transmissions, such as those used to control a UA and to downlink real-time video, must use frequency bands that are approved for use by the operating agency. The FCC authorizes civil operations. Some operating frequencies are unlicensed and can be used freely (e.g., 900 MHz, 2.4 GHz, and 5.8 GHz) without FCC approval. All other frequencies require a user-specific license for all civil users, except federal agencies, to be obtained from the FCC. For further information, visit https://www.fcc.gov/licensing-databases/licensing.

D. Aeronautical Decision Making (ADM)

1. Aeronautical Decision Making is a unique environment

a) It is a systematic approach to the mental process used by pilots to consistently determine the best course of action in response to a given set of circumstances. It is what a pilot intends to do based on the latest information he or she has.

b) The importance of learning and understanding effective ADM skills cannot be overemphasized. While progress is continually being made in the advancement of pilot training methods, aircraft equipment and systems, and services for pilots, accidents still occur. Despite all the changes in technology to improve flight safety, one factor remains the same: the human factor which leads to errors. It is estimated that approximately 80 percent of all aviation accidents are related to human factors and the vast majority of these accidents occur during landing (24.1 percent) and takeoff (23.4 percent). [Figure 2-1]

c) ADM is a systematic approach to risk assessment and stress management. To understand ADM is to also understand how personal attitudes can influence decision-making and how those attitudes can be modified to enhance safety in the flight deck. It is important to understand the factors that cause humans to make decisions and how the decision-making process not only works, but can be improved.

d) Steps for good decision-making are:

(1) Identifying personal attitudes hazardous to safe flight
(2) Learning behavior modification techniques
(3) Learning how to recognize and cope with stress
(4) Developing risk assessment skills
(5) Using all resources
(6) Evaluating the effectiveness of one's ADM skills

e) The ADM process addresses all aspects of decision making in a solo or crew environment and identifies the steps involved in good decision making. These steps for good decision making are as follows:

(1) Identifying Personal Attitudes Hazardous to Safe Flight. Hazardous attitudes can affect unmanned operations if the remote PIC is not aware of the hazards, leading to such things as: getting behind the aircraft/situation, operating without adequate fuel/battery reserve, loss of positional or situational awareness, operating outside the envelope, and failure to complete all flight planning tasks, preflight inspections, and checklists. Operational pressure is a contributor to becoming subject to these pit-falls.

(2) Learning Behavior Modification Techniques. Continuing to utilize risk assessment procedures for the operation will assist in identifying risk associated with the operation. Conducting an attitude assessment will identify situations where a hazardous attitude may be present.

(3) Learning How to Recognize and Cope with Stress. Stress is ever present in our lives and you may already be familiar with situations that create stress in aviation. However, UAS operations may create stressors that differ from manned aviation. Such examples may include: working with an inexperienced crewmember, lack of standard crewmember training, interacting with the public and city officials, and understanding new regulatory requirements. Proper planning for the operation can reduce or eliminate stress, allowing you to focus more clearly on the operation.

(4) Developing Risk Assessment Skills. As with any aviation operation, identifying associated hazards is the first step. Analyzing the likelihood and severity of the hazards occurring establishes the probability of risk. In most cases, steps can be taken to mitigate, even eliminate, those risks. Actions such as using visual observers (VO), completing a thorough preflight inspection, planning for weather, familiarity with the airspace, proper aircraft loading, and performance planning can mitigate identified risks. Figure A-1, Hazard Identification and Risk Assessment Process Chart, is an example of a risk assessment tool. Others are also available for use.

f) Evaluating the Effectiveness of One's ADM Skills.

(1) Successful decision making is measured by a pilot's consistent ability to keep himself or herself, any persons involved in the operation, and the aircraft in good condition regardless of the conditions of any given flight. As with manned operations, complacency and overconfidence can be risks, and so there are several checklists and models to assist in the decision making process. Use the IMSAFE checklist to ensure you are mentally and physically prepared for the flight. Use the DECIDE model to help you continually evaluate each operation for hazards and analyze risk. Paragraph A.5.5 and the current edition of AC 60-22, Aeronautical Decision Making, can provide additional information on these models and others.

2. Effective team communication

a) Using All Available Resources with More Than One Crewmember (CRM). A characteristic of CRM is creating an environment where open communication is encouraged and expected, and involves the entire crew to maximize team performance. Many of the same resources that are available to manned aircraft operations are available to UAS operations. For example, remote PICs can take advantage of traditional CRM techniques by utilizing additional crewmembers, such as VOs and other ground crew. These crewmembers can provide information about traffic, airspace, weather, equipment, and aircraft loading and performance. Examples of good CRM include:

(1) Communication procedures; One way to accomplish this is to have the VO maintain visual contact with the small UA and maintain awareness of the surrounding airspace, and then communicate flight status and any hazards to the remote PIC and person manipulating the controls so that appropriate action can be taken. Then, as conditions change, the remote PIC should brief the crew on the changes and any needed adjustments to ensure a safe outcome of the operation.

(2) Communication methods; The remote PIC, person manipulating the controls, and VO must work out a method of communication, such as the use of a hand-held radio or other effective means, that would not create a distraction and allows them to understand each other. The remote PIC should evaluate which method is most appropriate for the operation and should be determined prior to flight.

(3) Other resources; Take advantage of information from a weather briefing, air traffic control (ATC), the FAA, local pilots, and landowners. Technology can aid in decision making and improve situational awareness. Being able to collect the information from these resources and manage the information is key to situational awareness and could have a positive effect on your decision making.

3. Task management

a) Tasks vary depending on the complexity of the operation. Depending upon the area of the operations, additional crewmembers may be needed to safely operate. Enough crewmembers should be utilized to ensure no one on the team becomes overloaded. Once a member of the team becomes overworked, there's a greater possibility of an incident/accident.

4. Crew Resource Management (CRM)

a) While CRM focuses on pilots operating in crew environments, many of the concepts apply to single-pilot operations. Many CRM principles have been successfully applied to single-pilot aircraft and led to the development of Single-Pilot Resource Management (SRM). SRM is defined as the art and science of managing all the resources (both on-board the aircraft and from outside sources) available to a single pilot (prior to and during flight) to ensure the successful outcome of the flight. SRM includes the concepts of ADM, risk management (RM), task management (TM), automation management (AM), controlled flight into terrain (CFIT) awareness, and situational awareness (SA). SRM training helps the pilot maintain situational awareness by managing the automation and associated aircraft control and navigation tasks. This enables the pilot to accurately assess and manage risk and make accurate and timely decisions.

b) SRM is all about helping pilots learn how to gather information, analyze it, and make decisions. Although the flight is coordinated by a single person and not an onboard flight crew, the use of available resources such as auto-pilot and air traffic control (ATC) replicates the principles of CRM.

5. Situational awareness

a) Situational awareness is the accurate perception and understanding of all the factors and conditions within the five fundamental risk elements (flight, pilot, aircraft, environment, and type of operation that comprise any given aviation situation) that affect safety before, during, and after the flight. Monitoring radio communications for traffic, weather discussion, and ATC communication can enhance situational awareness by helping the pilot develop a mental picture of what is happening.

b)   Maintaining situational awareness requires an understanding of the relative significance of all flight related factors and their future impact on the flight. When a pilot understands what is going on and has an overview of the total operation, he or she is not fixated on one perceived significant factor. Not only is it important for a pilot to know the aircraft's geographical location, it is also important he or she understand what is happening. For instance, while flying above Richmond, Virginia, toward Dulles Airport or Leesburg, the pilot should know why he or she is being vectored and be able to anticipate spatial location. A pilot who is simply making turns without understanding why has added an additional burden to his or her management in the event of an emergency. To maintain situational awareness, all of the skills involved in ADM are used.

6. Hazardous attitudes

a)   Being fit to fly depends on more than just a pilot's physical condition and recent experience. For example, attitude affects the quality of decisions. Attitude is a motivational predisposition to respond to people, situations, or events in a given manner. Studies have identified five hazardous attitudes that can interfere with the ability to make sound decisions and exercise authority properly: anti-authority, impulsivity, invulnerability, macho, and resignation.

b)   Hazardous attitudes can affect unmanned operations if the remote PIC is not aware of the hazards, leading to such things as: getting behind the aircraft/situation, operating without adequate fuel/battery reserve, loss of positional or situational awareness, operating outside the envelope, and failure to complete all flight planning tasks, preflight inspections, and checklists. Operational pressure is a contributor to becoming subject to these pit-falls.

c)   Learning Behavior Modification Techniques.

(1)   Continuing to utilize risk assessment procedures for the operation will assist in identifying risk associated with the operation. Conducting an attitude assessment will identify situations where a hazardous attitude may be present.

Hazardous Attitudes and Antidotes

Anti-authority – Don't tell me.

– Follow the rules, they are usually right

Impulsivity – Do something – do it now.

– Not so fast, think first

Invulnerability – It won't happen to me.

– It could happen to me.

Macho – I can do it.

– Taking chances is foolish.

Resignation – What's the use?

– I can make a difference.

7. Hazard identification and risk assessment

    a) Hazard identification

        (1) Hazards in the sUAS and its operating environment must be identified, documented, and controlled. The analysis process used to define hazards needs to consider all components of the system, based on the equipment being used and the environment it is being operated in. The key question to ask during analysis of the sUAS and its operation is, "what if?" sUAS remote PICs are expected to exercise due diligence in identifying significant and reasonably foreseeable hazards related to their operations.

(2) Risk analysis and assessment

    (a) The risk assessment should use a conventional breakdown of risk by its two components: likelihood of occurrence and severity.

(3) Severity and likelihood criteria

    (a) There are several tools which could be utilized in determining severity and likelihood when evaluating a hazard. One tool is a risk matrix. Several examples of these are presented in Figure A-2, Safety Risk Matrix Examples. The definitions and construction of the matrix is left to the sUAS remote PIC to design. The definitions of each level of severity and likelihood need to be defined in terms that are realistic for the operational environment. This ensures each remote PIC's decision tools are relevant to their operations and operational environment, recognizing the extensive diversity which exists. An example of severity and likelihood definitions is shown in Table A-1, Sample Severity and Likelihood Criteria.

(4) Risk acceptance

(a) In the development of risk assessment criteria, sUAS remote PICs are expected to develop risk acceptance procedures, including acceptance criteria and designation of authority and responsibility for risk management decision making. The acceptability of risk can be evaluated using a risk matrix, such as those illustrated in Figure A-2. Table A-2, Safety Risk Matrix—Example shows three areas of acceptability.

(b) Unacceptable (Red). Where combinations of severity and likelihood cause risk to fall into the red area, the risk would be assessed as unacceptable and further work would be required to design an intervention to eliminate that associated hazard or to control the factors that lead to higher risk likelihood or severity.

(c) Acceptable (Green). Where the assessed risk falls into the green area, it may be accepted without further action. The objective in risk management should always be to reduce risk to as low as practicable regardless of whether or not the assessment shows that it can be accepted as is.

(d) Acceptable with Mitigation (Yellow). Where the risk assessment falls into the yellow area, the risk may be accepted under defined conditions of mitigation. An example of this situation would be an assessment of the impact of an sUAS operation near a school yard. Scheduling the operation to take place when school is not in session could be one mitigation to prevent undue risk to the children that study and play there. Another mitigation could be restricting people from the area of operations by placing cones or security personnel to prevent unauthorized access during the sUAS flight operation.

		A	B	C	D	E
		Negligible	Minor	Moderate	Significant	Severe
E	Very Likely	Low Med	Medium	Med Hi	High	High
D	Likely	Low	Low Med	Medium	Med Hi	High
C	Possible	Low	Low Med	Medium	Med Hi	Med Hi
B	Unlikely	Low	Low Med	Low Med	Medium	Med Hi
A	Very Unlikely	Low	Low	Low Med	Medium	Medium

b) Other risk assessment tools for flight and operational risk management:

(1) Other tools can also be used for flight or operational risk assessments and can be developed by the remote PICs themselves. The key thing is to ensure that all potential hazards and risks are identified and appropriate actions are taken to reduce the risk to persons and property not associated with the operations.

c) Reducing risk

Severity		1	2	3	4	5
Catastrophic Extreme	E	1E	2E		4E	5E
Major Critical	D	1D	2D	3D		5D
Moderate	C	1C	2C	3C	4C	
Minor	B	1B	2B	3B	4B	5B
Negligible	A	1A	2A	3A	4A	5A
		1	2	3	4	5
		Rare Improbable	Remote Unlikely	Occasional	Probable Likely	Frequent Almost certain

Likelihood

138

(1) Risk analyses should concentrate not only on assigning levels of severity and likelihood, but on determining why these particular levels were selected. This is referred to as root cause analysis, and is the first step in developing effective controls to reduce risk to lower levels. In many cases, simple brainstorming sessions among crewmembers is the most effective and affordable method of finding ways to reduce risk. This also has the advantage of involving people who will ultimately be required to implement the controls developed.

(2) It is also very easy to get quite bogged down in trying to identify all hazards and risks. That is not the purpose of a risk assessment. The focus should be upon those hazards which pose the greatest risks. As stated earlier, by documenting and compiling these processes, a remote PIC can build an arsenal of safety practices that will add to the safety and success of future operations.

d) As with any aviation operation, identifying associated hazards is the first step. Analyzing the likelihood and severity of the hazards occurring establishes the probability of risk. In most cases, steps can be taken to mitigate, even eliminate, those risks. Actions such as using visual observers (VO), completing a thorough preflight inspection, planning for weather, familiarity with the airspace, proper aircraft loading, and performance planning can mitigate identified risks. Figure A-1, Hazard Identification and Risk Assessment Process Chart, is an example of a risk assessment tool. Others are also available for use.

e) As previously discussed, identifying hazards and associated risk is key to preventing risk and accidents. If a pilot fails to search for risk, it is likely that he or she will neither see it nor appreciate it for what it represents. Unfortunately, in aviation, pilots seldom have the opportunity to learn from their small errors in judgment because even small mistakes in aviation are often fatal. In order to identify risk, the use of standard procedures is of great assistance. One guide in the form of a checklist that helps the pilot examine areas of interest in his or her preflight planning is a framework called PAVE. Elements of PAVE are:

(1) Pilot-in-command (PIC)
(2) Aircraft
(3) Environment
(4) External pressures

f) With the PAVE checklist, pilots have a simple way to remember each category to examine for risk prior to each flight. Once a pilot identifies the risks of a flight, he or she needs to decide whether the risk or combination of risks can be managed safely and successfully. If not, make the decision to cancel the flight. If the pilot decides to continue with the flight, he or she should develop strategies to mitigate the risks. One way a pilot can control the risks is to set personal minimums for items in each risk category.

g) Using the Personal Minimums (PAVE) Checklist for Risk Management, I will set personal minimums based upon my specific flight experience, health habits, and tolerance for stress, just to name a few. After identifying hazards, I will then input them into the Hazard Identification and Risk Management Process Chart (Figure A-1).

  (1) P: Personal: Am I healthy for flight and what are my personal minimums based upon my experience operating this sUAS? During this step, I will often use the IMSAFE checklist in order to perform a more in-depth evaluation:

    (a) *Illness – Am I suffering from any illness or symptom of an illness which might affect me in flight?*
    (b) *Medication – Am I currently taking any drugs (prescription or over-the-counter)?*
    (c) *Stress – Am I experiencing any psychological or emotional factors which might affect my performance?*
    (d) *Alcohol – Have I consumed alcohol within the last 8 to 24 hours?*
    (e) *Fatigue – Have I received sufficient sleep and rest in the recent past?*
    (f) *Eating – Am I sufficiently nourished?*

  (2) A: Aircraft: Have I conducted a preflight check of my sUAS (aircraft, control station (CS), takeoff and landing equipment, etc.) and determined it to be in a condition for safe operation? Is the filming equipment properly secured to the aircraft prior to flight?

  (3) V: EnVironment: What is the weather like? Am I comfortable and experienced enough to fly in the forecast weather conditions? Have I considered all of my options and left myself an "out?" Have I determined alternative landing spots in case of an emergency?

  (4) E: External Pressures: Am I stressed or anxious? Is this a flight that will cause me to be stressed or anxious? Is there pressure to complete the flight operation quickly? Am I dealing with an unhealthy safety culture? Am I being honest with myself and others about my personal operational abilities and limitations?

h) Controlling risk

(1) After hazards and risks are fully understood through the preceding steps, risk controls must be designed and implemented. These may be additional or changed procedures, additional or modified equipment, the addition of VOs, or any of a number of other changes.

i) Residual and substitute risk

(1) Residual risk is the risk remaining after mitigation has been completed. Often, this is a multistep process, continuing until risk has been mitigated down to an acceptable level necessary to begin or continue operation. After these controls are designed but before the operation begins or continues, an assessment must be made of whether the controls are likely to be effective and/or if they introduce new hazards to the operation.

(2) The latter condition, introduction of new hazards, is referred to as substitute risk, a situation where the cure is worse than the disease. The loop seen in Figure A-1 that returns back to the top of the diagram depicts the use of the preceding hazard identification, risk analysis, and risk assessment processes to determine if the modified operation is acceptable.

j) Starting the operation

(1) Once appropriate risk controls are developed and implemented, then the operation can begin.

E. Physiology

1. Physiological considerations and their effects on safety, such as dehydration and heatstroke

a) A number of health factors and physiological effects can be linked to flying. Some are minor, while others are important enough to require special attention to ensure safety of flight. In some cases, physiological factors can lead to inflight emergencies. Some important medical factors that a pilot should be aware of include hypoxia, hyperventilation, middle ear and sinus problems, spatial disorientation, motion sickness, carbon monoxide (CO) poisoning, stress and fatigue, dehydration, and heatstroke. Other subjects include the effects of alcohol and drugs, anxiety, and excess nitrogen in the blood after scuba diving.

b) Dehydration: Dehydration is the term given to a critical loss of water from the body. Causes of dehydration are hot flight decks and flight lines, wind, humidity, and diuretic drinks—coffee, tea, alcohol, and caffeinated soft drinks. Some common signs of dehydration are headache, fatigue, cramps, sleepiness, and dizziness.

c) The first noticeable effect of dehydration is fatigue, which in turn makes top physical and mental performance difficult, if not impossible. Flying for long periods in hot summer temperatures or at high altitudes increases the susceptibility to dehydration because these conditions tend to increase the rate of water loss from the body.

d) To help prevent dehydration, drink two to four quarts of water every 24 hours. Since each person is physiologically different, this is only a guide. Most people are aware of the eight-glasses-a-day guide: If each glass of water is eight ounces, this equates to 64 ounces, which is two quarts. If this fluid is not replaced, fatigue progresses to dizziness, weakness, nausea, tingling of hands and feet, abdominal cramps, and extreme thirst.

e) The key for pilots is to be continually aware of their condition. Most people become thirsty with a 1.5 quart deficit or a loss of 2 percent of total body weight. This level of dehydration triggers the "thirst mechanism." The problem is that the thirst mechanism arrives too late and is turned off too easily. A small amount of fluid in the mouth turns this mechanism off and the replacement of needed body fluid is delayed.

(1) Other steps to prevent dehydration include:

(a) *Carrying a container in order to measure daily water intake.*
(b) *Staying ahead—not relying on the thirst sensation as an alarm. If plain water is not preferred, add some sport drink flavoring to make it more acceptable.*
(c) *Limiting daily intake of caffeine and alcohol (both are diuretics and stimulate increased production of urine).*

f) Heatstroke

(1) Heatstroke is a condition caused by any inability of the body to control its temperature. Onset of this condition may be recognized by the symptoms of dehydration, but also has been known to be recognized only upon complete collapse. To prevent these symptoms, it is recommended that an ample supply of water be carried and used at frequent intervals on any long flight, whether thirsty or not. The body normally absorbs water at a rate of 1.2 to 1.5 quarts per hour. Individuals should drink one quart per hour for severe heat stress conditions or one pint per hour for moderate stress conditions. If the aircraft has a canopy or roof window, wearing light-colored, porous clothing and a hat will help provide protection from the sun. Keeping the flight deck well ventilated aids in dissipating excess heat.

2. Drug and alcohol use

a) Alcohol impairs the efficiency of the human body. [Figure 17-8] Studies have shown that consuming alcohol is closely linked to performance deterioration. Pilots must make hundreds of decisions, some of them time-critical, during the course of a flight. The safe outcome of any flight depends on the ability to make the correct decisions and take the appropriate actions during routine occurrences, as well as abnormal situations. The influence of alcohol drastically reduces the chances of completing a flight without incident. Even in small amounts, alcohol can impair judgment, decrease sense of responsibility, affect coordination, constrict visual field, diminish memory, reduce reasoning ability, and lower attention span. As little as one ounce of alcohol can decrease the speed and strength of muscular reflexes, lessen the efficiency of eye movements while reading, and increase the frequency at which errors are committed. Impairments in vision and hearing can occur from consuming as little as one drink.

Type Beverage	Typical Serving (oz)	Pure Alcohol Content (oz)
Table wine	4.0	.48
Light beer	12.0	.48
Aperitif liquor	1.5	.38
Champagne	4.0	.48
Vodka	1.0	.50
Whiskey	1.25	.50

0.01–0.05% (10–50 mg)	average individual appears normal
0.03–0.12%* (30–120 mg)	mild euphoria, talkativeness, decreased inhibitions, decreased attention, impaired judgment, increased reaction time
0.09–0.25% (90–250 mg)	emotional instability, loss of critical judgment, impairment of memory and comprehension, decreased sensory response, mild muscular incoordination
0.18–0.30% (180–300 mg)	confusion, dizziness, exaggerated emotions (anger, fear, grief), impaired visual perception, decreased pain sensation, impaired balance, staggering gait, slurred speech, moderate muscular incoordination
0.27–0.40% (270–400 mg)	apathy, impaired consciousness, stupor, significantly decreased response to stimulation, severe muscular incoordination, inability to stand or walk, vomiting, incontinence of urine and feces
0.35–0.50% (350–500 mg)	unconsciousness, depressed or abolished reflexes, abnormal body temperature, coma, possible death from respiratory paralysis (450 mg or above)

* Legal limit for motor vehicle operation in most states is 0.08 or 0.10% (80–100 mg of alcohol per dL of blood).

b) The alcohol consumed in beer and mixed drinks is ethyl alcohol, a central nervous system depressant. From a medical point of view, it acts on the body much like a general anesthetic. The "dose" is generally much lower and more slowly consumed in the case of alcohol, but the basic effects on the human body are similar. Alcohol is easily and quickly absorbed by the digestive tract. The bloodstream absorbs about 80 to 90 percent of the alcohol in a drink within 30 minutes when ingested on an empty stomach. The body requires about 3 hours to rid itself of all the alcohol contained in one mixed drink or one beer.

c) While experiencing a hangover, a pilot is still under the influence of alcohol. Although a pilot may think he or she is functioning normally, motor and mental response impairment is still present. Considerable amounts of alcohol can remain in the body for over 16 hours, so pilots should be cautious about flying too soon after drinking.

d) Altitude multiplies the effects of alcohol on the brain. When combined with altitude, the alcohol from two drinks may have the same effect as three or four drinks. Alcohol interferes with the brain's ability to utilize oxygen, producing a form of histotoxic hypoxia. The effects are rapid because alcohol passes quickly into the bloodstream. In addition, the brain is a highly vascular organ that is immediately sensitive to changes in the blood's composition. For a pilot, the lower oxygen availability at altitude and the lower capability of the brain to use the oxygen that is available can add up to a deadly combination.

e) Intoxication is determined by the amount of alcohol in the bloodstream. This is usually measured as a percentage by weight in the blood. 14 CFR part 91 requires that blood alcohol level be less than .04 percent and that 8 hours pass between drinking alcohol and piloting an aircraft. A pilot with a blood alcohol level of .04 percent or greater after 8 hours cannot fly until the blood alcohol falls below that amount. Even though blood alcohol may be well below .04 percent, a pilot cannot fly sooner than 8 hours after drinking alcohol.

f) Drug use

(1) The Federal Aviation Regulations include no specific references to medication usage. Two regulations, though, are important to keep in mind Title 14 of the CFR part 61, section 61.53 prohibits acting as pilot-in-command or in any other capacity as a required pilot flight crewmember, while that person:

(a) *Knows or has reason to know of any medical condition that would make the person unable to meet the requirement for the medical certificate necessary for the pilot operation, or*

(b) *Is taking medication or receiving other treatment for a medical condition that results in the person being unable to meet the requirements for the medical certificate necessary for the pilot operation*

(2) Further, 14 CFR part 91, section 91.17 prohibits the use of any drug that affects the person's faculties in any way contrary to safety.

(3) There are several thousand medications currently approved by the U.S. Food and Drug Administration (FDA), not including OTC (over the counter) drugs. Virtually all medications have the potential for adverse side effects in some people. Additionally, herbal and dietary supplements, sport and energy boosters, and some other "natural" products are derived from substances often found in medications that could also have adverse side effects. While some individuals experience no side effects with a particular drug or product, others may be noticeably affected. The FAA regularly reviews FDA and other data to assure that medications found acceptable for aviation duties do not pose an adverse safety risk. Drugs that cause no apparent side effects on the ground can create serious problems at even relatively low altitudes. Even at typical general aviation altitudes, the changes in concentrations of atmospheric gases in the blood can enhance the effects of seemingly innocuous drugs that can result in impaired judgment, decision-making, and performance. In addition, fatigue, stress, dehydration, and inadequate nutrition can increase an airman's susceptibility to adverse effects from various drugs, even if they appeared to tolerate them in the past. If multiple medications are being taken at the same time, the adverse effects can be even more pronounced.

(4) Another important consideration is that the medical condition for which a medication is prescribed may itself be disqualifying. The FAA will consider the condition in the context of risk for medical incapacitation, and the medication as well for cognitive impairment, and either or both could be found unacceptable for medical certification and never mix drugs with alcohol because the effects are often unpredictable.

(5) The dangers of illegal drugs also are well documented. Certain illegal drugs can have hallucinatory effects that occur days or weeks after the drug is taken. Obviously, these drugs have no place in the aviation community.

(6) 14 CFR prohibits pilots from performing crewmember duties while using any medication that affects the body in any way contrary to safety. The safest rule is not to fly as a crewmember while taking any medication, unless approved to do so by the FAA. If there is any doubt regarding the effects of any medication, consult an AME before flying.

g) Prior to each and every flight, all pilots must do a proper physical self-assessment to ensure safety. A great mnemonic, covered in Chapter 2 on Aeronautical Decision-Making, is IMSAFE, which stands for Illness, Medication, Stress, Alcohol, Fatigue, and Emotion.

h) For the medication component of IMSAFE, pilots need to ask themselves, "Am I taking any medicines that might affect my judgment or make me drowsy? For any new medication, OTC or prescribed, you should wait at least 48 hours after the first dose before flying to determine you do not have any adverse side effects that would make it unsafe to operate an aircraft. In addition to medication questions, pilots should also consider the following:

    (1) Do not take any unnecessary or elective medications;
    (2) Make sure you eat regular balanced meals;
    (3) Bring a snack for both you and your passengers for the flight;
    (4) Maintain good hydration - bring plenty of water;
    (5) Ensure adequate sleep the night prior to the flight; and
    (6) Stay physically fit.

3. Prescription and over the counter medication

a) Some of the most commonly used OTC drugs, antihistamines and decongestants, have the potential to cause noticeable adverse side effects, including drowsiness and cognitive deficits. The symptoms associated with common upper respiratory infections, including the common cold, often suppress a pilot's desire to fly, and treating symptoms with a drug that causes adverse side effects only compounds the problem. Particularly, medications containing diphenhydramine (e.g., Benadryl) are known to cause drowsiness and have a prolonged half-life, meaning the drugs stay in one's system for an extended time, which lengthens the time that side effects are present.

b) Many medications, such as tranquilizers, sedatives, strong pain relievers, and cough suppressants, have primary effects that may impair judgment, memory, alertness, coordination, vision, and the ability to make calculations. [Figure 17-9] Others, such as antihistamines, blood pressure drugs, muscle relaxants, and agents to control diarrhea and motion sickness, have side effects that may impair the same critical functions. Any medication that depresses the nervous system, such as a sedative, tranquilizer, or antihistamine, can make a pilot more susceptible to hypoxia.

c) Over-the-counter analgesics, such as acetylsalicylic acid (aspirin), acetaminophen (Tylenol), and ibuprofen (Advil), have few side effects when taken in the correct dosage. Although some people are allergic to certain analgesics or may suffer from stomach irritation, flying usually is not restricted when taking these drugs. However, flying is almost always precluded while using prescription analgesics, such as drugs containing propoxyphene (e.g., Darvon), oxycodone (e.g., Percodan), meperidine (e.g., Demerol), and codeine, since these drugs are known to cause side effects, such as mental confusion, dizziness, headaches, nausea, and vision problems.

d) Stimulants are drugs that excite the central nervous system and produce an increase in alertness and activity. Amphetamines, caffeine, and nicotine are all forms of stimulants. Common uses of these drugs include appetite suppression, fatigue reduction, and mood elevation. Some of these drugs may cause a stimulant reaction, even though this reaction is not their primary function. In some cases, stimulants can produce anxiety and mood swings, both of which are dangerous when flying.

e) Depressants are drugs that reduce the body's functioning in many areas. These drugs lower blood pressure, reduce mental processing, and slow motor and reaction responses. There are several types of drugs that can cause a depressing effect on the body, including tranquilizers, motion sickness medication, some types of stomach medication, decongestants, and antihistamines. The most common depressant is alcohol.

f) Some drugs that are classified as neither stimulants nor depressants have adverse effects on flying. For example, some antibiotics can produce dangerous side effects, such as balance disorders, hearing loss, nausea, and vomiting. While many antibiotics are safe for use while flying, the infection requiring the antibiotic may prohibit flying. In addition, unless specifically prescribed by a physician, do not take more than one drug at a time, and never mix drugs with alcohol because the effects are often unpredictable.

Substance	Generic Or Brand Name	Treatment for	Possible Side Effects
Alcohol	Beer Liquor Wine	N/A	Impaired judgment and perception Impaired coordination and motor control Reduced reaction time Impaired sensory perception Reduced intellectual functions Reduced tolerance to G-forces Inner-ear disturbance and spatial disorientation (up to 48 hours) Central nervous system depression
Nicotine	Cigars Cigarettes Pipe tobacco Chewing tobacco Snuff	N/A	Sinus and respiratory system infection and irritation Impaired night vision Hypertension Carbon monoxide poisoning (from smoking)
Amphetamines	Ritalin Obetrol Eskatrol	Obesity (diet pills) Tiredness	Prolonged wakefulness Nervousness Impaired vision Suppressed appetite Shakiness Excessive sweating Rapid heart rate Sleep disturbance Seriously impaired judgment
Caffeine	Coffee Tea Chocolate No-Doz	N/A	Impaired judgment Reduced reaction time Sleep disturbance Increased motor activity and tremors Hypertension Irregular heart rate Rapid heart rate Body dehydration (through increased urine output) Headaches
Antacid	Alka-2 Di-Gel Maalox	Stomach acids	Liberations of carbon dioxide at altitude (distension may cause acute abdominal pain and may mask other medical problems)
Antihistamines	Coricidin Contac Dristan Dimetapp Omade Chlor-Trimeton Diphenhydramine	Allergies Colds	Drowsiness and dizziness (sometimes recurring) Visual disturbances (when medications also contain antispasmodic drugs)
Aspirin	Bayer Bufferin Alka-Seltzer	Headaches Fevers Aches Pains	Irregular body temperature Variation in rate and depth of respiration Hypoxia and hyperventilation (two aspirin can contribute to) Nausea, ringing in ears, deafness, diarrhea, and hallucinations when taken in excessive dosages Corrosive action on the stomach lining Gastrointestinal problems Decreased clotting ability of the blood (clotting ability could be the difference between life and death in a survival situation)

4. Hyperventilation

a) Hyperventilation is the excessive rate and depth of respiration leading to abnormal loss of carbon dioxide from the blood. This condition occurs more often among pilots than is generally recognized. It seldom incapacitates completely, but it causes disturbing symptoms that can alarm the uninformed pilot. In such cases, increased breathing rate and anxiety further aggravate the problem. Hyperventilation can lead to unconsciousness due to the respiratory system's overriding mechanism to regain control of breathing.

b) Pilots encountering an unexpected stressful situation may subconsciously increase their breathing rate. If flying at higher altitudes, either with or without oxygen, a pilot may have a tendency to breathe more rapidly than normal, which often leads to hyperventilation.

5. Stress and fatigue

a) Stress is the body's response to physical and psychological demands placed upon it. The body's reaction to stress includes releasing chemical hormones (such as adrenaline) into the blood and increasing metabolism to provide more energy to the muscles. Blood sugar, heart rate, respiration, blood pressure, and perspiration all increase. The term "stressor" is used to describe an element that causes an individual to experience stress. Examples of stressors include physical stress (noise or vibration), physiological stress (fatigue), and psychological stress (difficult work or personal situations).

b) Stress falls into two broad categories: acute (short term) and chronic (long term). Acute stress involves an immediate threat that is perceived as danger. This is the type of stress that triggers a "fight or flight" response in an individual, whether the threat is real or imagined. Normally, a healthy person can cope with acute stress and prevent stress overload. However, ongoing acute stress can develop into chronic stress.

c) Chronic stress can be defined as a level of stress that presents an intolerable burden, exceeds the ability of an individual to cope, and causes individual performance to fall sharply. Unrelenting psychological pressures, such as loneliness, financial worries, and relationship or work problems can produce a cumulative level of stress that exceeds a person's ability to cope with the situation. When stress reaches these levels, performance falls off rapidly. Pilots experiencing this level of stress are not safe and should not exercise their airman privileges. Pilots who suspect they are suffering from chronic stress should consult a physician.

d) AC1072: Stress is ever present in our lives and you may already be familiar with situations that create stress in aviation. However, UAS operations may create stressors that differ from manned aviation. Such examples may include: working with an inexperienced crewmember, lack of standard crewmember training, interacting with the public and city officials, and understanding new regulatory requirements. Proper planning for the operation can reduce or eliminate stress, allowing you to focus more clearly on the operation.

e) Fatigue: fatigue is frequently associated with pilot error. Some of the effects of fatigue include degradation of attention and concentration, impaired coordination, and decreased ability to communicate. These factors seriously influence the ability to make effective decisions. Physical fatigue results from sleep loss, exercise, or physical work. Factors such as stress and prolonged performance of cognitive work result in mental fatigue.

  (1) Like stress, fatigue falls into two broad categories: acute and chronic. Acute fatigue is short term and is a normal occurrence in everyday living. It is the kind of tiredness people feel after a period of strenuous effort, excitement, or lack of sleep. Rest after exertion and 8 hours of sound sleep ordinarily cures this condition.

  (2) A special type of acute fatigue is skill fatigue. This type of fatigue has two main effects on performance:

    (a) *Timing disruption—appearing to perform a task as usual, but the timing of each component is slightly off. This makes the pattern of the operation less smooth because the pilot performs each component as though it were separate, instead of part of an integrated activity.*

    (b) *Disruption of the perceptual field—concentrating attention upon movements or objects in the center of vision and neglecting those in the periphery. This is accompanied by loss of accuracy and smoothness in control movements. Acute fatigue has many causes, but the following are among the most important for the pilot:*

      (i) *Mild hypoxia (oxygen deficiency)*

      (ii) *Physical stress*

      (iii) *Psychological stress*

      (iv) *Depletion of physical energy resulting from psychological stress (v)* *Sustained psychological stress* *Sustained psychological stress accelerates the glandular secretions that prepare the body for quick reactions during an emergency. These secretions make the circulatory and respiratory systems work harder, and the liver releases energy to provide the extra fuel needed for brain and muscle work. When this reserve energy supply is depleted, the body lapses into generalized and severe fatigue. Acute fatigue can be prevented by proper diet and adequate rest and sleep. A well-balanced diet prevents the body from needing to consume its own tissues as an energy source. Adequate rest maintains the body's store of vital energy.*

f) Chronic fatigue, extending over a long period of time, usually has psychological roots, although an underlying disease is sometimes responsible. Continuous high-stress levels produce chronic fatigue. Chronic fatigue is not relieved by proper diet and adequate rest and sleep and usually requires treatment by a physician. An individual may experience this condition in the form of weakness, tiredness, palpitations of the heart, breathlessness, headaches, or irritability. Sometimes chronic fatigue even creates stomach or intestinal problems and generalized aches and pains throughout the body. When the condition becomes serious enough, it leads to emotional illness.

g) If suffering from acute fatigue, stay on the ground. If fatigue occurs in the flight deck, no amount of training or experience can overcome the detrimental effects. Getting adequate rest is the only way to prevent fatigue from occurring. Avoid flying without a full night's rest, after working excessive hours, or after an especially exhausting or stressful day. Pilots who suspect they are suffering from chronic fatigue should consult a physician.

h) If suffering from acute fatigue, stay on the ground. If fatigue occurs in the flight deck, no amount of training or experience can overcome the detrimental effects. Getting adequate rest is the only way to prevent fatigue from occurring. Avoid flying without a full night's rest, after working excessive hours, or after an especially exhausting or stressful day. Pilots who suspect they are suffering from chronic fatigue should consult a physician.

6. Factors affecting vision

a) Of all the senses, vision is the most important for safe flight. Most of the things perceived while flying are visual or heavily supplemented by vision. As remarkable and vital as it is, vision is subject to limitations, such as illusions and blind spots. The more a pilot understands about the eyes and how they function, the easier it is to use vision effectively and compensate for potential problems. Of all the senses, vision is the most important for safe flight. Most of the things perceived while flying are visual or heavily supplemented by vision. As remarkable and vital as it is, vision is subject to limitations, such as illusions and blind spots. The more a pilot understands about the eyes and how they function, the easier it is to use vision effectively and compensate for potential problems. light energy into electrical impulses that travel through nerves to the brain. The brain interprets the electrical signals to form images. There are two kinds of light-sensitive cells in the eyes: rods and cones.

b) The cones are responsible for all color vision, from appreciating a glorious sunset to discerning the subtle shades in a fine painting. Cones are present throughout the retina, but are concentrated toward the center of the field of vision at the back of the retina. There is a small pit called the fovea where almost all the light sensing cells are cones. This is the area where most "looking" occurs (the center of the visual field where detail, color sensitivity, and resolution are highest).

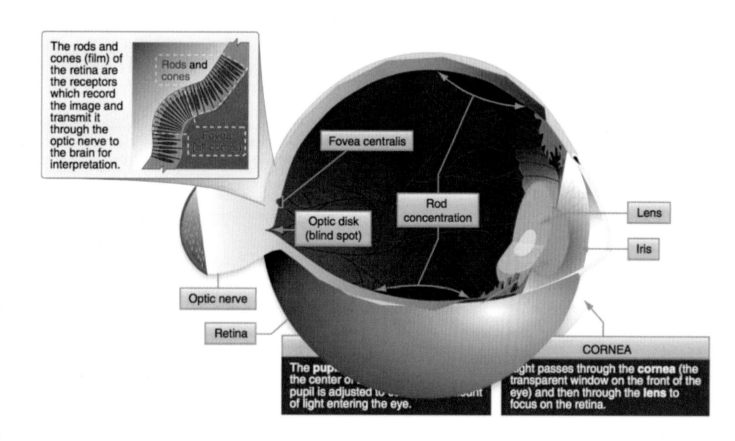

The rods and cones (film) of the retina are the receptors which record the image and transmit it through the optic nerve to the brain for interpretation.

Rods and cones

Fovea centralis

Optic disk (blind spot)

Rod concentration

Lens

Iris

Optic nerve

Retina

CORNEA

The pup... the center o... pupil is adjusted to ... of light entering the eye.

...ght passes through the **cornea** (the transparent window on the front of the eye) and then through the **lens** to focus on the retina.

c) While the cones and their associated nerves are well suited to detecting fine detail and color in high light levels, the rods are better able to detect movement and provide vision in dim light. The rods are unable to discern color but are very sensitive at low-light levels. The trouble with rods is that a large amount of light overwhelms them, and they take longer to "reset" and adapt to the dark again. There are so many cones in the fovea that are at the very center of the visual field but virtually has no rods at all. So in low light, the middle of the visual field is not very sensitive, but farther from the fovea, the rods are more numerous and provide the major portion of night vision.

d) There are three types of vision: photopic, mesopic, and scotopic. Each type functions under different sensory stimuli or ambient light conditions.

(1) Photopic vision provides the capability for seeing color and resolving fine detail (20/20 or better), but it functions only in good illumination. Photopic vision is experienced during daylight or when a high level of artificial illumination exists.

(2) Mesopic vision is achieved by a combination of rods and cones and is experienced at dawn, dusk, and during full moonlight. Visual acuity steadily decreases as available light decreases and color perception changes because the cones become less effective. Mesopic viewing period is considered the most dangerous period for viewing. As cone sensitivity decreases, pilots should use off-center vision and proper scanning techniques to detect objects during low-light levels.

(3) Scotopic vision is experienced under low-light levels and the cones become ineffective, resulting in poor resolution of detail. Visual acuity decreases to 20/200 or less and enables a person to see only objects the size of or larger than the big "E" on visual acuity testing charts from 20 feet away. In other words, a person must stand at 20 feet to see what can normally be seen at 200 feet under daylight conditions. When using scotopic vision, color perception is lost and a night blind spot in the central field of view appears at low light levels when the cone-cell sensitivity is lost.

Types of Vision						
Types of vision used	Light level	Technique of viewing	Color perception	Receptors used	Acuity best	Blind spot
Photopic	High	Central	Good	Cones	20/20	Day
Mesopic	Medium/Low	Both	Some	Cones/Rods	Varies	Day/Night
Scotopic	Low	Scanning	None	Rods	20/200	Day/Night

e) Empty-field myopia is a condition that usually occurs when flying above the clouds or in a haze layer that provides nothing specific to focus on outside the aircraft. This causes the eyes to relax and seek a comfortable focal distance that may range from 10 to 30 feet. For the pilot, this means looking without seeing, which is dangerous. Searching out and focusing on distant light sources, no matter how dim, helps prevent the onset of empty-field myopia.

f) Night vision: There are many good reasons to fly at night, but pilots must keep in mind that the risks of night flying are different than during the day and often times higher. [Figure 17-16] Pilots who are cautious and educated on night-flying techniques can mitigate those risks and become very comfortable and proficient in the task.

g) Night blind spot: It is estimated that once fully adapted to darkness, the rods are 10,000 times more sensitive to light than the cones, making them the primary receptors for night vision. Since the cones are concentrated near the fovea, the rods are also responsible for much of the peripheral vision. The concentration of cones in the fovea can make a night blind spot in the center of the field of vision. To see an object clearly at night, the pilot must expose the rods to the image. This can be done by looking 5° to 10° off center of the object to be seen. This can be tried in a dim light in a darkened room. When looking directly at the light, it dims or disappears altogether. When looking slightly off center, it becomes clearer and brighter.

h) Situational awareness: Situational awareness is the accurate perception and understanding of all the factors and conditions within the five fundamental risk elements (flight, pilot, aircraft, environment, and type of operation that comprise any given aviation situation) that affect safety before, during, and after the flight. Monitoring radio communications for traffic, weather discussion, and ATC communication can enhance situational awareness by helping the pilot develop a mental picture of what is happening.

(1) Maintaining situational awareness requires an understanding of the relative significance of all flight related factors and their future impact on the flight. When a pilot understands what is going on and has an overview of the total operation, he or she is not fixated on one perceived significant factor. Not only is it important for a pilot to know the aircraft's geographical location, it is also important he or she understand what is happening. For instance, while flying above Richmond, Virginia, toward Dulles Airport or Leesburg, the pilot should know why he or she is being vectored and be able to anticipate spatial location. A pilot who is simply making turns without understanding why has added an additional burden to his or her management in the event of an emergency. To maintain situational awareness, all of the skills involved in ADM are used.

7. Fitness for flight

a) There are several techniques to help manage the accumulation of life stresses and prevent stress overload. For example, to help reduce stress levels, set aside time for relaxation each day or maintain a program of physical fitness. To prevent stress overload, learn to manage time more effectively to avoid pressures imposed by getting behind schedule and not meeting deadlines.

F. Maintenance and inspection procedures

1. Basic maintenance

a) sUAS maintenance includes scheduled and unscheduled overhaul, repair, inspection, modification, replacement, and system software upgrades of the sUAS and its components necessary for flight. Whenever possible, the operator should maintain the sUAS and its components in accordance with manufacturer's instructions. The aircraft manufacturer may provide the maintenance program, or, if one is not provided, the applicant may choose to develop one. See paragraph 7.3.5 for suggested benefits of recordkeeping.

(1) Scheduled maintenance. The sUAS manufacturer may provide documentation for scheduled maintenance of the entire UA and associated system equipment. There may be components of the sUAS that are identified by the manufacturer to undergo scheduled periodic maintenance or replacement based on time-in-service limits (such as flight hours, cycles, and/or the calendar-days). All manufacturer scheduled maintenance instructions should be followed in the interest of achieving the longest and safest service life of the sUAS.

(a) *If there are no scheduled maintenance instructions provided by the sUAS manufacturer or component manufacturer, the operator should establish a scheduled maintenance protocol. This could be done by documenting any repair, modification, overhaul, or replacement of a system component resulting from normal flight operations, and recording the time-in-service for that component at the time of the maintenance procedure. Over time, the operator should then be able to establish a reliable maintenance schedule for the sUAS and its components.*

(b) Unscheduled maintenance. During the course of a preflight inspection, the remote PIC may discover that an sUAS component is in need of servicing (such as lubrication), repair, modification, overhaul, or replacement outside of the scheduled maintenance period as a result of normal flight operations or resulting from a mishap. In addition, the sUAS manufacturer or component manufacture may require an unscheduled system software update to correct a problem. In the event such a condition is found, the remote PIC should not conduct flight operations until the discrepancy is corrected.

2. Pre-flight inspection

a) Before each flight, the remote PIC must inspect the sUAS to ensure that it is in a condition for safe operation, such as inspecting for equipment damage or malfunction(s). The preflight inspection should be conducted in accordance with the sUAS manufacturer's inspection procedures when available (usually found in the manufacturer's owner or maintenance manual) and/or an inspection procedure developed by the sUAS owner or operator.

   (1) Creating an inspection program. As an option, the sUAS owner or operator may wish to create an inspection program for their UAS. The person creating an inspection program for a specific sUAS may find sufficient details to assist in the development of a suitable inspection program tailored to a specific sUAS in a variety of industry programs.

   (2) Scalable preflight inspection. The preflight check as part of the inspection program should include an appropriate UAS preflight inspection that is scalable to the UAS, program, and operation to be performed prior to each flight. An appropriate preflight inspection should encompass the entire system in order to determine a continued condition for safe operation prior to flight.

   (3) Title 14 CFR Part 43 Appendix D Guidelines. Another option and best practice may include the applicable portions of part 43 appendix D as an inspection guideline correlating to the UA only. System-related equipment, such as, but not limited to, the CS, data link, payload, or support equipment, are not included in the list in appendix D. Therefore, these items should be included in a comprehensive inspection program for the UAS.

b) Preflight inspection items. Even if the sUAS manufacturer has a written preflight inspection procedure, it is recommended that the remote PIC ensure that the following inspection items are incorporated into the preflight inspection procedure required by part 107 to help the remote PIC determine that the sUAS is in a condition for safe operation. The preflight inspection should include a visual or functional check of the following items:

(1) Visual condition inspection of the UAS components;
(2) Airframe structure (including undercarriage), all flight control surfaces, and linkages;
(3) Registration markings, for proper display and legibility;
(4) Moveable control surface(s), including airframe attachment point(s);
(5) Servo motor(s), including attachment point(s);
(6) Propulsion system, including power plant(s), propeller(s), rotor(s), ducted fan(s), etc.;
(7) Verify all systems (e.g., aircraft and control unit) have an adequate energy supply for the intended operation and are functioning properly;
(8) Avionics, including control link transceiver, communication/navigation equipment, and antenna(s);
(9) Calibrate UAS compass prior to any flight;
(10) Control link transceiver, communication/navigation data link transceiver, and antenna(s);
(11) Display panel, if used, is functioning properly;
(12) Check ground support equipment, including takeoff and landing systems, for proper operation;
(13) Check that control link correct functionality is established between the aircraft and the CS;
(14) Check for correct movement of control surfaces using the CS;
(15) Check onboard navigation and communication data links;
(16) Check flight termination system, if installed;
(17) Check fuel for correct type and quantity;
(18) Check battery levels for the aircraft and CS;
(19) Check that any equipment, such as a camera, is securely attached;
(20) Verify communication with UAS and that the UAS has acquired GPS location from at least four satellites;
(21) Start the UAS propellers to inspect for any imbalance or irregular operation;
(22) Verify all controller operation for heading and altitude;
(23) If required by flight path walk through, verify any noted obstructions that may interfere with the UAS; and
(24) At a controlled low altitude, fly within range of any interference and recheck all controls and stability.

3. Techniques to mitigate mechanical failures of all elements used in sUAS operations such as the battery and or any devices used to operate the sUAS.

a) In the interest of assisting varying background levels of sUAS knowledge and skill, below is a chart offering conditions that, if noticed during a preflight inspection or check, may support a determination that the UAS is not in a condition for safe operation. Further inspection to identify the scope of damage and extent of possible repair needed to remedy the unsafe condition may be necessary prior to flight.

Condition	Action
1. **Structural or skin cracking**	Further inspect to determine scope of damage and existence of possible hidden damage that may compromise structural integrity. Assess the need and extent of repairs that may be needed for continued safe flight operations.
2. **Delamination of bonded surfaces**	Further inspect to determine scope of damage and existence of possible hidden damage that may compromise structural integrity. Assess the need and extent of repairs that may be needed for continued safe flight operations.
3. **Liquid or gel leakage**	Further inspect to determine source of the leakage. This condition may pose a risk of fire resulting in extreme heat negatively impacting aircraft structures, aircraft performance characteristics, and flight duration. Assess the need and extent of repairs that may be needed for continued safe flight operations.
4. **Strong fuel smell**	Further inspect to determine source of the smell. Leakage exiting the aircraft may be present and/or accumulating within a sealed compartment. This condition may pose a risk of fire resulting in extreme heat negatively impacting aircraft structures, aircraft performance characteristics, and flight duration. Assess the need and extent of repairs that may be needed for continued safe flight operations.
5. **Smell of electrical burning or arcing**	Further inspect to determine source of the possible electrical malfunction. An electrical hazard may pose a risk of fire or extreme heat negatively impacting aircraft structures,

	aircraft performance characteristics, and flight duration. Assess the need and extent of repairs that may be needed for continued safe flight operations.
6. **Visual indications of electrical burning or arcing (black soot tracings, sparking)**	Further inspect to determine source of the possible electrical malfunction. An electrical hazard may pose a risk of fire or extreme heat negatively impacting aircraft structures, aircraft performance characteristics, and flight duration. Assess the need and extent of repairs that may be needed for continued safe flight operations.
7. **Noticeable sound (decibel) change during operation by the propulsion system**	Further inspect entire aircraft with emphasis on the propulsion system components (i.e., motors and propellers) for damage and/or diminished performance. Assess the need and extent of repairs that may be needed for continued safe flight operations.
8. **Control inputs not synchronized or delayed**	Discontinue flight and/or avoid further flight operations until further inspection and testing of the control link between the ground control unit and the aircraft. Ensure accurate control communications are established and reliable prior to further flight to circumvent possible loss of control resulting in the risk of a collision or flyaway. Assess the need and extent of repairs that may be needed for continued safe flight operations.
9. **Battery casing distorted (bulging)**	Further inspect to determine integrity of the battery as a reliable power source. Distorted battery casings may indicate impending failure resulting in abrupt power loss and/or explosion. An electrical hazard may be present, posing a risk of fire or extreme heat negatively impacting aircraft structures, aircraft performance characteristics, and flight duration. Assess the need and extent of repairs that may be needed for continued safe flight operations.
10. **Diminishing flight time capability (electric powered propulsion systems)**	Further inspect to determine integrity of the battery as a reliable power source. Diminishing battery capacity may indicate impending failure due to exhausted service life, internal, or external damage. An electrical hazard may

	be present, posing a risk of fire or extreme heat negatively impacting aircraft structures, aircraft performance characteristics, and flight duration. Assess the need and extent of repairs that may be needed for continued safe flight operations.
11. Loose or missing hardware/fasteners	Further inspect to determine structural integrity of the aircraft and/or components with loose or missing hardware/fasteners. Loose or missing hardware/fasteners may pose a risk of negatively impacting flight characteristics, structural failure of the aircraft, dropped objects, loss of the aircraft, and risk to persons and property on the grounds. For continued safe flight operations, secure loose hardware/fasteners. Replace loose hardware/fasteners that cannot be secured. Replace missing hardware/fasteners.

4. Appropriate record keeping

a) Benefits of record keeping.

b) sUAS owners and operators may find recordkeeping to be beneficial. This could be done by documenting any repair, modification, overhaul, or replacement of a system component resulting from normal flight operations, and recording the time-in-service for that component at the time of the maintenance procedure. Over time, the operator should then be able to establish a reliable maintenance schedule for the sUAS and its components. Recordkeeping that includes a record of all periodic inspections, maintenance, preventative maintenance, repairs, and alterations performed on the sUAS could be retrievable from either hardcopy and/or electronic logbook format for future reference. This includes all components of the sUAS, including: small UA, CS, launch and recovery equipment, C2 link equipment, payload, and any other components required to safely operate the sUAS. Recordkeeping of documented maintenance and inspection events reinforces owner/operator responsibilities for airworthiness through systematic condition for safe flight determinations. Maintenance and inspection recordkeeping provides retrievable empirical evidence of vital safety assessment data defining the condition of safety-critical systems and components supporting the decision to launch. Recordkeeping of an sUAS may provide essential safety support for commercial operators that may experience rapidly accumulated flight operational hours/cycles. Methodical maintenance and inspection data collection can prove to be very helpful in the tracking of sUAS component service life, as well as systemic component, equipage, and structural failure events.

5. Persons that may perform Maintenance on an sUAS

a) Performing maintenance.

(1) In some instances, the sUAS or component manufacturer may require certain maintenance tasks be performed by the manufacturer or by a person or facility (personnel) specified by the manufacturer. It is highly recommended that the maintenance be performed in accordance with the manufacturer's instructions. However, if the operator decides not to use the manufacturer or personnel recommended by the manufacturer and is unable to perform the required maintenance, the operator should consider the expertise of maintenance personnel familiar with the specific sUAS and its components. In addition, though not required, the use of certificated maintenance providers are encouraged, which may include repair stations, holders of mechanic and repairman certificates, and persons working under the supervision of these mechanics and repairman.

b) If the operator or other maintenance personnel are unable to repair, modify, or overhaul an sUAS or component back to its safe operational specification, then it is advisable to replace the sUAS or component with one that is in a condition for safe operation. It is important that all required maintenance be completed before each flight, and preferably in accordance with the manufacturer's instructions or, in lieu of that, within known industry best practices.

c) In the interest of assisting varying background levels of sUAS knowledge and skill, below is a chart offering conditions that, if noticed during a preflight inspection or check, may support a determination that the UAS is not in a condition for safe operation. Further inspection to identify the scope of damage and extent of possible repair needed to remedy the unsafe condition may be necessary prior to flight.

QUIZ QUESTIONS - Operations

1. Which of the following events is considered a flyaway?
   A. Unmanned aircraft does not respond to control inputs and does not execute known lost link maneuvers
   B. Loss of link between the Remote PIC and the unmanned aircraft
   C. Loss of communication link between the Remote PIC and ATC

2. Fatigue can be either
   A. physiological or psychological
   B. physical or mental
   C. acute or chronic

3. A common cause of sUAS flyaway events is
   A. frequency interference
   B. loss of GPS signals
   C. persons standing close to the control station antenna

4. You have just landed at a towered airport and the tower tells you to contact ground control when clear of the runway. You are considered clear of the runway when
   A. the aircraft cockpit is clear of the hold line
   B. the tail of the aircraft is clear of the runway edge
   C. all parts of the aircraft have crossed the hold line

5. Which of the following sources of information should you consult first when determining what maintenance should be performed on an sUAS or its components
   A. Local pilot best practices
   B. 14 CFR Part 107
   C. Manufacturer guidance

6. What is the best way for the remote PIC to minimize the risk of radio frequency interference during sUAS operations?
   A. Never transmit on aviation frequency ranges during flight operations
   B. Monitor frequency use with a spectral analyzer
   C. Avoid the use of cellphones in the vicinity of the control station

7. Under what condition should the operator of a small unmanned aircraft establish a scheduled maintenance protocol?
   A. When the manufacturer does not provide a maintenance schedule
   B. When the FAA requires you to, following an accident
   C. Small unmanned aircraft systems do not require maintenance

8. During the preflight inspection who is responsible for determining the aircraft is safe for flight?
   A. The owner or operator
   B. The remote pilot-in-command
   C. The certificate mechanic who performed the annual inspection

9. Which would most likely result in hyperventilation
   A. The excessive consumption of alcohol
   B. Emotional tension, anxiety or fear
   C. An extremely slow rate of breathing and insufficient oxygen

10. Upon GPS signal loss, the remote Pilot should immediately
    A. contact ATC and declare an emergency
    B. perform the planned lost link contingency procedure
    C. operate the sUAS normally, noting to account for any mode or control changes that occur if GPS is lost

11. After landing at a tower controlled airport, a pilot should contact ground control
    A. when advised by the tower
    B. prior to turning off the runway
    C. after reaching a taxiway that leads directly to the parking area

12. What action should the remote PIC take upon GPS signal loss?
    A. Perform the planned flyaway emergency procedure
    B. Follow normal sUAS operational procedure, noting any mode or control changes that normally occur if GPS is lost.
    C. Land the unmanned aircraft immediately prior to loss of control

13. Which will almost always affect your ability to fly?
    A. Prescription analgesics and antihistamines
    B. Over-the-counter analgesics and antihistamines
    C. Antibiotics and anesthetic drugs

14. What antidotal phrase can help reverse the hazardous attitude of "antiauthority"?
    A. Rules do not apply for this situation
    B. I know what I am doing
    C. Follow the rules

15. Which of the following lithium batteries should not be used
    A. A battery with a bulge on one of the sides of its case
    B. A partially discharged battery that is warm from recent prior use
    C. A new battery that has only been charged once, several charging cycles are required prior to normal use.

16. The responsibility for ensuring that an sUAS is maintained in an airworthy condition is primarily that of the
    A. Owner or operator
    B. Remote pilot-in-command
    C. mechanic who performs the work

17. When flying HAWK N666CB, the proper phraseology for initial contact with Whitted ATC Tower is
   A. Whitted, HAWK SIX SIX SIX CEE BEE requesting to operate within Class D, west of the field.
   B. Whitted Tower, HAWK SIX SIX SIX CHARLIE BRAVO five NM west of the airport, request permission to enter Class D airspace for unmanned aircraft operations below four hundred AGL, three NM west of the airport
   C. Whitted Tower, Triple Six Charlie Bravo, five NM west, operating in Class D below four hundred AGL west of the airport

18. Who is responsible for determining whether a pilot is fit to fly for a particular flight even though he or she holds a current medical certificate
   A. The FAA
   B. The medical examiner
   C. The Pilot

19. Fatigue can be recognized
   A. as being in an impaired state
   B. easily by an experienced pilot
   C. by an ability to overcome sleep deprivation

20. What action should be taken by the Remote PIC during a sUAS flyaway event?
   A. Immediately notify any/all crewmembers, bystanders, and ATC (if applicable)
   B. Immediately notify the NTSB
   C. Immediately notify any/all crewmembers, local law enforcement personnel, and bystanders

21. How should an sUAS preflight inspection be accomplished for the first flight of the day?
   A. Quick walk around with a check of gas and oil
   B. Thorough and systematic means recommended by the manufacturer
   C. Any sequence as determined by the pilot-in-command

22. In which of the following scenarios is a remote PIC not required to perform a preflight inspection of their sUAS?
   A. Preflight inspections are required before each flight, thus no scenario precludes such an inspection
   B. If the subsequent flight occurs immediately, following a flight before which an inspection was made
   C. Preflight inspections are only required for the first flight of the day so any other flight does not require such an inspection

23. What is the proper response by the remote PIC if experiencing a lost link situation?
   A. Wait for the unit to reestablish link while notifying local law enforcement of possible dangers to non-participants
   B. Turning the control stations off and then back on to attempt the reestablishment of the link
   C. Notify all available crew and ATC (if applicable) while executing the briefed lost link procedure

24. What is the recommended communication procedure when operating in the vicinity of Cooperstown Airport?

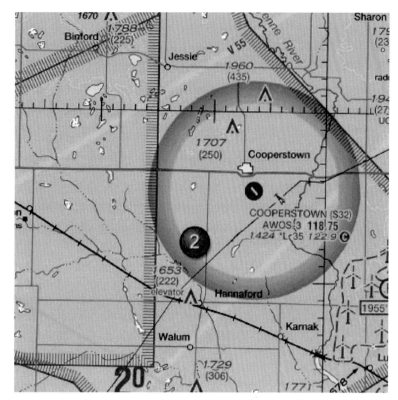

A. Broadcast intentions when 10 miles out and monitor transmissions on the CTAF/ MULTICOM frequency, 122.9 MHz

B. Contact UNICOM when 10 miles out on 122.8 MHz

C. Circle the airport in a left turn prior to entering traffic monitoring transmissions on 122.9 MULTICOM frequency is always 122.9 MHz and the correct procedure is to broadcast intentions when 10 miles from the airport

25. What is the recommended communications procedure for a landing at Currituck County Airport?

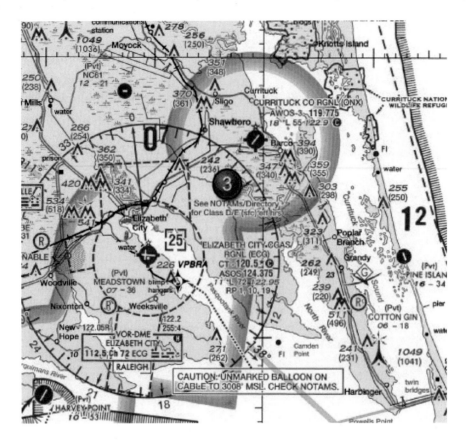

    A. Contact Elizabeth City FSS for airport advisory service

    B. Transmit intentions on 122.9 MHz when 10 miles out and give position reports in the traffic pattern.

    C. Contact New Bern FSS for area traffic information

26. To avoid missing important steps, always use the

    A. appropriate checklists

    B. placarded airspeeds

    C. airworthiness certificate

27. You have been hired as a Remote Pilot in command by a local TV news with a small unmanned aircraft. You expressed a safety concern and the station manager has instructed you to " Fly First, ask questions later" What type of hazardous attitude does this attitude represent?

    A. Invulnerability

    B. Machoism

    C. Impulsivity

28. The correct method of stating 4,500 feet MSL to ATC is

    A. FOUR POINT FIVE

    B. FOUR THOUSAND FIVE HUNDRED

    C. FORTY-FIVE HUNDRED FEET MSL

29. Absence of the sky condition and visibility on an ATIS broadcast indicates that
    A. weather conditions are at or above VFR minimums
    B. the ceiling is at least 5,000 feet and visibility is 5 miles or more
    C. the sky conditions are clear and visibility is unrestricted

30. Safety is an important element for a remote pilot to consider prior to operating an unmanned aircraft system. To prevent the final "link" in the accident chain, a remote pilot must consider which methodology?
    A. Risk management
    B. Crew resource management
    C. Safety management system

31. Inbound to an airport with no tower, FSS or UNICOM in operation, a pilot should self-announce on MULTICOM frequency
    A. 123
    B. 122.7
    C. 122.9

32. When a stressful situation is encountered in flight, an abnormal increase in the volume of air breathed in and out can cause a condition known as
    A. hyperventilation
    B. aerosinusitis
    C. aerotitis

33. A local TV station has hired a remote pilot to operate their small UA to cover breaking news stories. The remote pilot has had multiple near misses with obstacles on the ground and two small UAS accidents. What would be a solution for the news station to improve their operating safety culture?
    A. The news station should implement a policy of no more than five crashes/ incidents within 6 months
    B. The news station should recognize hazardous attitudes and situations and develop standard operating procedures that emphasize safety
    C. the news station does not need to make any changes; there are times that an accident is unavoidable

34. As standard operating practice all inbound and local traffic approaching or near an airport without a control tower should continuously monitor the appropriate facility from a distance of
    A. 25 miles
    B. 20 miles
    C. 10 miles

35. Automatic Terminal Information Service (ATIS) is the continuous broadcast of recorded information concerning
    A. pilots of radar-identified aircraft whose aircraft is in dangerous proximity to terrain or to an obstruction
    B. nonessential information to reduce frequency congestion
    C. non-control information in selected high-activity terminal areas. ATIS is the continuous broadcast of recorded non-control information in selected high-activity terminal areas

36. How often is the remote PIC required to inspect the sUAS to ensure that it is in condition for safe operation?
    A. Before each flight
    B. Annually
    C. monthly

37. When should the battery for an unmanned aircraft be replaced?
    A. Once recharged more than 10 times in the preceding 30 days
    B. per the guidelines of the sUAS manufacturer or the battery manufacturer, whichever is more restrictive
    C. Per the guidelines of the sUAS manufacturer or the battery manufacturer whichever is least restrictive

38. An ATC radar facility issues the following advisory to a pilot flying on a heading of 090 degrees: "UNMANNED AIRCRAFT OPERATIONS 3'O CLOCK, 2 MILES..." Where should the remote PIC (also visual observer) look for this traffic in reference to the UA?
    A. North
    B. South
    C. West

39. An ATC radar facility issues the following advisory to a manned pilot flying north in a calm wind: "UNMANNED AIRCRAFT OPERATIONS 9'O CLOCK, 2 MILES..." Where should the remote PIC (also visual observer) look for this traffic in reference to the UA?
    A. North
    B. East
    C. West

40. Which statement is not correct concerning crew resource management in sUAS operations
    A. Individuals who are exhibiting signs of hazardous attitudes should be approach about the issue
    B. The Remote PIC and all crewmembers should communicate any observed hazards or concerns to one another
    C. Crewmembers cannot, under any circumstances, challenge the decisions of the remote PIC

41. When setting up the location of the control station and placement of crewmembers for an afternoon flight, which of the following would be most appropriate for ensuring that vision is not impaired by the environment?
    A. The operation should be set up so that the remote PIC and crewmembers can face west
    B. the operation should be set up so that the Remote PIC and crewmembers are facing any reflective objects in the area
    C. The operation should be set up so that the remote PIC and crewmembers can face east

42. Risk management, as part of the aeronautical decision making (ADM) process, relies on which features to reduce the risks associated with each flight
    A. Situational awareness, problem recognition, and good judgement
    B. Application of stress management and risk element procedures
    C. The mental process of analyzing all information in a particular situation and making a timely decision on what action to take

43. Damaged lithium batteries can cause
    A. a change in aircraft center of gravity
    B. an inflight fire
    C. increased endurance

44. Identify the hazardous attitude or characteristic a Remote Pilot in Command displays while taking risks in order to impress others
    A. machoism
    B. Impulsivity
    C. invulnerability

45. When setting up the location of the control station and placement of crewmembers for a flight over snowy terrain, which of the following would be most appropriate for ensuring that vision is not impaired by the environment?
    A. The operation should be set up so that the crewmembers are most comfortable
    B. The operation should be set up so that the crewmembers face the directions in which the terrain most closely matches the color of unmanned aircraft
    C. The operation should be set up so that the remote PIC and crewmembers will face minimum glare from the snow

46. As a pilot, flying for long period in hot summer temperatures increases the susceptibility of dehydration since the
    A. dry air at altitude tends to increase the rate of water loss from the body
    B. moist air at altitude helps retain the body's moisture
    C. temperature decreases with altitude

47. Scheduled maintenance should be performed in accordance with the
    A. stipulations in 14 CFR Part 43
    B. manufactures" suggested procedures
    C. Contractor requirements

48. When adapting crew resource management (CRM) concepts to the operation of a small unmanned aircraft, CRM must be integrated into
    A. the communications only
    B. all phases of the operation
    C. the flight portion only

49. You are a remote pilot in command for a co-op energy service provider. You plan to use your unmanned aircraft to inspect powerlines in the remote area 15 hours away from your home office. After the drive, fatigue impacts your abilities to complete your assignment on time. What kind of fatigue is this?
    A. Acute fatigue
    B. Chronic Fatigue
    C. Exhaustion

50. Hazardous attitudes occur to every pilot to some degree at some time. What are some of these hazardous attitudes?
  A. Poor risk management and lack of stress management
  B. Poor situational awareness, snap judgements and lack of a decision-making process
  C. Antiauthority, impulsivity, macho, resignation and invulnerability

51. When should pilots state their position on the airport when calling the tower for takeoff?
  A. when departing from a runway intersection
  B. when visibility is less than 1 mile
  C. when parallel runways are in use

52. While preparing your sUAS for flight, you notice that one of the propeller blades has a nick. What action should you take?
  A. If the nick is less than 1/4 the length of the blade, it is safe to operate without replacement
  B. Remove and replace the propeller; consult manufacturer guidelines for repair, if any
  C. Repair by filing the nick to a smooth curve or with adhesive approved for use on the propeller material

53. A visual observer notices a manned aircraft approaching the area in which sUAS operations are taking place, flying just north of the area from west to east. What call could the remote PIC/ visual observer make on CTAF to alert the manned pilot?
  A. Zephyr Hills traffic unmanned aircraft Xray Yankee Zulu, operating five NM south of airport at or below 400 AGL, located at the three-o clock positon of the Cessna just north of our position Zephyrhills traffic
  B. Zephyr Hills traffic, unmanned aircraft at three o clock of manned aircraft in the area, Zephyrhills traffic
  C. Zephyr Hills traffic, unmanned aircraft Xray Yankee Zulu to Cessna in the area, look for UAS at your three-o clock position, we are about a mile south

54. What services will a FSS provide?
  A. Fuel pricing
  B. Clearance to taxi for takeoff
  C. Assistance during an emergency

55. The effective use of all available resources - human, hardware and information -prior to and during flight to ensure the successful outcome of the operation is called
  A. risk management
  B. crew resource management
  C. safety management system

56. Fatigue is one of the most treacherous hazards to flight safety
  A. as it may not be apparent until serious errors are made
  B. because it results in slow performance
  C. as it may be a function of physical robustness or mental activity

57. An extreme case of a pilot getting behind the aircraft can lead to operational pitfall of
   A. loss of workload
   B. loss of situational awareness
   C. Internal stress

58. During your preflight inspection, you discover that the casing of your sUAS battery has expanded beyond its normal dimensions. What actions will you take?
   A. Throw it away with your household trash
   B. Follow the manufacturer's guidance
   C. Use it as long as it will still hold a charge

59. The Common Traffic Advisory Frequency (CTAF) is used for manned aircraft to
   A. announce ground and flight intentions
   B. request air traffic control clearance
   C. request fuel services

60. At Coeur D'Alene, which frequency should be used as a Common Traffic Advisory Frequency (CTAF) to monitor airport traffic (use the next two images for this question)?

IDAHO   31

- -

COEUR D'ALENE–PAPPY BOYINGTON FLD (COE) 9 NW UTC–8(–7DT)

GREAT FALLS

N47°46.46' W116°49.18'

2320 B S4 **FUEL** 100, JET A OX 1, 2, 3, 4 Class IV, ARFF Index A NOTAM FILE COE H–1C, L–13B

RWY 05–23: H7400X100 (ASPH–GRVD) S–57, D–95, 2S–121, 2D–165 HIRL 0.6% up NE IAP

RWY 05: MALSR (NSTD). PAPI(P4R)—GA 3.0° TCH 56'.

RWY 23: REIL. PAPI(P4R)—GA 3.0° TCH 50'.

RWY 01–19: H5400X75 (ASPH) S–50, D–83, 2S–105, 2D–150

MIRL 0.3% up N

RWY 01: REIL. PAPI(P2L)—GA 3.0° TCH 39'. Rgt tfc.

RWY 19: PAPI(P2L)—GA 3.0° TCH 41'.

RUNWAY DECLARED DISTANCE INFORMATION

RWY 01: TORA–5400 TODA–5400 ASDA–5400 LDA–5400

RWY 05: TORA–7400 TODA–7400 ASDA–7400 LDA–7400

RWY 19: TORA–5400 TODA–5400 ASDA–5400 LDA–5400

RWY 23: TORA–7400 TODA–7400 ASDA–7400 LDA–7400

AIRPORT REMARKS: Attended Mon–Fri 1500–0100Z‡. For after hrs fuel-self svc avbl or call 208–772–6404, 208–661–4174, 208–661–7449, 208–699–5433. Self svc fuel avbl with credit card. 48 hr PPR for unscheduled ops with more than 30 passenger seats call arpt manager 208–446–1860. Migratory birds on and invof arpt Oct–Nov. Remote cntl airstrip is 2.3 miles west AER 05. Arpt conditions avbl on AWOS. Rwy 05 NSTD MALSR, thld bar extends 5' byd rwy edge lgts each side. ACTIVATE MIRL Rwy 01–19, HIRL Rwy 05–23, REIL Rwy 01 and Rwy 23, MALSR Rwy 05—CTAF. PAPI Rwy 01. Rwy 19, Rwy 05, and Rwy 23 opr continuously.

WEATHER DATA SOURCES: AWOS-3 135.075 (208) 772–8215.

HIWAS 108.8 COE.

COMMUNICATIONS: CTAF/UNICOM 122.8

RCO 122.05 (BOISE RADIO)

Ⓡ SPOKANE APP/DEP CON 132.1

AIRSPACE: CLASS E svc continuous.

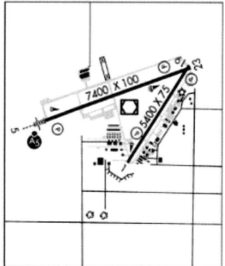

173

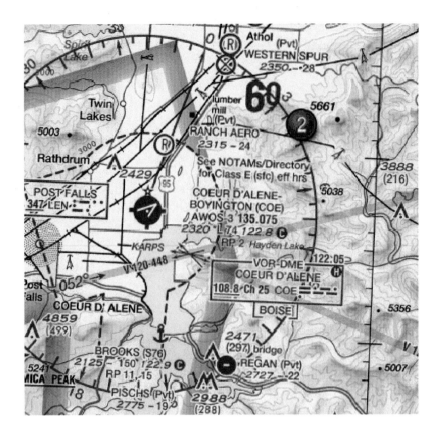

A. 122.05 MHz

B. 135.075 MHz

C. 122.8 MHz

61. The accurate perception and understanding of all the risk element factors and conditions is
   A. situational awareness
   B. judgment
   C. aeronautical decision making

62. What is the best way to mitigate risk?
   A. SMS plan
   B. Weekly meetings
   C. Establishing an operational procedure guideline

63. What can help a pilot mitigate stress?
   A. Increasing stress tolerance
   B. Removing stress from personal life
   C. Breathing into a paper bag

64. What can affect your performance?
   A. Prescription medications
   B. Over the counter medications
   C. Over the counter and prescribed medications

65. The aircraft call sign N169US will be spoken in this way:
   A. November one six niner uniform sierra
   B. November one six niner unmanned system
   C. November one hundred sixty-nine uniform sierra

SAMPLE TEST QUESTIONS

1. A professional wildlife photographer operates an sUAS from a moving truck to capture aerial images of migrating birds in remote wetlands. The drive of the truck does not serve any crewmember role in the operation. Is this sUAS operation in compliance with 14 CFR Part 107
    A. Compliant with Part 107
    B. Not compliant with Part 107
    C. Not compliant with state and local traffic laws

2. You have accepted football tickets in exchange for using your sUAS to videotape a future construction zone. What FAA regulation is this sUAS operation subject to?
    A. 14 CFR Part 101
    B. 14 CFR Part 107
    C. This operation is not subject to FAA regulations

3. To avoid a possible collision with a manned airplane, you estimate that your small unmanned aircraft climbed to an altitude greater than 600 feet AGL. to whom must you report the deviation?
    A. The National Transportation Safety Board
    B. Upon request of the Federal Aviation Administration
    C. Air Traffic Control

4. What do the blue shaped lines indicate throughout this sectional excerpt?

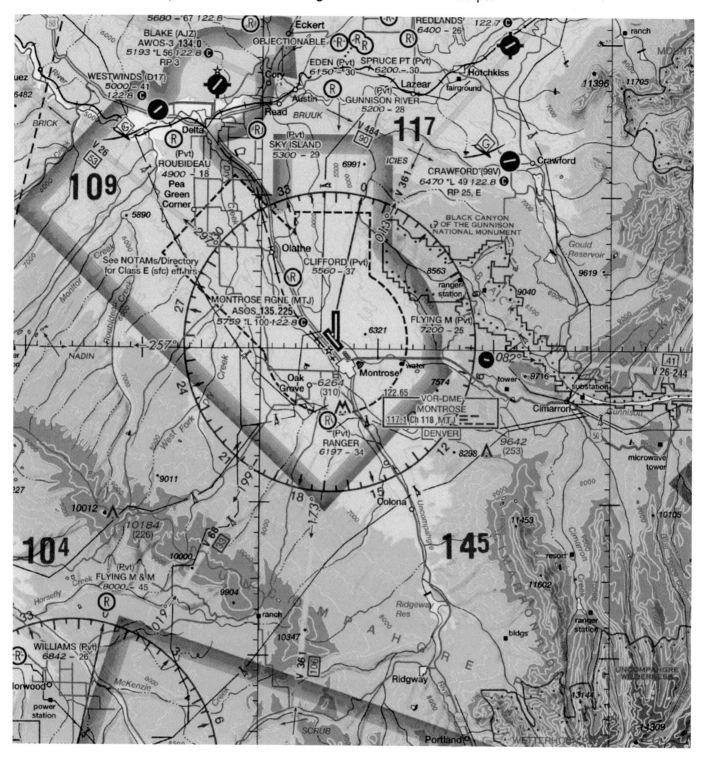

    A. Victor Airways

    B. Airline corridors

    C. Military Training routes

5. Which aircraft has right-of-way over other traffic

    A. An sUAS

    B. An airplane

    C. A quadcopter

6. As you are flying your sUAS, valued at $1000, over a home to photograph it for real estate sales purposes, the sUAS has a failure causing it to fall onto an awning, causing some minor damage. The fair market value of the awning is $800 but it can be repaired for $400. What type of report is required?
    A. No report is required
    B. An sUAS accident report to the FAA, within 10 days of operation
    C. An sUAS incident report to the FAA, within 10 days of the operation

7. When must a current remote pilot certificate be in the pilot's personal possession or readily accessible in the aircraft?
    A. When acting as a crew chief during launch and recovery
    B. Anytime when acting as pilot-in-command or as a required crewmember
    C. Only when a payload is carried

8. Which of the following individuals may process an application for a Part 107 remote pilot certificate with an sUAS rating?
    A. Commercial Balloon pilot
    B. Designated Pilot examiner
    C. Remote Pilot in command

9. While operating a small unmanned aircraft system (sUAS), you experience a flyaway and several people suffer injuries. Which of the following injuries requires reporting to the FAA?
    A. An injury requiring an overnight hospital stay
    B. Scrapes and cuts bandaged on site
    C. Minor bruises.

10. Which of the following types of operations are excluded from the requirements in 14 CFR Part 107?
    A. Quadcopter capturing aerial imagery for crop monitoring
    B. UAS used for motion picture filming
    C. Model aircraft for hobby use

11. No person may attempt to act as a crewmember of a sUAS with
    A. .04 percent by weight or more alcohol in the blood
    B. 0.004 percent by weight or more alcohol in the blood
    C. .4 percent by weight or more alcohol in the blood

12. When requesting a waiver, the required documents should be presented to the FAA at least how many days prior to the planned operation?
    A. 90 days
    B. 30 days
    C. 10 days

13. Within how many days must an sUAS accident be reported to the FAA?
    A. 90 days
    B. 10 days
    C. 30 days

14. In accordance with 14 CFR Part 107, except when within a 400 foot radius of a structure, at what maximum altitude can you operate sUAS?

    A. 400 feet AGL

    B. 600 feet AGL

    C. 500 feet AGL

15. To satisfy medical requirements, all sUAS crewmembers must

    A. hold a valid third-class medical certificate

    B. complete a physical with an Aviation Medical examiner

    C. be free of any physical or mental condition that would interfere with the safe operation of the small unmanned aircraft system

16. When using a small unmanned aircraft in a commercial operation, who is responsible for informing the participants about emergency procedure?

    A. the lead visual observer

    B. the FAA inspection-in-charge

    C. Remote Pilot in Command

17. Power company employees use an sUAS to inspect a long stretch of high voltage powerlines. due to muddy condition, their vehicle must stay beside the road and the crew must use binoculars to maintain visual line of sight with the aircraft. is this sUAS operation in compliance with 14 CFR Part 107?

    A. No, the operation is not in compliance with Part 107

    B. Yes, the operation is in compliance with Part 107

    C. There is not enough information to make a determination

18. Who is ultimately responsible for preventing a hazardous situation before an accident occurs?

    A. Person manipulating the controls

    B. Remote Pilot in Command

    C. Visual Observer

19. Within what airspace is Coeur D' Alene Pappy Boyington Fld located?

COEUR D'ALENE–PAPPY BOYINGTON FLD   (COE)   9 NW   UTC–8(–7DT)

N47°46.46' W116°49.18'

2320   B   S4   **FUEL** 100, JET A   OX 1, 2, 3, 4   Class IV, ARFF Index A   NOTAM FILE COE

RWY 05–23: H7400X100 (ASPH–GRVD)   S–57, D–95, 2S–121, 2D–165   HIRL   0.6% up NE

GREAT FALLS
H–1C, L–13B
IAP

RWY 05: MALSR (NSTD). PAPI(P4R)—GA 3.0° TCH 56'.

RWY 23: REIL. PAPI(P4R)—GA 3.0° TCH 50'.

RWY 01–19: H5400X75 (ASPH)   S–50, D–83, 2S–105, 2D–150

MIRL   0.3% up N

RWY 01: REIL. PAPI(P2L)—GA 3.0° TCH 39'. Rgt tfc.

RWY 19: PAPI(P2L)—GA 3.0° TCH 41'.

RUNWAY DECLARED DISTANCE INFORMATION

RWY 01:	TORA–5400	TODA–5400	ASDA–5400	LDA–5400
RWY 05:	TORA–7400	TODA–7400	ASDA–7400	LDA–7400
RWY 19:	TORA–5400	TODA–5400	ASDA–5400	LDA–5400
RWY 23:	TORA–7400	TODA–7400	ASDA–7400	LDA–7400

AIRPORT REMARKS: Attended Mon–Fri 1500–0100Z‡. For after hrs fuel-self svc avbl or call 208–772–6404, 208–661–4174, 208–661–7449, 208–699–5433. Self svc fuel avbl with credit card. 48 hr PPR for unscheduled ops with more than 30 passenger seats call arpt manager 208–446–1860. Migratory birds on and invof arpt Oct–Nov. Remote cntl airstrip is 2.3 miles west AER 05. Arpt conditions avbl on AWOS. Rwy 05 NSTD MALSR, thld bar extends 5' byd rwy edge lgts each side. ACTIVATE MIRL Rwy 01–19, HIRL Rwy 05–23, REIL Rwy 01 and Rwy 23, MALSR Rwy 05—CTAF. PAPI Rwy 01, Rwy 19, Rwy 05, and Rwy 23 opr continuously.

WEATHER DATA SOURCES: AWOS-3 135.075 (208) 772–8215.

HIWAS 108.8 COE.

COMMUNICATIONS: CTAF/UNICOM 122.8

RCO 122.05 (BOISE RADIO)

(R) SPOKANE APP/DEP CON 132.1

AIRSPACE: CLASS E svc continuous.

RADIO AIDS TO NAVIGATION: NOTAM FILE COE.

(T) VORW/DME 108.8   COE   Chan 25   N47°46.42' W116°49.24'   at fld. 2320/19E.   HIWAS.

DME portion unusable:

220°–240° byd 15 NM   280°–315° byd 15 NM blo 11,000'.

POST FALLS NDB (MHW) 347   LEN   N47°44.57' W116°57.66'   053° 6.0 NM to fld.

ILS 110.7   I–COE   Rwy 05   Class ID.   Localizer unusable 25° left and right of course.

A. Class E
B. Class B
C. Class D

20. How would a remote PIC "Check NOTAMs" as noted in the CAUTION box regarding the unmarked balloon?

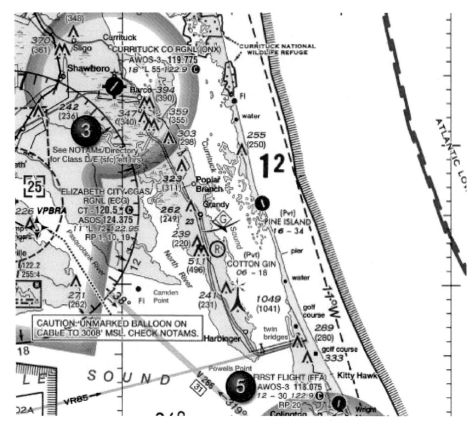

A. By obtaining a briefing via an online source such as 1800WXbrief.com
B. By utilizing the B4UFLY mobile application
C. By contacting the FAA district office

21. The airspace surrounding the Gila Bend AF AUX Airport (GXF) (area 6) is classified as

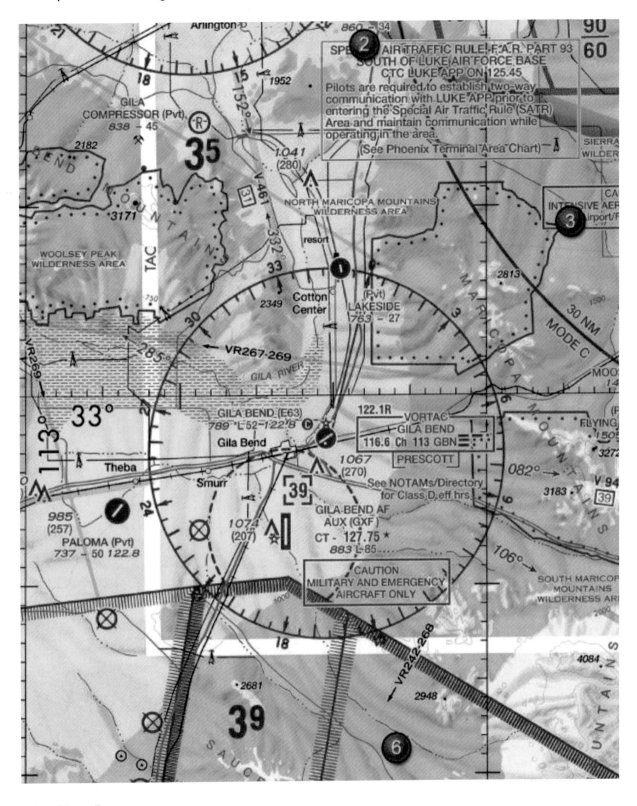

A. Class B
B. Class D
C. Class C

22. The "taxiway ending" marker
    A. indicates taxiway does not continue
    B. identifies area where aircraft are prohibited
    C. provides general taxiing direction to named taxiway

23. Entries into traffic patterns by manned aircraft while descending create specific collision hazards and
    A. should be used whenever possible
    B. are illegal
    C. should be avoided

24. One of the purposes for issuing a Temporary Flight Restriction (TFR) is to
    A. announce Parachute Jump areas
    B. identify Airport Advisory areas
    C. protect public figures

25. When turning onto a taxiway from another taxiway, what is the purpose of the taxiway directional sign?
    A. Indicates designation and direction of taxiway leading out of an intersection
    B. Indicates direction to take off runway
    C. Indicates designation and direction of exit taxiway from runway

26. You plan to operate a 33 lb SUAS to capture aerial imagery over real estate for use in sales listings. What FAA regulation is this sUAS operation subject to?
    A. 14 CFR Part 101
    B. 14 CFR Part 107
    C. This operation is not subject to FAA regulations

27. What action, if any, is appropriate if the remote pilot deviates from Part 107 during an emergency?
    A. File a detained report to the FAA Administrator, upon request
    B. Take no special action since you are pilot-in-command
    C. File a report to the FAA Administrator, as soon as possible

28. You are operating a 1280 g (2.8 lb) quadcopter for your own enjoyment. What FAA regulation is this sUAS operation subject to?
    A. 14 CFR Part 107
    B. 14 CFR Part 101
    C. This operation is not subject to FAA regulations

29. According to 14 CFR Part 107, what is required to operate a small unmanned aircraft within 30 minutes after official sunset
    A. Use of a transponder
    B. Use of lighted anti-collision lights
    C. Must be operated in a rural area

30. Which preflight action is specifically required of the pilot prior to each flight?
    A. Assess the operating environment including local weather conditions, local airspace and any flight restrictions, the location of persons and property on the surface, and other ground hazards
    B. Check the aircraft logbooks for appropriate entries
    C. Visually inspect the pilot certificates of all crew members

31. Remote Pilots are required to complete the following operational area surveillance prior to sUAS flight
    A. Select an operational area that is populated
    B. Keep the operational area free of and at an appropriate distance from all non-participants
    C. Make a plan to keep non-participants in viewing distance for the whole operation

32. As a remote pilot with an sUAS rating, under which situation can you deviate from 14 CFR Part 107?
    A. In response to an in-flight emergency
    B. When conducting public operations during a search mission
    C. Flying for enjoyment with family and friends

33. Whose sole task during an sUAS operation is to watch the sUAS and report potential hazards to the rest of the crew?
    A. Remote pilot-in-command
    B. Visual Observer
    C. Person manipulating the controls

34. When must a current remote pilot certificate be in the pilot's personal possession or readily accessible in the aircraft?
    A. Anytime when acting as pilot-in-command or as a required crewmember
    B. When acting as a crew chief during launch and recovery
    C. Only when a payload is carried

35. Each person who holds a pilot certificate, a US driver's license, or a medical certificate shall present it for inspection upon the request for the Administrator, the National Transportation Safety board, or any
    A. authorized representative of the Department of State
    B. federal, state, or local law enforcement officer
    C. authorized Administrator of the Department of Transportation

36. Unless otherwise authorized, what is the maximum airspeed at which a person may operate an sUAS below 400 feet?
    A. 100 mph
    B. 80 mph
    C. 200 knots

37. In accordance with 14 CFR Part 107, you may operate an sUAS from a moving vehicle when no property is carried for compensation or hire
    A. Over suburban areas
    B. Over a sparsely populated area
    C. Over a parade or other social event

38. While monitoring the Cooperstown CTAF you hear an aircraft announce that they are midfield left downwind to RWY 13. Where would the aircraft be relative to the runway?

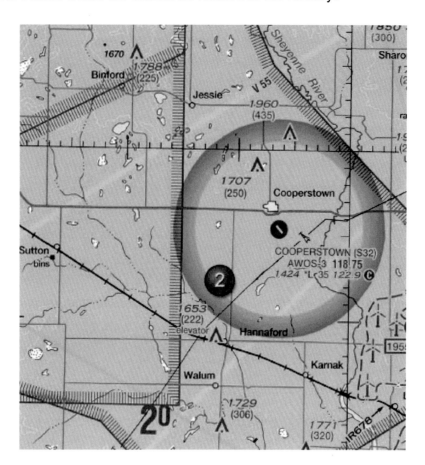

A. The Aircraft is South

B. The aircraft is East

C. The aircraft is south

39. What does the line of longitude at area 7 measure?

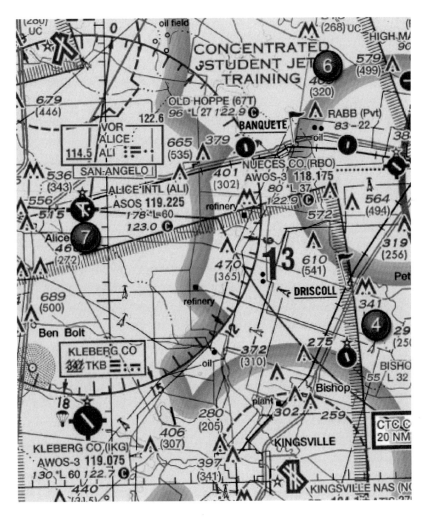

A. The degrees of longitude east and west of the line that passed through Greenwich, England
B. The degrees of longitude east and west of the Prime Meridian
C. The degrees of longitude north and south from the equator

40. One of the purposes for issuing a Temporary Flight Restriction (TFR) is to
A. announce Parachute Jump areas
B. identify Airport Advisory areas
C. protect public figures

41. The floor of Class B airspace overlying Hicks Airport (T67) north-northwest of Fort Worth Meacham Field is

    A. 4,000 feet MSL
    B. at the surface
    C. 3,200 feet MSL

42. The recommended entry position for manned aircraft to enter an airport traffic pattern is
    A. 45 degrees to the base leg just below traffic pattern altitude
    B. to enter 45 degrees at the midpoint of the downwind left at traffic pattern altitude
    C. to cross directly over the airport at traffic pattern altitude and join the downwind leg

43. You have received authorization to operate an sUAS at an airport. When flying the sUAS, the ATC tower instructs you to stay clear of all runways. Which situation would indicate that you are complying with this request.
    A. You are on the double dashed yellow line side of markings near the runway
    B. You are over the dashed white lines in the center of the pavement
    C. You are on the double solid yellow line side of markings near the runway

44. The minimum distance from clouds required for sUAS part 107 operations is
   A. clear of clouds
   B. 500 feet above, 1,000 feet horizontally
   C. 500 feet below, 2,000 feet horizontally

45. The development of thermals depends upon
   A. a counterclockwise circulation of air
   B. solar heating
   C. temperature inversions

46. Thunderstorms which generally produce the most intense hazard to aircraft are
   A. squall line thunderstorms
   B. steady state thunderstorms
   C. warm front thunderstorms

47. An air mass moving inland from the coast in winter is likely to result in
   A. fog
   B. rain
   C. frost

48. Which factor would tend to increase the density altitude at a given airport referenced in the weather briefing?
   A. An increase in barometric pressure
   B. A decrease in relative humidity
   C. An increase in ambient temperature

49. What situation is most conducive to the formation of radiation fog?
   A. Moist, tropical air moving over cold offshore water
   B. The movement of cold air over much warmer water
   C. Warm, moist air over low, flatland areas on clear, calm nights

50. Which weather phenomenon is always associated with a thunderstorm?
   A. Heavy rain
   B. Hail
   C. Lightning

51. Upon your preflight evaluation of weather, the forecasts you reference state there is an unstable air mass approaching your location. Which would not be a concern for your impending operation?
   A. Thunderstorms
   B. Stratiform clouds
   C. Turbulent conditions

52. An increase in load factor will cause an unmanned aircraft to
   A. stall at a higher airspeed
   B. have a tendency to spin
   C. be more difficult to control

53. When range and economy of operation are the principal goals, the remote pilot must ensure that the sUAS will be operated at the recommended
    A. specific endurance
    B. long range cruise performance
    C. equivalent airspeed

54. Maximum endurance is obtained at the point of minimum power to maintain the aircraft
    A. in steady, level flight
    B. in a long range descent
    C. at its slowest possible indicated airspeed

55. The angle of attack at which an airfoil stalls which
    A. increase if the CG is moved forward
    B. change with an increase in gross weight
    C. remain the same regardless of gross weight

56. You are operating an sUAS that does not have GPS or an installed altimeter. How can you determine the altitude you are operating?
    A. Operating a second sUAS that has an altimeter to gain a visual perspective of 400 feet from the air
    B. Gaining a visual perspective of what 400 feet looks like on the ground before the flight
    C. Operating the sUAS in close proximity of a tower known to be 400 feet tall

57. The amount of excess load that can be imposed on the wing of an airplane depends upon the
    A. position of the CG
    B. speed of the airplane
    C. abruptness at which the load is applied

58. What could be a consequence of operating a small unmanned aircraft above its maximum allowable weight?
    A. shorter endurance
    B. increased maneuverability
    C. faster speed

59. According to 14 CFR Part 107, who is responsible for determining the performance of a small unmanned aircraft?
    A. Remote pilot-in-command
    B. Manufacturer
    C. Owner or operator

60. Before each flight the remote PIC must ensure that:
    A. objects carried on the sUAS are secure
    B. ATC has granted clearance
    C. the site supervisor has approved the flight

ANSWER KEYS

Regulations (Section 1)

1. A
You may operate an sUAS from a moving vehicle if you are in a sparsely populated area and the driver does not serve as the remote PIC, person manipulating the controls, or visual observer. Reference: 14 CFR 107.25

2. C
You may not operate a small unmanned aircraft directly over another person unless that person is directly involved in the operation (such as a visual observer or other crewmember) or within a safe cover, such as inside a stationery vehicle or a protective structure that would protect a person from harm if the small unmanned aircraft were to crash into that structure. Reference: 14 CFR 107.39

3. C
This scenario is not compliant with Part 107. You may not operate over non-participants without safe cover and you may not drop objects in a manner that creates hazard.

4. A
A remote pilot-in-command must be used during Part 107 sUAS operations. A visual observer is optional. The person manipulating the controls may be the remote PIC, or must be operating under the direct supervision of the remote PIC.
Reference:14 CFR 107.19

5. B
A person may not operate or act as a remote pilot-in-command or visual observer in the operation of more than one unmanned aircraft at the same time.

6. B
An unmanned aircraft means an aircraft operated without the possibility of direct human intervention from within or on the aircraft. Reference: 14 CFR 107.1, 107.3, AC 107-2

7. C
No items may be dropped from the small unmanned aircraft in a manner that creates undue hazard to persons or property.
Reference: 14 CFR 107.23

8. B
The sUAS cannot be flown faster than a ground speed of 87 knots (100mph) and must be operated below 400 feet.
Reference: 14 CFR 107.51

9. A
Except in an emergency, no person may operate an aircraft contrary to an ATC clearance or instruction.
Reference: 14 CFR 107.21

10. B

"Owners must register the sUAS if it is greater than 0.55 lbs, less than 55 pounds and operated under the provisions of the 14 CFR Part 107.
Reference: 14 CFR 107.13"

11. C

"When sUAS operations are conducted during civil twilight, the sUAS must be equipped with anti-collision lights that are capable of being visible for at least 3 statute miles.
Reference: 14 CFR 107.29"

12. A

"Lithium batteries that are installed in an sUAS for power during the operation are not considered a hazardous material under Part 107. However, spare (uninstalled) lithium batteries would meet the definition of hazardous material and may not be carried on the sUAS.
Reference: AC 107-2"

13. B

"In case of an in-flight emergency, the remote PIC is permitted to deviate from any rule of Part 107 to the extent necessary to respond to that emergency.
Reference: 14 CFR 107.21"

14. A

"Although not required by Part 107, the FAA encourages applicants to submit their application at least 90 days prior to the start of the proposed operation. The FAA will strive to complete review and adjudication of waiver within 90 days; however, the time required for the FAA to make a determination regarding waiver requests will vary based on the complexity of the request.
Reference: AC 107-2"

15. C

"The remote PIC must report any sUAS accident to the FAA, within 10 days of the operation, if a serious injury to any person or any loss of consciousness occurs. It would be considered a serious injury if a person requires hospitalization.
Reference: 14 CFR 107.9, AC 107-2"

16. C

"Remote pilot certificate holders with an sUAS rating must meet the recurrent training requirements after 24 months. This retraining can be satisfied by completing the online FAA course or taking the FAA knowledge exam.
Reference: 14 CFR Part 107.63 and 107.65; AC 107-2"

17. B

"The sUAS must remain within visual line of sight (VLOS) of flight crewmembers. The VLOS requirement would not prohibit actions such as scanning the airspace or briefly looking down at the sUAS control station. Should the remote PIC or person manipulating the controls lose VLOS of the small UA, he or she must regain VLOS as soon as possible.
Reference: 14 CFR 107.31"

18. B

"The remote pilot application must be submitted to a Flight Standards District Office (FSDO), a designated pilot examiner (DPE), an airman certification representative for a pilot school, a certified flight instructor (CFI), or other person authorized by the Administrator to process the application.
Reference: 14 CFR 107.63 and 61.56"

19. C

"The remote PIC or person manipulating the flight controls of an sUAS must comply with the ""do not operate while impaired"" regulations.
Reference: 14 CFR 107.19 (b), 107.19(d) and 107.57"

20. C

"Owners must register the sUAS if it is greater than 0.55 lbs, less than 55 pounds and operated under the provisions of the 14 CFR Part 107.
Reference: 14 CFR 107.13"

21. C

"Each remote pilot shall, before each flight, assess the operating environment including local weather condition, local airspace and any flight restrictions, the location of persons and property on the surface, and other ground hazards.
Reference: 14 CFR 107.49"

22. B

"As little as one ounce of liquor, one bottle of beer, or four ounces of wine can impair flying skills.
Reference: AIM 8-1-1"

23. A

"The remote PIC must be able to maneuver the sUAS to avoid a collision and prevent other aircraft from having to take evasive action.
Reference: 14 CFR 107.37"

24. A

14 CFR Part 107 does not apply to model aircraft that meet the criteria in 14 CFR 101.41, amateur rockets, moored balloons or unmanned free balloons, kites, operations conducted outside the United States, public aircraft operations, and air carrier operations.

25. B

"The sUAS must be registered by a person who is at least 13 years of age
Reference: 14 CFR 107.13, 91.2013"

26. C

"A remote pilot-in-command, owner, or person manipulating the flight controls of a small unmanned aircraft must, upon request, make available to the administrator: (1) the remote pilot certificate with a small UAS rating; and (2) any other document, record, or report required.
Reference: 14 CFR 107.7"

27. A

"A person who does not hold a remote pilot certificate or a remote pilot that has not met the recurrent testing/training requirements of part 107 may operate the sUAS under Part 107, as long as he or she is directly supervised by a remote PIC and the remote PIC has the ability to immediately take direct control of the sUAS.
Reference: 14 CFR 107.12"

28. B

"This sUAS operation is subject to 14 CFR part 107 because the aerial imagery is for the furtherance of a business, making it commercial in nature.
Reference: 14 CFR 107.3"

29. A

"The remote PIC must complete a preflight familiarization, inspection, and other actions, such as crewmember briefings, prior to beginning flight operations.
Reference: 14 CFR 107.49 "

30. B

"the sUAS cannot be flown higher than 400 feet AGL unless flown within a 400-foot radius of a structure and is not flown higher than 400 feet above the structure's immediate upper-most limit.
Reference: 14 CFR 107.51"

31. C

"The FAA has stated that they will not provide waivers for beyond VLOS during the carriage of goods for hire. Also, moving vehicles (land or sea) are not authorized to be used during flights upon which goods are carried for hire.
Reference: AC 107-2"

32. C

"Each remote PIC who deviates from a rule in Part 107 must, upon request of the FAA administrator, send a written report of that deviation to the Administrator
Reference: 14 CFR 107.21"

33. A

"Report any sUAS accident to the FAA within 10 days if it results in serious injury, loss of consciousness, or repairs costing over $500.
Reference: 14 CFR 107.9"

34. B

"14 CFR 65.20 states that any person who falsifies or makes a fraudulent entry in a logbook, report or record is subject to the suspension or revocation of any airman or ground instructor certificate or rating held by that person.
Reference: 14 CFR 107.6"

35. A

"No person may act as a pilot-in0command (PIC), or in any other capacity as a required pilot flight crewmember when operating a sUAS unless he or she has in possession or readily accessible a current-pilot certificate.
Reference: 14 CFR 107.7"

36. B

"A remote pilot may not act as pilot-in-command of an sUAS at night. A remote pilot must land by the end of evening twilight.
Reference: 14 CFR 107.29"

37. A

"Each remote PIC who deviates from a rule in Part 107 must, upon request of the FAA administrator, send a written report of that deviation to the Administrator
Reference: 14 CFR 107.21"

38. C

"No person may manipulate the flight controls of a small unmanned aircraft system or act as a remote pilot-in-command, visual observer, or direct participant in the operation of the small unmanned aircraft if he or she knows or has reason to know that he or she has a physical or mental condition that would interfere with the safe operation of the small un manned aircraft system.
Reference: 14 CFR 107.17 "

39. A

"A refusal to submit to a test to indicate the percentage by weight of alcohol in the blood, when requested by a law enforcement officer, or a refusal to furnish or authorize the release of the test results requested by the Administrator, is grounds for denial os an application for a remote pilot certificate with a small UAS rating for a period of up to 1 year after the date of that refusal; or suspension or revocation of a remote pilot certificate with a small UAS rating.
Reference: 14 CFR 107.59"

40. B

"No person may act, or attempt to act, as a crewmember of a civil aircraft while having .04 percent or more, by weight alcohol in the blood.
Reference: 14 CFR 107.27,91.17"

41. C

"The remote PIC must hold a Part 107 remote pilot certificate with an sUAS rating before conducting any sUAS operation
Reference: 14 CFR 107.12"

42. C

"The sUAS cannot be flown faster than a ground speed of 87 knots (100mph).
Reference: 14 CFR 107.51"

43. A

"The visual observer (when asked by the remote PIC) maintains visual line of sight with sUAS and reports any potential hazards to the remote PIC and person manipulating the controls.
Reference: 14 CFR 107.33"

44. A

"small unmanned aircraft (sUAS) means an unmanned aircraft weighing less than 55 pounds on takeoff, including everything that is on board or otherwise attached to the aircraft.
Reference: 14 CFR 107.1,AC 107-2"

45. C

"Operation of an sUAS is permitted from a moving land or waterborne vehicle over a sparsely populated (or unpopulated) area.
Reference: 14 CFR 107.25"

46. A

"Operation of an sUAS is permitted from a moving land or waterborne vehicle over a sparsely populated (or unpopulated) area.
Reference: 14 CFR 107.25"

47. B

"If the remote PIC determines that the operation cannot be conducted within the regulatory structure of Part 107, he or she is responsible for applying for a Certificate of Waiver (COW) and proposing a safe alternative to the operation. This COW with allow an sUAS operation to deviate from certain provisions to Part 107 as long as the FAA finds that the proposed operation can be safely conducted under the terms of that Certificate of Waiver.
Reference: 14 CFR 107.200"

48. A

"Report any sUAS accident to the FAA within 10 days if it results in serious injury, loss of consciousness, or repairs costing over $500.
Reference: 14 CFR 107.9"

49. C

"Part 107 regulates commercial sUAS operations.
Reference: 14 CFR 107.41 and 107.1"

50. A

"You may not operate a small unmanned aircraft directly over another person unless that person is directly involved in the operation (such as a visual observer or other crewmember) or within a safe cover, such as inside a stationery vehicle or a protective structure that would protect a person from harm if the small unmanned aircraft were to crash into that structure.
Reference: 14 CFR 107.39"

51. B

"No person may manipulate the flight controls of a small unmanned aircraft system or act as a remote pilot-in-command, visual observer, or direct participant in the operation of the small unmanned aircraft if he or she knows or has reason to know that he or she has a physical or mental condition that would interfere with the safe operation of the small un manned aircraft system.
Reference: 14 CFR 107.17 "

52. B

"The remote PIC also has a responsibility to remain clear of and yield right of way to all other aircraft, manned or unmanned, and avoid other potential hazards that may affect the remote PIC's operation of the aircraft.
Reference: 14 CFR 107.37"

53. A

"No report is required because the damage can be repaired for less than $500. A report is required only when damage to any property, other than the small UA, is greater than $500 to repair or replace the property (whichever is lower). The cost of the sUAS is not considered when determining if an event is considered to be an accident or incident.
Reference: 14 CFR 107.9, AC 107-2"

54. C

"The remote PIC is ultimately responsible for assessing the needs of the operation and preparing sufficient support crewmembers to ensure the safety of the operation.
Reference: 14 CFR 107.12"

55. B

"The holder of a remote pilot certificate who has made a change in his or her permanent mailing address may not, after 30 days from the date moved, exercise the privileges of his or her certificate unless he or she has notified in writing the FAA Airmen Certificate Branch
Reference: 14 CFR 107.77"

56. A

"No person may act or attempt to act as a crewmember of a sUAS within 8 hours after the consumption of any alcoholic beverage. Remember ""8 hours bottle to throttle""
Reference: 14 CFR 107.27, 91.17"

57. B

"The sUAS cannot be flown higher than 400 feet AGL unless flown within a 400-foot radius of a structure and is not flown higher than 400 feet above the structure's immediate upper-most limit.
Reference: 14 CFR 107.51"

58. B

"A non-certified person may manipulate the controls of the sUAS only if he or she is under the direct supervision of the remote PIC.
Reference: 14 CFR 107.12"

59. C

"The remote pilot operating an sUAS must yield right-of-way to all other manned aircraft, including aircraft operating on the surface of the aircraft.
Reference: 14 CFR 107.37"

60. A

"Part 107 sUAS operations require minimum visibility of 3 SM and the minim distance from clouds must be no less than 500 feet below the cloud and 2000 feet horizontally from the cloud. To maintain 500 feet below the cloud, you must have a 900 foot ceiling to be able to operate to the maximum 400 AGL, or a ceiling that would allow the sUAS to operate at a lower AGL altitude.
Reference: 14 CFR 107.51"

61. C

"this sUAS operation is not subject to FAA sUAS regulations because the sUAS operation is recreational in nature. Part 101 details the regulations pertinent to model aircraft and hobby operations.
Reference: 14 cfr Part 107.3"

62. C

"The remote PIC is ultimately responsible for assessing the needs of the operation and preparing sufficient support crewmembers to ensure the safety of the operation.
Reference: 14 CFR 107.12"

63. B

"You may not operate a small unmanned aircraft directly over another person unless that person is directly involved in the operation (such as a visual observer or other crewmember) or within a safe cover, such as inside a stationery vehicle or a protective structure that would protect a person from harm if the small unmanned aircraft were to crash into that structure.
Reference: 14 CFR 107.39"

64. A

"This sUAS operation is subject to 14 CFR Part 107 because the compensation (money or otherwise) makes the operation commercial in nature
Reference: 14 CFR 107.3"

65. B

"Prior to flight, the remote PIC must ensure that all persons directly participating in the small unmanned aircraft operation are informed about the operating conditions, emergency procedures, contingency procedures, roles and responsibilities, and potential hazards.
Reference: 14 CFR 107.49, AC 107-2"

66. B

"An autonomous operation does not negate the requirement for a remote PIC. An autonomous operation is generally considered an operation in which the remote pilot inputs a flight plan into the CS, which send it to the autopilot on the small UA.
Reference: AC 107-2"

67. A
"This scenario is not compliant with Part 107. Visual aids such as binoculars may be used only momentarily to enhance situational awareness. they may not be used during the duration of the operation.
Reference: 14 CFR 107.31"

68. B
"A conviction for the violation of any Federal or State statute relating to the growing, processing, manufacture, sale, disposition, possession, transportation, or importation of narcotic drugs, marijuana, or depressant or stimulant drugs or substances is grounds for suspension or revocation of a remote pilot certificate with a small UAS rating.
Reference: 14 CFR 107.57"

69. B
"A remote pilot may not act as pilot-in-command of an sUAS at night. Night is defined as the time between the end of evening civil twilight and the beginning of morning civil twilight. Morning civil twilight is the period 30 minutes prior to sunrise until sunrise. This means you can launch your sUAS operation 30 minutes prior to sunrise.
Reference: 14 CFR 107.29"

70. A
"Part 107 addresses sUAS operations of certain civil small unmanned aircraft within the National Airspace System.
Reference: 14 CFR Part 107"

71. B
"A remote pilot-in-command, owner, or person manipulating the flight controls of a small unmanned aircraft system must, upon request, make available to the Administrator: (1) the remote pilot certificate with a small UAS rating; and (2) any other document, record, or report required.
Reference: 14 CFR 107.7"

72. A
"The Pilot's Handbook of Aeronautical Knowledge (FAA-H-8083-25) provide information on the physiological effects of alcohol, prescription drugs, and over-the-counter medications.
Reference: FAA-H-8083-25"

73. C
"A conviction for the violation of any Federal or State statute relating to the growing, processing, manufacture, sale, disposition, possession, transportation, or importation of narcotic drugs, marijuana, or depressant or stimulant drugs or substances is grounds for denial of an application for a remote pilot certificate with a small UAS rating for a period of up to 1 year after the date of that act.
Reference: 14 CFR 107.57"

1. B

"No person may operate a small unmanned aircraft in prohibited or restricted areas unless that person has permission from the using or controlling agency, as appropriate.
Reference: Sectional Chart Legend, 14 CFR 107.45"

2. A

"Both the Aeronautical Information Manual (AIM) and the Pilot's Handbook of Aeronautical Knowledge (FAA-H-8083-25) contain explanations of airport signs and markings
Reference: AIM Chapter 2, Section 3"

3. A

"Onawa, IA (K36) is in the bottom right quadrant of the sectional excerpt. It is outside any shading or lines, which indicates the airport is in Class G airspace up to 1200 feet AGL
Reference: Sectional Chart Legend"

4. B

"All activity within an Alert Area shall be conducted in accordance with FAA regulations, without waiver, and pilots of participating aircraft, as well as pilots transiting the area, shall be equally responsible for collision avoidance
Reference: AIM 3-4-6"

5. C

"No person may operate a small unmanned aircraft in class B, Class C, or class D airspace or within the lateral boundaries of the surface area of Class E airspace designated for an airport unless that person has prior authorization from ATC
Reference: 14 CFR 107.41"

6. C

"VFR Military training routes at and below 1500 feet AGL (will no segment above 1500) will be identified by four digit numbers, eg VR1351. VR above and below 1500 feet AGL (segments of these routes may be below 1500) will be identified by three digit numbers, eg VR 426. Small UAS must operate below 400 feet. This 4 digit Military Training Route indicates operations below 1500 feet AGL, which could present a hazard to the sUAS operations.
Reference: AIM 3-5-2"

7. B

"The chart supplement US includes airport details, including remarks unique to that airport. Figure 52 shown an abbreviated remark for Lincoln Airport ""Birds invof aipt""
Reference: Chart Supplement"

8. A

"When approaching the holding line from the side with the continuous lines, a pilot should not cross the holding line without ATC clearance at a controlled airport, or without making sure of adequate separation from other aircraft at uncontrolled airports.
Reference: AIM 2-3-5"

9. A

"The dimensions of Class D airspace are as needed for each individual circumstance. The airspace may include extensions necessary for IFR arrival and departure paths.
Reference: AIM 3-2-5"

10. C

"The chart supplement US includes airport details, including the airspace the airport lies in. Figure 31 shows Coeur D' Alene airport within Class E airspace.
Reference: Chart Supplement"

11. A

"Runway hold markings are indicated by two double dashed and two solid yellow lines. You are considered to be on the taxiway on the double solid yellow line side while you are considered to be on the runway if on the double dashed yellow line side.
Reference: AIM 2-3-4"

12. B

"When a manned aircraft is approaching to land at an airport in Class G airspace without an operating control tower, each pilot of an airplane will make all turns to the left unless the airport displays approved light signals of visual markings indicating that turns should be made to the right (which will be detailed in the Chart Supplement US)
Reference: 14 CFR 91.126"

13. A

"The ""98"" north of area 7 is the line of longitude east and west of the line that passes through Greenwich, England.
Reference: FAA-H-8083-25"

14. A

"Refer to Appendix 1, Legend 1. Airports having control towers are shown in blue, all others in magenta.
Reference: Sectional Chart Legend."

15. C

"The GXF airport is surrounded by a dashed blue line which indicates it is within Class D airspace.
Reference: Sectional Chart"

16. A

Restricted areas can be penetrated but only with the permission of the controlling agency. No person may operate an aircraft within a restricted area contrary to the restrictions imposed unless he/she has the permission of the using or controlling agency. Penetration of restricted areas without authorization from the using or controlling agency may be fatal to the aircraft and its occupants
Reference: 14 CFR 107.45, AIM 3-4-3

17. B

"Effective scanning is accomplished with a series of short, regularly spaced eye movements that bring successive areas of the sky into the central visual field. Each movement that brings successive areas of the sky into the central visual field. Each movement should not exceed 10 degrees and each area should be observed at least one second to enable detection.
Reference: AIM 8-1-6"

18. A

"FDC NOTAMs are issued by the National Flight Data Center and contain regulatory information such as Temporary Flight Restrictions.
Reference: FAA-H-8083-25"

19. C

"On final approach to runway 9, the aircraft will be heading from east to west on a 090 heading. Thus aircraft of the airport.
Reference: AIM 4-1-5"

20. B

"According to the Chart, the ATC control tower frequency is 120.50
Reference: Sectional Chart Legend."

21. A

"Hayward executive is located in Class D airspace up to but not including 1500 feet MSL as depicted by the blue segmented line surrounding it. Note that Class C begins at 1500 feet MSL in that sector and goes up to the bottom of the overlying Class B (noted by the ""T"" in the altitude description""
Reference: AIM 3-2-5"

22. B

"TFRs are imposed in order to:
   1. Protect persons and property in the air or on the surface from an existing or imminent flight associated hazard
   2. Provide a safe environment for the operation of disaster relief aircraft
   3. Prevent an unsafe congestion of sightseeing aircraft above an incident
   4. Protect the President, Vice President, or other public figures, and,
   5. Provide a safe environment for space agency operations.
   Pilots are expected to check appropriate NOTAMs during flight planning when conducting flight in an area where a TFR is in effect
Reference: FAA-H-8083-25"

23. A

"Refer to Appendix 1, Legend 1. The top number, printed in bold, is the height of the obstruction above mean sea level. The second number, printed in parentheses, is the height of the obstruction above ground level. The obstruction is shown as 1548 feel MSL and 1534 feet AGL.
Reference: Sectional Chart Legend"

24. A

"Refer to Appendix 1, Legend 1. On figure 24, area 3, the group obstruction near the 009 degree radial has the word ""stacks"" below 454. The bold number (454) indicates the height of the obstruction above mean sea level.
Reference: Sectional Chart Legend."

25. B

"On-airport areas that are used for certain cargo functions, including screening, must be a security identification display area (SIDA). A SIDA is that portion of an airport within the US, specified in the security program, in which individuals must display an airport-issued or approved ID and carry out other security measures.
Reference: 49 CFR 1544"

26. A

"Graticules on sectional charts are the lines dividing each 30 minutes of latitude and each 30 minutes of longitude. Each tick mark represents one minute of latitude or longitude. Latitude increases northward, west longitude increases going westward. The Garrison (Pvt) airport is located approximately 47 degrees 40''N latitude and 101 degrees 26'00''W longitude.
Reference: FAA-H-8083-25"

27. C

"Notice to Airmen (NOTAMs provide the most current information available) They provide time-critical information on airports and changes that affect the NAS.
Reference: FAA-H-8083-25"

28. C

"The hill has a height of 4,960 MSL. Therefore, an sUAS may be flown up to 400 feet AGL which is 5,360 feet. The floor of airspace such as Class E in in AGL not MSL.
Reference: Sectional Chart Legend, 14 CFR 107.51"

29. A

"Refer to Appendix 1, Legend 1. Anderson airport is in the bottom right quadrant of the sectional. The lack of shading around the airport indicates it is in Class G airspace. Small UAS operates in Class G airspace may be conducted without ATC permissions. However, remote pilots should exercise vigilance to ensure they cause no interruption to aircraft traffic.
Reference: Sectional Chart Legend"

30. B

"The Chart Supplement US is a publication for pilots containing information about airports, seaplane bases, and heliports open to the public including communications data, navigational facilities and certain special notices and procedures.
Reference: FAA-H-8083-25"

31. C

"Remote Pilots should report collisions between aircraft and wildlife so the authorities can take measures to mitigate future incidents.
Reference: AIM 7-4-5"

32. A

"The runway number is the whole number nearest one-tenth the magnetic azimuth of the centerline of the runway, measured clockwise from magnetic north. For example: 272 degrees = RWY 27; 087 degrees = RWY 9
Reference: AIM 2-3-3 "

33. A
"The 'Pvt' after the airport names indicates Sky Way Airport is a restricted or non-public use airport.
Reference: Sectional Chart"

34. B
"Notice to Airmen (NOTAMs provide the most current information available) and can be found by visiting www.faa.org or obtained at a flight service station (FSS). A comprehensive weather briefing can be obtained as part of a standard preflight briefing.
Reference: FAA-H-8083-25"

35. A
"Mandatory instructions signs are used to denote an entrance to a runway or critical area and areas where an aircraft is prohibited from entering. The runway holding position sing is located at the holding position on taxiways that intersect a runway or on runways that intersect other runways.
Reference: AIM 2-3-8"

36. C
"Entries into traffic patterns while descending create specific collision hazards and should be avoided.
Reference: AIM 4-4-15"

37. A
"The Barnes County Airport is depicted inside the magenta shading, which is controlled airspace from 700 feet AGL up to but not including 18,000 feet. Therefore, the airspace below 700 feet AGL is class G.
Reference: AIM 3-2-1"

38. B
"The notices to Airmen Publication (NTAP) is published by Air Traffic Publications every 28 days and contains all current NOTAM (D)s and FDC NOTAMs (except FDC NOTAMs for TFRs) available for publication.
Reference: FAA-H-8083-25"

39. A
"Most skeletal structures are supported by guy wires which are very difficult to see in good weather and can be invisible at dusk or during periods of reduced visibility. These wires can extend about 1,500 feet horizontally from a structure; therefore, all skeletal structures should be avoided horizontally by at least 2,000 feet.
Reference: AIM 7-5-3"

40. C
"The ""47"" at area 4 is the line of latitude north and south from the equator.
Reference: FAA-H-8083-35"

41. A
"Meridians of longitude encircle the earth from pole to pole, and all meridians cross the equator at right angles
Reference: FAA-H-8083-25"

42. A
"The taxiway directional sign identifies the designation(s) of the intersecting taxiway(s) leading out of the intersection that a pilot would normally be expected to turn onto or hold short of.
Reference: AIM 2-3-10"

43. C
"Contact with ATC must be made when operating within Class D airport, which is indicated by the blue airport and the blue dashed line surrounding it. The radius of Class D in the case is 4 NM, which is the command standard radius, although configuration of Class D is individually tailored for some airports.
Reference: Sectional Chart Legend, 14 CFR 107.41, AIM 3-2-5"

44. B
"No person may operate a small unmanned aircraft in Class B, Class C or Class D airspace or within, the lateral boundaries of the surface area of Class E airspace designated for an airport unless that person has prior authorization from Air Traffic Control (ATC)
Reference: 14 CFR 107.41"

45. A
"To measure the latitude and longitude, begin with looking for the hatched black lines with degree numbers on them. Just southeast of ECG there is the 36 degrees latitude line (running east/ west) and the 76 degrees longitude line (running north/ south). Count the ticks on the latitude line which is approximately 16 - these are the number of minutes yielding N 36 degrees 16' (north because the airport is north of the equator). Next, count the ticks west of the longitude line. There are approximately 10, therefore this is W76 degrees 10' (west because the airport is west of the prime meridian).
Reference: Sectional Chart Legend."

46. C
"The sectional chart excerpt includes a blue box note 4 SM southeast of the ECG airport that says ""
Caution: Unmarked balloon on cable to 3008' MSL. Check NOTAMs.
Reference: Sectional Chart Legend"

47. B
The common traffic advisory frequency (CTAF) is used for carrying out airport advisory practices and/or position reporting at an uncontrolled airport (which may also occur during hours when a tower is closed). The CTAF may be a UNICOM, MULTICOM, FSS or tower frequency and is identified in the appropriate aeronautical publications. On charts, CTAF is indicated by a solid dot with the letter "C" inside. When the control tower operates part time and a UNICOM frequency is provided, use the UNICOM frequency.

48. B
"Runway 6 faces northeast on a 060 heading thus arriving aircraft will be on final approach southwest of the airport. Since you are operating south of the airport, you would want to avoid areas west (which would be closer to the final approach course) and north (closer to the airport and possibly the final approach course for runway 6)
Reference: AIM 4-1-5"

49. A

"Runway holding position markings on taxiways identify the locations on a taxiway where an aircraft is supposed to stop when it does not have clearance to proceed onto the runway.
Reference: AIM 2-3-5"

50. A

"The wire rich environment is typically below 1000 feet. Not all wires are marked and they can be nearly invisible when viewed from different angles. Remote pilots must exercise vigilance when operating near helicopters, moored balloons and others places where wires are frequently present.
Reference: SAFO 10015"

51. C

"TFRs are imposed in order to:
1. Protect persons and property in the air or on the surface from an existing or imminent flight associated hazard
2. Provide a safe environment for the operation of disaster relief aircraft
3. Prevent an unsafe congestion of sightseeing aircraft above an incident
4. Protect the President, Vice President, or other public figures, and,
5. Provide a safe environment for space agency operations.
Pilots are expected to check appropriate NOTAMs during flight planning when conducting flight in an area where a TFR is in effect
Reference: FAA-H-8083-25"

52. A

"The magenta shading around Jamestown airport indicates the floor of the class E airspace starts 700 feet above the surface. No person may operate a small unmanned aircraft in class B, Class C or Class D airspace or within the lateral boundaries of the surface area of class E airspace designated for an airport unless that person has prior authorization from ATC.
Reference: 14 CFR 107.41, FAA-H-8083-25"

53. B

"Taxiway ending markers are used to indicate that the taxiway foes not continue
Reference: AIM 2-3-4"

54. B

"No person may operate a small unmanned aircraft that interferes with operations and traffic patterns at any airport, heliport or seaplane base.
Reference: 14 CFR 107.43"

55. A

"If taking off of runway 35, the aircraft will be departing to the north on a 360 degree heading. With right traffic, it will turn right towards the northeast on the crosswind leg.
Reference: AIM 4-1-5"

56. A

"The Aeronautical Information Manual (AIM) is the official guide to basic flight information and ATC procedures
Reference: AIM"

57. C

"The thick blue lines on the sectional chart indicate the boundaries of the overlying Class B airspace. Within each segment, the floor and ceiling are denoted by one number over a second number or the letters SFC. The floor of the class B airspace is 4,000 feet MSL.
Reference: AIM 13-2-3"

58. A

"Within the outer magenta circle of Savannah Class C airspace, there is a number 41 directly above the number 13. These numbers depict the floor and ceiling of the Class C airspace, the floor being 1,300 feet MSL and the ceiling being 4,100 feet MSL.
Reference: AIM 3-2-4"

59. C

"The recommended entry position for an airport traffic pattern is 45 degrees to the midpoint of the downwind left at traffic pattern altitude
Reference: AIM 4-3-3"

60. A

"A military operations area (MOA) contains military training activities such as acrobatics and calls for extreme caution. Any flight service station (FSS) within 100 miles of the area will provide, information concerning MOA hours of operation. Prior to entering an active MOA, pilots should contact the controlling agency for traffic advisories, noted in the legend for special use airspace.
Reference: AIM 3-4-5"

61. B

"Cooperstown Airport depicts one runway; RWY 13 means the aircraft will be headed 130 degrees upon landing. ""Left downwind"" means the aircraft is currently to the left side, heading opposite and midway of the landing runway. This would place the aircraft east of the landing runway
Reference: AIM 4-1-5"

62. A

"Hold Position signs have white inscription on red background
Reference: AIM 2-3-5"

63. C

"The no entry sign prohibits an aircraft from entering an area. Typically, this sing would be located on a taxiway intended to be used in only one direction or at the intersection of vehicle roadways with runways, taxiways or aprons where the roadway may be mistaken as a taxiway or other aircraft movement surface.
Reference: AIM 2-3-8"

64. C

"The elevation of the top of the obstacle is shown as 903 feet above mean sea level (MSL). Small UAS operations may not exceed 400 AGL. Moreover, the sUAS may be operated higher than 400 feet AGL if the sUAS is flown within a 400-foot radius of the structure and doesn't not fly higher than 400 feet above the structure's immediate uppermost limit.
Reference: Sectional Chart Legend, 14 CFR 107.51"

65. A

"Georgetown Airport is outside the magenta shaded area, which indicates the floor of Class E airspace is at 1,200 feet AGL. The airport elevation is given in the airport data as 2, 623 feet MSL. Therefore, the class E airspace above Georgetown Airport is 3,823 feet MSL (2,623 +1,200)
Reference: Sectional Chart"

66. B

"The FAA near mid-air collision report indicates that 81% of the incidents occurred in clear skies and unrestricted visibility conditions.
Reference: FAA-H-8083-25"

67. B

"The flag symbol represents a visual checkpoint used by manned aircraft to identify the position to initiate their contact with Norfolk approach control. As a defined checkpoint, a higher volume of air traffic should be expected there
Reference: Sectional Chart Legend, FAA-H-8083-25"

68. C

"The routes established between VORs are depicted by blue-tinted bands showing the airway number following the letter ""V"", and are called ""Victor airways"". Remote pilots should exercise vigilance in looking for other aircraft when operating near these high-density areas.
Reference: Sectional Chart Legend."

69. A

"Operations within Class C airspace requires two-way radio communications, a transponder, and an encoding altimeter.
Reference: FAA-H-8083-25"

70. A

"Notices to Airmen (NOTAMs) provide time-critical aeronautical information either temporary in nature or not sufficiently known in advance to permit publication on aeronautical charts or in other operational publications.
Reference: FAA-H-8083-25"

71. C

"The town of Hinton is north of Sioux City airport. Winnebago is south of Sioux City airport. This route is through the Class D airspace, depicted with the dashed blue line. You will need to contact ATC before conducting this flight.
Reference: Sectional Chart Legend"

72. A

"A NOTAM may be issued for reasons including hazards, such as air shows. The NOTAM will include the location and time for the affected region. UAS operations should stay away from these locations during the timeframe defined by the NOTAM.
Reference: FAA-H-8083-25"

73. A

"Restricted areas are identified on sectional charts with an 'R' followed by a number. You can find information about restricted areas on the back of the sectional chart.
Reference: FAA-H-8083-25"

74. C

"When aircraft are approaching each other head-on, or nearly so, each pilot of each aircraft (regardless of category or size) shall alter course to the right.
Reference: AC 107-2"

75. A

"Military Operations Areas (MOA) are depicted on sectional charts with a shaded, hashed magenta line. You can find information about the MOA on the back of the sectional, including times of operation, altitudes affected, and the controlling agency.
Reference: AIM 3-4-5"

76. B

"Tomlinson Airport is in the top left corner of Figure 26, and lies outside any colored circles. This indicates the airport is within Class E airspace from 1,200 feet AGL up to but not including 18,000 feet MSL.
Reference: AIM 3-2-5"

77. B

"The normal radius of the Class C outer area will be 20 NM. This is the area where separation is provided after two-way communication is established. It is only a requirement to contact ATC before entering the 10 NM Class C airspace depicted on the sectional chart.
Reference: FAA-H-8083-25"

78. B

"Class D airspace is depicted with the dashed blue circle, the ceiling defined by the number in brackets.
Reference: AIM 3-2-5"

79. A

"Notices to Airmen (NOTAMs) provide the most current information available. They provide time-critical information on airports and changes that affect the NAS. Answer (B) is incorrect because the Chart Supplements U.S. is only revised every 8 weeks. Answer (C) is incorrect because the FAA systematically issues ACs to inform the aviation public of non-regulatory material.
Reference: FAA-H-8083-25"

80. C

"Class C requires two-way radio communications equipment, a transponder, and an encoding altimeter.
Reference: FAA-H-8083-25"

1. B

"Ice pellets always indicate freezing rain at higher altitude
Reference: AC 00-6"

2. A

"Part 107 sUAS operations require the minimum distance of the small unmanned aircraft from clouds must be no less than 500 feet below the cloud and 2,000 feet horizontally from the cloud.
Reference: 14 CFR 107.51"

3. C

"Fog is more likely to form when the temperature and dew point convergence. A difference between these two temperatures of 3 degrees C (or 5 degrees F) is indicative of possible fog formation.
Reference: AC 00-6"

4. C

"A thunderstorm is, in general, a local storm invariably produced by a cumulonimbus cloud, and is always accompanied by lightning and thunder.
Reference: AC 00-6"

5. C

"The propeller produces thrust in proportion to the mass of air being accelerated through the rotating blades. If the air is less dense, propeller efficiency is decreased.
Reference: FAA-H-8083-25"

6. A

"Characteristics of a moist unstable air mass include cumuliform clouds, showery precipitation, rough air (turbulence), and good visibility (except in blowing obstructions)
Reference: AC 00-6"

7. B

"A condition favorable for rapid accumulation of clear icing is freezing rain below a frontal surface.
Reference: AC 00-6"

8. A

"Wind direction always changes across a front
Reference: AC 00-6"

9. B

"Characteristics of a stable air mass include stratiform clouds and fog, continuous precipitation, smooth air, and fair to poor visibility in haze and smoke.
Reference: FAA-H-8083-25"

10. C

"An individual microburst will seldom last longer than 15 minutes from the time it strikes the ground until dissipation. However, there may be multiple microbursts in the area.
Reference: AIM 7-1-25"

11. A

"Between 1000Z and 1200Z, the visibility at KMEM is forecast to be 3 statute miles (BECMG 1012... 3SM)
Reference: AC 00-45"

12. C

"SH" stands for showers and "RA" stands for rain.
Reference: AC 00-45"

13. C

"Crewmembers must operate sUAS Part 107 operations with a minimum visibility, as observed from the location of the control station, no less than 3 statute miles.
Reference: 14 CFR 107.51"

14. B

"From 1600Z until the end of the forecast, wind will be variable in direction at 6 knots (VRB06KT)
Reference: AC 00-45"

15. A

"The difference between the existing lapse rate of a given mass of air and the adiabatic rates of cooling in upward moving air determines if the air is stable or unstable.
Reference: AC 00-6"

16. B

"On a hot day, the air becomes ""thinner"" or lighter, and its density is equivalent to a higher altitude in the standard atmosphere, thus the term ""high density altitude""
Reference: AC 00-6"

17. B

"Steam fog forms in the winter when cold, dry air passes from land areas over comparatively warm ocean waters. Low level turbulence can occur and icing can become hazardous in a steam fog.
Reference: AC 00-6"

18. A

"The wind is reported as a five digit group (six digits if speed is over 99 knots). The first three digits is the direction the wind is blowing from rounded to the nearest tens of degrees relative to true (not magnetic) north, or ""VRB"" if the direction is variable. The next two digits is the speed in knots or if over 99 knots, the next three digits. If the wind is gusty, it is reported as a ""G"" after the speed followed by the highest gust reported. The abbreviation ""KT"" is appended to denote the use of knots for wind speed. The wind group for KJFK is 18004KT which means the wind from 180 degrees at 4 knots.
Reference: AC 00-45"

19. B

"Downdrafts characterize the dissipating stage of the thunderstorm cell and the storm dies rapidly.
Reference: AC 00-6"

20. A

"Unmanned aircraft often have limited performance and therefore in high wind conditions, it may consume more power to maintain position or other maneuvers than in calm air. If the wind is strong enough, the sUAS's performance might not be able to adequately counter the wind, making it impossible to fly back to you for recovery.
Reference: FAA-H-8083-25, 14 CFR Part 107.49"

21. C

"Conditions favorable for radiation fog are clear sky, little or no wind, and small temperature/ dew point spread (high relative humidity). Radiation fog is restricted to land because water surfaces cool little from nighttime radiation.
Reference: AC 00-6"

22. A

"All altimeter settings are corrected to sea level, unequal heating of the Earth's surface causes pressure differences.
Reference: AC 00-6"

23. C

"A squall line is a non-frontal, narrow band of active thunderstorms. The line may be too long to easily detour and too wide and severe to penetrate. It often contains severe steady state thunderstorms and presents the single, most intense weather hazard to aircraft
Reference: AC 00-6"

24. A

"For a cumulonimbus cloud or thunderstorm to form the air must have:
    1. Sufficient water vapor
    2. An unstable lapse rate
    3. An initial upward boost (lifting) to start the storm process in motion
Reference: AC 00-6"

25. B

"The key feature of the cumulus stage is an updraft. Precipitation beginning to fall from the cloudbase is the signal that a downdraft has developed also and a cell has entered the mature stage.
Reference: AC 00-6"

26. C

"Weather factors can greatly influence sUAS performance and safety of flight
Reference: AC 107-2"

27. C

"Advection fog forms when moist air moves over colder ground or water. It is most common along coastal areas, but often develops deep in continental areas. Advection fog deepens as wind speed increases up to about 15 knots. Wind much stronger than 15 knots lifts the fog into a layer of low stratus or stratocumulus. Upslope fog forms as a result of moist, stable air being cooked adiabatically as it moves up sloping terrain. Once upslope wind ceases, the fog dissipates.
Reference: AC 00-6"

28. A

"All thunderstorms hazards reach their greatest intensity during the mature stage.
Reference: AC 00-6"

29. A

"A squall line is a non-frontal, narrow band of active thunderstorms. The line may be too long to easily detour and too wide and severe to penetrate. It often contains severe steady state thunderstorms and presents the single, most intense weather hazard to aircraft
Reference: AC 00-6"

30. B

"Two conditions are necessary for structural icing in flight
    1. The aircraft must be flying through visible water such as rain or cloud droplets, and
    2. the temperature at the point where the moisture strikes the aircraft must be 0 degrees C (32 degrees F) or colder.
Reference: AC 00-6"

31. A

"If the temperature is above standard the density altitude will be higher than pressure altitude.
Reference: FAA-H-8083-25"

32. C

"Unstable conditions are characterized by cumulus clouds, turbulence, showery precipitations and good visibility.
Reference: AC 00-6"

33. A

"Dry areas get hotter than moist area. Dry fields or dry ground of any nature are better thermal sources than mist areas. This applies to woods or forests, which are poor sources of thermals because of the large amount of moisture given off by foliage.
Reference: AC 00-6"

34. A

"Between 2000Z and 2200Z there is a 40% probability (PROB) that is the visibility will drop to 1 SM due to a thunderstorm (TS) and moderate rain (RA).
Reference: AC 00-6"

35. C

"Thermals are updrafts in convective currents dependent on solar heating. A temperature inversion would result in stable air with very little, if any, convective activity.
Reference: AC 00-6"

36. B

"Characteristics of a stable air mass include stratiform clouds and fog, continuous precipitation, smooth air, and fair to poor visibility in haze and smoke.
Reference: FAA-H-8083-25"

37. B

"Local condition, geological features, and other anomalies can change the wind direction and speed close to the Earth's surface, making it difficult to control and maneuver the sUAS.
Reference: FAA-H-8083-25"

38. A

"Advection fog forms when moist air moves over colder ground or water. It is most common along coastal areas. The fog frequently forms offshore as a result of cold water, then is carried inland by the wind.
Reference: AC 00-6"

39. B

"Advection fog forms when moist air moves over colder ground or water. It is most common along coastal areas. The fog frequently forms offshore as a result of cold water, then is carried inland by the wind.
Reference: AC 00-6"

40. A

"Wind shear is an invisible hazard associated with all thunderstorms. Shear turbulence has been encountered 20 miles laterally from a severe storm.
Reference: AC 00-6"

41. C

"The key feature of the cumulus stage is an updraft. Precipitation beginning to fall from the cloud base is the signal that a downdraft has developed also and a cell has entered the mature stage.
Reference: AC 00-6"

42. C

"Standard sea level pressure is 29.92 inches of mercury, standard sea level temperatures is 15 degree C.
Reference: FAA-H-8083-25"

43. A

"The current conditions at KMDW are 1-1/2 SM visibility (1-1/2 SM) with rain (RA), ceiling overcast at 700 feet (OVC007)
Reference: AC 00-6"

44. B

"You should request a standard briefing any time you are planning a flight and you have not received a previous briefing.
Reference: FAA-H-8083-25"

45. A

"When air near the surface is warm and moist, suspect instability. Surface heating, cooling aloft, converging or upslope winds, or an invading mass of colder air may lead to instability and cumuliform clouds
Reference: AC 00-6"

46. A

"Temperature is one of the most easily recognized discontinuities across a front
Reference: AC 00-6"

47. B

"ASOS is designed to support aviation operations and weather forecast activities. The ASOS will provide continuous minute-by-minute observations and perform the basic observing functions necessary to generate an aviation routine weather report (METAR) and other aviation weather information.
Reference: AIM 7-1-11"

48. B

"A lightning strike can puncture the skin of an aircraft, damage communication and navigation equipment, or hit the remote pilot or crew on the ground.
Reference: AC 00-6"

49. C

"A combination of high temperature, high humidity, and high altitude result in a density altitude higher than the pressure altitude which in turn, results in reduced aircraft performance.
Reference: FAA-H-8083-25"

50. A

"Thunderstorms and heavy rain are common, although not always, associated with cold fronts.
Reference: AC 00-6"

51. C

"Every physical process of weather is accompanied by, or is the result of, unequal heating of the Earth's surface
Reference: AC 00-6"

52. A

"Thunderstorm hazards reach their greatest intensity during the mature stage, which is when precipitation begins.
Reference: AC 00-6"

53. A

"Part 107 require the minimum distance of the sUAS from clouds must be no less than 500 feet below the cloud. The towers depicted 4 NM east of K36 are 292 feet AGL. 292 + 500 = 792 feet AGL.
Reference: 14 CFR 107.51"

54. B

"A squall line is a nonfrontal, narrow band of active thunderstorms. The line may be too long to easily detour and too wide and severe to penetrate. It often contains severe steady-state thunderstorms and presents the single, most intense weather hazard to aircraft.
Reference: AC 00-6"

55. C

"Regardless of the location, crewmembers must conduct sUAS Part 107 operations with a minimum visibility, as observed from the location of the control station, no less than 3 statute miles.
Reference: 14 CFR 107.51"

56. C

"A continuous line of thunderstorms, or squall line, may form along or ahead of the front. Squall lines present a serious hazard to pilots as squall type thunderstorms are intense and move quickly. Squalls can occur at any altitude - they are not unique to high- or low-altitude operations.
Reference: AC 00-6"

57. A

"Any convective SIGMET implies severe or greater turbulence, severe icing, and low-level wind shear. The forecast may be issued for any of the following; severe thunderstorms due to:
    1. Surface winds greater than or equal to 50 knots, or
    2. Hail at the surface greater than or equal to 3/4 inch in diameter, or
    3. Tornadoes, embedded thunderstorms, lines of thunderstorms.
Reference: AC 00-45"

58. C

"An increase in air temperature or humidity, or a decrease in air pressure (which results in a higher density altitude) will significantly decrease both power output and propeller efficiency. If an air mass is humid, there is more water in it, therefore, less oxygen.
Reference: AC 00-6"

59. A

"As water vapor condenses or sublimates on condensation nuclei, liquid or ice particles begin to grow. Some condensation nuclei have an affinity for water and can induce condensation or sublimation even when air is almost, but not completely, saturated. Answer (B) is incorrect because the presence of water vapor does not result in clouds, fog, or dew unless condensation occurs. Answer (C) is incorrect because it is possible to have 100% humidity without the occurrence of condensation, which is necessary for clouds, fog, or dew to form.
Reference: AC 00-6"

60. B

"The combination of moisture and temperature determine the stability of the air and the resulting weather. Cool, dry air is very stable and resists vertical movement, which leads to good and generally clear weather.
Reference: AC 00-6"

61. B

"Part 107 require the minimum distance of the sUAS from clouds must be no less than 500 feet below the cloud. The towers depicted 8 NM SW of CRP are 1,104 feet MSL. 1,104 + 500 = 1,604 feet MSL.
Reference: 14 CFR 107.51"

62. A

"When the temperature of the air rises with altitude, a temperature inversion exists. Inversion layers are commonly shallow layers of smooth, stable air close to the ground. The temperature of the air increases with altitude to a certain point, which is the top of the inversion. The air at the top of the layer acts as a lid, keeping weather and pollutants trapped below. If the relative humidity of the air is high, it can contribute to the formation of clouds, fog, haze, or smoke resulting in diminished visibility in the inversion layer.
Reference: AC 00-6"

63. B

"The entry RAB35 means that rain began 35 minutes past the hour. Answer (A) is incorrect because mist is reported as BR. Answer (C) is incorrect because there is no format for reporting an altimeter change in a METAR.
Reference: AC 00-45"

64. A

"Wind shear is a sudden, drastic change in wind speed and/or direction over a very small area. Wind shear can subject an aircraft to violent updrafts and downdrafts, as well as abrupt changes to the horizontal movement of the aircraft. While wind shear can occur at any altitude, low-level wind shear is especially hazardous due to the proximity of an aircraft to the ground.
Reference: AC 00-6"

65. B

"On cool, clear, calm nights, the temperature of the ground and objects on the surface can cause temperatures of the surrounding air to drop below the dew point. When this occurs, the moisture in the air condenses and deposits itself on the ground, buildings, and other objects like cars and aircraft. This moisture is known as dew and sometimes can be seen on grass and other objects in the morning. If the temperature is below freezing, the moisture is deposited in the form of frost.
Reference: AC 00-6"

66. C

"Part 107 require the minimum distance of the sUAS from clouds must be no less than 500 feet below the cloud. 800 cloud - 500 = 300 feet AGL.
Reference: 14 CFR 107.51"

67. A

"The zone between two different air masses is a frontal zone or front. Across this zone, temperature, humidity and wind often change rapidly over short distances.
Reference: AC 00-6"

1. A

"Any mounted equipment should be balanced in a manner that does not adversely affect the center of gravity or result in unsafe performance.
Reference: AC 107-2"

2. A

"Loading the aircraft outside of limitations (weight, balance, or both) may lead to moments that exceed the capabilities of the flight controls/ engine (s), thus possibly leading to loss of control or other performance anomalies
Reference: FAA-H8083-1"

3. B

"The airfoil will stall if the critical angle of attach is exceeded.
Reference: FAA-H-8083-3"

4. B

"The maximum endurance condition is obtained at the point of minimum power required since this would require the lowest fuel flow or battery to keep the sUAS in steady, level flight. Maximum range condition occurs where the proportion between speed and power required is greatest.
Reference: FAA-H-8083-25"

5. A

"Total range is dependent on both fuel available and specific range. When range and economy of operation are the principal goals, the remote pilot must ensure that the sUAS is operated at the recommended long range cruise condition. By this procedure, the sUAS will be capable of its maximum design-operating radius, or can achieve lesser flight distances with a maximum of fuel reserve at the destination
Reference: FAA-H-8083-25"

6. C

"The manufacturer is the best source of performance data and information, if available
Reference: FAA-H-8083-25"

7. B

"Refer to Figure 2 and use the following steps
    1. Enter the chart at a 60 degree angle of bank and proceed upward to the curved reference line.
    2. From the point of intersection, move to the left side of the chart and read a load factor of 2Gs.
    3. Multiply the aircraft weight by the load factor: 10x2=20 lbs or working from the table 10x2.0 (load factor) = 20 lbs
Reference: FAA-H-8083-25"

8. A

"The effect of runway slope on launch distance is due to the component of weight along the inclined path of the aircraft. An upslope would contribute an accelerating force component. In the case of an upslope, the retarding force component adds to drag and rolling friction to reduce the net accelerating force.
Reference: FAA-H-8083-25"

9. C

"Unmanned airplane performance can be decreased due to an increase in load factor when the airplane is operated in maneuvers other than straight and level flight.
Reference: FAA-H-8083-25"

10. C

"The most critical conditions of launch performance are the result of some combination of high gross weight, altitude, temperature and unfavorable wind. In all cases the remote pilot must make and accurate prediction of take-off distance from the performance data of the AFM/ POH, regardless of the runway available, and strive for polished, professional launch procedures.
Reference: FAA-H-8083-25"

11. A

"Prior to each flight, the remote PIC must ensure that any object attached to or carried by the small unmanned aircraft is secure and does not adversely affect the flight characteristics or controllability of the aircraft
Reference: AC 107-2"

12. B

"Stall speed increases in proportion to the square root of the load factor. Thus, with a load factor of 4, an aircraft will stall, at a speed which is double the normal stall speed.
Reference: FAA-H-8083-25"

13. C

"To determine altitude, with the sUAS on the ground, the remote pilot and VO should pace off 400 feet from the sUAS to get a visual perspective of the sUAS at that distance, wherein the remote pilot and VO maintain that visual perspective or closer while the sUAS is in flight
Reference: AC 107-2"

14. A

"Referencing Appendix 1, Figure 2, use the following steps:
    1.Enter the chart at a 30 degree angle of bank and proceed upward to the curved reference line. From the point of intersection, move to the left side of the chart and read an approximate load factor of 1.2 Gs.
    2.Multiply the aircraft weight by the load factor: 33*1.2=39.6 lbs Or, working from the table:33*1.154 (load factor)= 38.1 lbs.
Reference: FAA-H-8083-25"

15. B

"when the angle of attack is increased to between 18 and 20 degrees (critical angle of attack) on most airfoils the airstream can no longer follow the upper curvature of the wing because of the excessive change in direction. The airfoil will stall if the critical angle of attack is exceeded. The airspeed at which stall occurs will be determined by weight and load factor, but the stall angle of attack is the same.
Reference: FAA-H-8083-25"

16. A

"Without a GPS or manufacturer performance data, you can determine speed of the sUAS when it is flown between two or more fixed points, taking into account wind speed and direction between each point, then noting the power settings of the sUAS to operate at or less than 87 knots ground speed. This is a form of dead reckoning.
Reference: FAA-H-8083-25,AC 107-2"

17. B

"At slow speeds, the maximum available lifting force of the wing is only slightly greater than the amount necessary to support the weight of the sUAS. However, at high speeds, the capacity of the flight controls or a strong gust, may increase the load factor beyond safe limits,
Reference: FAA-H-8083-25"

18. A

"The angle of attack is the acute angle between the relative wind and the chord line of the wing.
Reference: FAA-H-8083-25"

19. C

"Excessive weight reduces the flight performance in almost every respect, including a shorter endurance. In addition, operating above the maximum weight limitation can compromise the structural integrity of an unmanned aircraft.
Reference: AC 107-2"

20. C

"Refer to Appendix 1, Legend 1. In addition to local resources, the sectional chart for that region should be consulted for information or the altitude of the terrain and structures. towers and other known obstructions are depicted with their altitude noted.
Reference: Sectional chart"

21. A

"Referencing Appendix 1, Figure 2, use the following steps:
    1.Enter the chart at a 30 degree angle of bank and proceed upward to the curved reference line. From the point of intersection, move to the left side of the chart and read an approximate load factor of 1.2 Gs.
    2.Multiply the aircraft weight by the load factor: 50*1.2= 60 lbs Or, working from the table: 50*1.154 (load factor)= 57.7 lbs.
Reference: FAA-H-8083-25"

22. B

"A change in speed during straight flight will not produce any appreciable change in load but when a change is made in the sUAS flight path, an additional load is imposed upon the structure. This is particularly true if a change in direction is made at high speeds with rapid, forceful control movements.
Reference: FAA-H-8083-25"

23. A

"Before any flight, verify that the unmanned aircraft is correctly loaded by determining the weight and balance condition. Review any available manufacturer weight and balance data and follow all restrictions and limitations.
Reference: FAA-H-8083-1"

24. C

"It is the responsibility of the remote PIC to use the most current weight and balance data when planning a flight and operating the sUAS.
Reference: FAA-H-8083-1"

25. B

"The remote PIC is responsible for ensuring that every flight can be accomplished safely, does not pose an undue hazard, and does not increase the likelihood of a loss of positive control.
Reference: 14 CFR 107.12"

26. A

"The purpose of the rudder is to control yaw. Answer (B) is incorrect because the ailerons control bank. Answer (C) is incorrect because pitch is controlled by the elevator.
Reference: FAA-H-8083-25"

27. A

"In addition to local resources, the sectional chart for that region should be consulted for information on the altitude of the terrain and structures. Towers and other known obstructions are depicted with their altitude noted.
Reference: Sectional Chart"

28. B

"Stall speed increases in proportion to the square root of the load factor. Thus, with a load factor of 4, an aircraft will stall at a speed which is double the normal stall speed.
Reference: FAA-H-8083-25"

1. A

"A flyaway is when the sUAS becomes uncontrollable and does not operate in a manner that would be expected in a normal or lost link flight situation.
Reference: 14 CFR Part 107"

2. C

"Fatigue can be either acute (short-term) or chronic (long-term). Acute fatigue, a normal occurrence of everyday living, is the tiredness felt after long periods of physical and mental strain, including strenuous muscular effort, immobility, heavy mental workload, strong emotional pressure, monotony, and lack of sleep. Chronic fatigue occurs when there is not enough time for a full recovery from repeated episodes of acute fatigue.
Reference: FAA-H-8083-25"

3. A

"Frequency interference is one of the most common causes of flyaways; therefore, remote PICs should assess the risk of such interference prior to and during flight. Extra caution is necessary when operating in the vicinity of other sUAS. The loss of GPS may degrade the sUAS capabilities slightly but should not cause a flyaway. It is not unusual for people to stand near the control station; it is highly unlikely for this to cause a flyaway.
Reference: AC 107-2"

4. C

"An aircraft exiting a runway is not clear of the runway until all parts of the aircraft have crossed the applicable holding position marking.
Reference: AIM 2-3-5"

5. C

"The preferred source of information is the manufacturer's guidance about maintenance schedule and instructions,
Reference: AC 107-2"

6. B

"Remote PICs should monitor the appropriate aviation frequency such as CTAF during flight operations and make announcement concerning sUAS operations as appropriate. Some sUAS require the use of cellphone or tablet computers for operation, therefore are acceptable for use in most cases. The best way to avoid frequency interference is to check local frequency spectrum use prior to flight and continue to monitor such use during flight by utilizing a frequency spectrum analyzer.
Reference: AC 107-2"

7. A

"Follow all manufacturer maintenance recommendations to achieve the longest safest service life of the sUAS. if the sUAS or component manufacturer does not provide scheduled maintenance instructions, it is recommended that you establish your own scheduled maintenance protocol.
Reference: AC 107-2"

8. B

"The remote PIC is responsible for determining whether that aircraft is in condition for safe flight.
Reference: FAA-H-8083-25"

9. B

"Hyperventilation is most likely to occur during period of stress or anxiety
Reference: AIM 8-1-3"

10. C

"Most sUAS are designed to fly normally with minimal impact on features or controllability if GPS signals are degraded or lost. Loss of GPS is not an emergency and is not considered to be a loss of link between the unmanned aircraft and the control station. If the failure of GPS does result in a flyaway or other dangerous situation, it should be treated as an emergency.
Reference: AC 107-2"

11. A

"A pilot who has just landed should not change from the tower frequency to the ground control frequency until directed to do so by the controller
Reference: AIM 4-3-14"

12. B

"Most sUAS are designed to fly normally with minimal impact on features or controllability if GPS signals are degraded or lost. Loss of GPS is not an emergency and is not considered to be a loss of link between the unmanned aircraft and the control station. If the failure of GPS does result in a flyaway or other dangerous situation, it should be treated as an emergency.
Reference: AC 107-2"

13. A

"Pilot performance can be seriously degraded by both prescribed and over-the-counter medications, as well as by the medical conditions for which they are taken. Flying is almost always precluded while using prescription analgesics since these drugs may cause side effects such as mental confusion, dizziness, headaches, nausea, and vision problems. Depressants, including antihistamines, lower blood pressure, reduce mental processing and slow motor and reaction responses.
Reference: FAA-H-8083-25"

14. C

"The antiauthority (don't tell me) attitude is found in people who do not like anyone telling them what to do. The antidote for this attitude is: follow the rules, they are usually right.
Reference: FAA-H-8083-25"

15. A

"Damaged batteries should never be used or charged. Lithium batteries do normally get warm during discharge. Avoid the use of hot batteries. New batteries should be treated per manufacturing instructions, but do not normally need several charge cycles to use.
Reference: SAFO 10017"

16. B

"No person may operate a sUAS unless it is in a condition for safe operation. Prior to each flight, the remote pilot-in-command must check the sUAS to determine whether it is in a condition for safe operation. No person may continue flight of the small unmanned aircraft when he or she knows or has reason to know that the small unmanned aircraft system is no longer in a condition for safe operation
Reference: 14 CFR 107.15"

17. B

"The term ""initial radio contact"" or ""initial call-up"" means the first radio call you make to a given facility, or the first call to a different controller or Flight Service specialist within a facility.
Use the following format:
      1. Name of the facility being called
      2. You full aircraft identification as filed in the flight plan
      3. Type of message to follow or your request if it is short
      4. The word ""over"" if required (typically omitted, except for communications via a remote communication outlet or in cases when it is necessary to confirm the end of a transmission
      Example: New York Radio, Mooney Three One One Echo, over
      When the aircrafts manufacturer's name or model is stated, the prefix ""N"" is dropped. The first two characters of the call sign may be dropped only after ATC calls you by your last three numbers
Reference: AIM 4-2-3"

18. C

"The pilot is responsible for determining whether he or she is fit to fly for a particular flight
Reference: FAA-H-8083-25"

19. A

"The fatigues pilot is an impaired pilot, and flying requires unimpaired judgement
Reference: FAA-H-8083-2"

20. A

"During a flyaway event sUAS may not react in ways that can be expected or predicted thus this is an emergency situation. The remote PIC should immediately communicate this emergency to crewmembers and ATC (if applicable) as well as any persons in the immediate area so as to minimize risk for injury. There is no obligation to contact the NTSB or law enforcement during a flyaway.
Reference: 14 CFR 107.19, 107.21"

21. B

"The preflight inspection should be a thorough and systematic means by which the remote PIC determines that the sUAS is ready for safe flight. Most aircraft flight manuals or Pilot's operating handbooks contain a section on preflight inspection that should be used for guidance in this
Reference: FAA-H-8083-25"

22. A

"The remote PIC must inspect the sUAS before each flight
Reference: 14 CFR 107.49"

23. C

"All participants in the sUAS operation and ATC (if operating within or near controlled airspace) should be notified of the lost link situation, an emergency should be declared. There is no obligation to contact law enforcement. It is never recommended to turn off the control station when the UA engines are running or if it is in flight.
Reference: AC 107-2, 14 CFR 107.21"

24. A

"MULTICOM frequency is always 122.9 MHz and the correct procedure is to broadcast intentions when 10 miles from the airport
Reference: AIM 4-1-9"

25. B

"When there is no tower, Flight service, or UNICOM station on the airport use MULTICOM frequency 122.9 for self-announce procedures. Such airports will be identified in the appropriate aeronautical information publications.
Reference: AIM 4-1-9"

26. A

"To avoid missing important steps, always use the appropriate checklists whenever, they are available. Consistent adherence to approved checklists is a sign if a disciplined and competent pilot.
Reference: FAA-H-8083-25"

27. C

"Impulsivity, as a hazardous attitude, has the motto ""Do it quickly"" The person frequently feels the need to do something, anything, immediately. He or she does not stop to think about the best alternative and does the first thing that comes to mind.
Reference: FAA-H-8083-25"

28. B

"Up to but not including 18,000 feet MSL, state the separate digits of the thousands, plus the hundreds, if appropriate. Example: ""4,500-four thousand, five hundred""
Reference: AIM 4-2-9"

29. B

"The absence of a sky condition or ceiling and/or visibility on ATIS indicates a ceiling of 5,000 feet or above and visibility of 5 miles or more.
Reference: AIM 4-1-13"

30. A

"Risk management is the part of the decision making process that relies on situational awareness, problem recognition, and good judgement to reduce the risks associated with each flight.
Reference: FAA-H-8083-25"

31. C

"Where there is no tower or UNICOM station on the airport, use MULTICOM frequency 122.9 for self-announce procedures.
Reference: AIM 4-1-9"

32. A

"An abnormal increase in the volume of air breathed in and out of the lungs flushes an excessive amount of carbon dioxide from the lings and blood, causing hyperventilation
Reference: AIM 8-1-3"

33. B

"A culture of safety must be established with all commercial sUAS operations. This safety culture may use a number of techniques including situational awareness, risk based aeronautical decision making (ADM) crew resource management (CRM) and safety management systems(SMS)
Reference: FAA-H-8083-25"

34. C

"Pilots of inbound traffic should monitor and communicate as appropriate on the designated CTAF from 10 miles to landing. Pilots of departing aircraft should monitor/ communicate on the appropriate frequency from start-up, during taxi and until 10 miles from the airport unless the regulations or local procedures require otherwise.
Reference: AIM 4-1-9"

35. C

"ATIS is the continuous broadcast of recorded non-control information in selected high activity terminal areas
Reference: AIM 4-1-13"

36. A

"The remote PIC must inspect the sUAS before each flight
Reference: 14 CFR 107.49"

37. B

"Follow all manufacturer maintenance recommendations to achieve the longest safest service life of the sUAS. By abiding by the more restrictive limitation or component life cycle the remote PIC will be assured of being in compliance of both the sUAS and battery manufactures' guidelines
Reference: AC 107-2"

38. A

"Traffic information will be given in azimuth from the aircraft in terms of the 12 hour clock. Thus each hour would constitute an angle of 30 degrees. If an aircraft is proceeding on a heading of 090 degrees (east) traffic located at 3'o clock position would be 90 degrees right of the nose, south of the aircraft. If the sUAS is being operated to the south of the aircraft, the aircraft itself is to the north of the operation.
Reference: AIM 4-1-15"

39. B

"An aircraft flying north in calm wind would be heading 360 degrees. When advised of traffic at the 9'O clock position, the pilot should look 90 degrees left of the nose, to the west but the Remote PIC and sUAS need to look to the east as they are to the west of the manned aircraft
Reference: AIM 4-1-15"

40. C

"Crewmembers should express any and all concerns about decisions of the remote PIC or other crewmembers at any time. Clearly, the remote PIC is in charge, but that doesn't not always make them right or invulnerable to errors, omissions, or other potentially hazardous instances
Reference: FAA-H-8083-25"

41. C

"if the operation is to take place in the afternoon, the sun will be setting towards the west and could impair the vision of those participating in the sUAS operation. Thus, when practical, the operation should be set up to minimize the impact of the the sun on being able to maintain the visual line of sight with the unmanned aircraft
Reference: FAA-H-8083-25, 14 CFR 107.31"

42. A

"Risk management is the part of the decision making process that relies on situational awareness, problem recognition, and good judgement to reduce the risks associated with each flight.
Reference: FAA-H-8083-25"

43. B

"Both lithium metal and lithium -ion batteries are highly flammable and capable of self-ignition when a battery short circuits or is overcharged, heated to extreme temperature, mishandled or otherwise defective
Reference: SAFO 10017"

44. A

"Machoism, as a hazardous attitude, has the motto ""I can do it, I'll show them"" The person tries to prove that he or she is better than anyone else. the person takes risks to impress others.
Reference: FAA-H-8083-25"

45. C

"If the operation is to take place in snow covered environment, awareness concerning how this may impact vision, such as a glare or the ability to see and operate the unmanned aircrafts against a featureless background. Thus, when practical, the operation should be set up to minimize the impact of the the sun on being able to maintain the visual line of sight with the unmanned aircraft
Reference: FAA-H-8083-25, 14 CFR 107.31"

46. A

"As a pilot, flying for long periods in hot summer temperatures or at high altitudes increases the susceptibility of dehydration since the dry air at altitude tends to increase the rate of water loss from the body. If this fluid is not replaced, fatigue progresses to dizziness, weakness, nausea, tingling of hands and feet, abdominal cramps, and extreme thirst.
Reference: FAA-H-8083-25"

47. B

"Follow all manufacturer maintenance recommendations to achieve the longest and safest service life of the sUAS. If the sUAS or component manufacturer does not provide scheduled maintenance instructions, it is recommended that you establish your own scheduled maintenance protocol.
Reference: AC 107-2"

48. B

"Crew resource management is the effective use of all available resources - human, hardware and information - prior to and during flight to ensure a successful outcome of the operation. The remote PIC must integrate crew resource management techniques into all phases of the sUAS operation.
Reference: FAA-H-8083-25"

49. A

Acute fatigue is short term and is normal occurrence in everyday living. It is the kind of tiredness people feel after a period of strenuous effort, excitement, or lack of sleep.

50. C

"ADM addresses the following five hazardous attitudes. antiauthority (don't tell me) impulsivity (do something quickly) invulnerability (it won't happen to me) machoism (I can do it) resignation (what's the use)
Reference: FAA-H-8083-25"

51. A

"Pilots should state their position on the airport, when calling the tower for takeoff from a runway intersection
Reference: AIM 4-3-10"

52. B

"When in doubt, remove and replace any damaged part. If repair is allowed, it should be outlines by the manufacturer. Remote PICs should consult with the manufacturer about such repair.
Reference: AC 107-2"

53. A

"using standard phraseology, remote PICs/ crew should clearly communicate the position of the sUAS operation in relation to a known geographic location and any other information that may help the manned aircraft be aware of and avoid conflicting with the sUAS
Reference: AIM 4-1-15, AC 107-2"

54. C

"Flight Service Stations (FSS's) are air traffic facilities that provide pilot briefings, enroute communications and VFR search-and-rescue services, assist lost aircraft and aircraft in emergency situations, relay ATC clearances, originate notice to Airmen, broadcast aviation weather and NAS information, receive and process IFR flight plans, and monitor NAVAIDs. In addition, FSS's take weather observations, issue airport advisories, advise customs and immigration of transborder flights, and provide En route flight advisory service (Flight watch) (in Alaska only)
Reference: AIM 4-1-3"

55. B

"Crew resource management is the effective use of all available resources - human, hardware and information - prior to and during flight to ensure a successful outcome of the operation.
Reference: AC 107-2"

56. A
"Fatigue is one of the most treacherous hazards to flight safety as it may not be apparent to a pilot until serious errors are made"
Reference: FAA-H-8083-25"

57. B
"Getting behind the aircraft" or falling can result in not knowing where you are, an inability to recognize deteriorating circumstances, and/or the misjudgment of the rate of deterioration
Reference: FAA-H-8083-25"

58. B
"Your first action should be to seek out the manufacturer's guidance about replacement or disposal. Do not use damaged batteries, as they may self-ignite during flight or if charged.
Reference: AC 107-2"

59. A
"CTAF is designed for the purpose of carrying out airport advisory practices and/or position reporting at an uncontrolled airport (which may also occur during hours when a tower is closed). The CTAF may be a UNICOM, MULTICOM, FSS, or tower frequency and is identified in the appropriate aeronautical publications. On the sectional chart, a solid dot with the letter "C" inside indicates Common Traffic Advisory Frequency. When the control tower operates part time and a UNICOM frequency is provided, use the UNICOM frequency.
Reference: AIM 4-1-9"

60. C
"CTAF is a frequency designed for the purpose of carrying out airport advisory practices and/or position reporting at an uncontrolled airport (which may also occur during hours when a tower is closed). The CTAF may be a UNICOM, MULTICOM, FSS, or tower frequency and is identified in the appropriate aeronautical publications. A solid dot with the letter "C" inside indicates CTAF. When the control tower operates part time and a UNICOM frequency is provided, use the UNICOM frequency.
Reference: AIM 4-1-9"

61. A
"Situational awareness is the accurate perception and understanding of all the factors and conditions within the five fundamental risk elements (flight, pilot, aircraft, environment, and type of operation that comprise any given aviation situation) that affect safety before, during, and after the flight.
Reference: FAA-H-8083-25"

62. C
"To fly safely, the pilot needs to assess the degree of risk and determine the best course of action to mitigate the risk.
Reference: FAA-H-8083-25"

63. B

"There are several techniques to help manage the accumulation of life stresses and prevent stress overload. For example, to help reduce stress levels, set aside time for relaxation each day or maintain a program of physical fitness. To prevent stress overload, learn to manage time more effectively to avoid pressures imposed by getting behind schedule and not meeting deadlines.
Reference: FAA-H-8083-25"

64. C

"Virtually all medications have the potential for adverse side effects in some people.
Reference: FAA-H-8083-25"

65. A

"Aircraft call signs should be spoken in their entirety, using the phonetic alphabet. Numbers are spoken individually.
Reference: AIM 4-2-3"

1. A

Category: Regulations

"You may operate an sUAS from a moving vehicle if you are in a sparsely populated area and the driver does not serve as the remote PIC, person manipulating the controls, or visual observer.
Reference: 14 CFR 107.25"

2. B

Category: Regulations

"This sUAS operation is subject to 14 CFR Part 107 because the compensation (money or otherwise) makes the operation commercial in nature
Reference: 14 CFR 107.3"

3. B

Category: Regulations

"Each remote PIC who deviates from a rule in Part 107 must, upon request of the FAA administrator, send a written report of that deviation to the Administrator
Reference: 14 CFR 107.21"

4. A

Category: Regulations

"Refer to Appendix 1, Legend 1. The routes established between VORs are depicted by blue-tinted bands showing the airway number following the letter ""V"", and are called ""Victor airways"". Remote pilots should exercise vigilance in looking for other aircraft when operating near these high density areas.
Reference: Sectional Chart Legend."

5. B

Category: Regulations

"The remote pilot operating an sUAS must yield right-of-way to all other manned aircraft, including aircraft operating on the surface of the aircraft.
Reference: 14 CFR 107.37"

6. A

Category: Regulations

"No report is required because the damage can be repaired for less than $500. A report is required only when damage to any property, other than the small UA, is greater than $500 to repair or replace the property (whichever is lower). The cost of the sUAS is not considered when determining if an event is considered to be an accident or incident.
Reference: 14 CFR 107.9, AC 107-2"

7. B

Category: Regulations

"No person may act as a pilot-in0command (PIC), or in any other capacity as a required pilot flight crewmember when operating a sUAS unless he or she has in possession or readily accessible a current-pilot certificate.
Reference: 14 CFR 107.7"

8. B

Category: Regulations

"The remote pilot application must be submitted to a Flight Standards District Office (FSDO), a designated pilot examiner (DPE), an airman certification representative for a pilot school, a certified flight instructor (CFI), or other person authorized by the Administrator to process the application.
Reference: 14 CFR 107.63 and 61.56"

9. A

Category: Regulations

"The remote PIC must report any sUAS accident to the FAA, within 10 days of the operation, if a serious injury to any person or any loss of consciousness occurs. It would be considered a serious injury if a person requires hospitalization.
Reference: 14 CFR 107.9, AC 107-2"

10. C

Category: Regulations

14 CFR Part 107 does not apply to model aircraft that meet the criteria in 14 CFR 101.41, amateur rockets, moored balloons or unmanned free balloons, kites, operations conducted outside the United States, public aircraft operations, and air carrier operations.

11. A

Category: Regulations

"No person may act, or attempt to act, as a crewmember of a civil aircraft while having .04 percent or more, by weight alcohol in the blood.
Reference: 14 CFR 107.27, 91.17"

12. A

Category: Regulations

"Although not required by Part 107, the FAA encourages applicants to submit their application at least 90 days prior to the start of the proposed operation. The FAA will strive to complete review and adjudication of waiver within 90 days; however, the time required for the FAA to make a determination regarding waiver requests will vary based on the complexity of the request.
Reference: AC 107-2"

13. B

Category: Regulations

"Report any sUAS accident to the FAA within 10 days if it results in serious injury, loss of consciousness, or repairs costing over $500.
Reference: 14 CFR 107.9"

14. A

Category: Regulations

"The sUAS cannot be flown higher than 400 feet AGL unless flown within a 400-foot radius of a structure and is not flown higher than 400 feet above the structure's immediate upper-most limit.
Reference: 14 CFR 107.51"

15. C

Category: Regulations

"No person may manipulate the flight controls of a small unmanned aircraft system or act as a remote pilot-in-command, visual observer, or direct participant in the operation of the small unmanned aircraft if he or she knows or has reason to know that he or she has a physical or mental condition that would interfere with the safe operation of the small un manned aircraft system.

Reference: 14 CFR 107.17 "

16. C

Category: Regulations

"Prior to flight, the remote PIC must ensure that all persons directly participating in the small unmanned aircraft operation are informed about the operating conditions, emergency procedures, contingency procedures, roles and responsibilities, and potential hazards.

Reference: 14 CFR 107.49, AC 107-2"

17. A

Category: Regulations

"This scenario is not compliant with Part 107. Visual aids such as binoculars may be used only momentarily to enhance situational awareness. they may not be used during the duration of the operation.

Reference: 14 CFR 107.31"

18. B

Category: Regulations   "The remote PIC is ultimately responsible for assessing the needs of the operation and preparing sufficient support crewmembers to ensure the safety of the operation.

Reference: 14 CFR 107.12"

19. A

Category: National Airspace System

"The chart supplement US includes airport details, including the airspace the airport lies in. Figure 31 shows Coeur D' Alene airport within Class E airspace.

Reference: Chart Supplement"

20. A

Category: National Airspace System

"Notice to Airmen (NOTAMs provide the most current information available) and can be found by visiting www.faa.org or obtained at a flight service station (FSS). A comprehensive weather briefing can be obtained as part of a standard preflight briefing.

Reference: FAA-H-8083-25"

21. B

Category: National Airspace System

"The GXF airport is surrounded by a dashed blue line which indicates it is within Class D airspace.

Reference: Sectional Chart"

22. A

Category: National Airspace System

"Taxiway ending markers are used to indicate that the taxiway foes not continue

Reference: AIM 2-3-4"

23. C

Category: National Airspace System

"Entries into traffic patterns while descending create specific collision hazards and should be avoided.
Reference: AIM 4-4-15"

24. C

Category: National Airspace System

"TFRs are imposed in order to:

    1. Protect persons and property in the air or on the surface from an existing or imminent flight associated hazard

    2. Provide a safe environment for the operation of disaster relief aircraft

    3. Prevent an unsafe congestion of sightseeing aircraft above an incident

    4. Protect the President, Vice President, or other public figures, and,

    5. Provide a safe environment for space agency operations.

Pilots are expected to check appropriate NOTAMs during flight planning when conducting flight in an area where a TFR is in effect
Reference: FAA-H-8083-25"

25. A

Category: National Airspace System

"The taxiway directional sign identifies the designation(s) of the intersecting taxiway(s) leading out of the intersection that a pilot would normally be expected to turn onto or hold short of.
Reference: AIM 2-3-10"

26. B

Category: Regulations

"This sUAS operation is subject to 14 CFR part 107 because the aerial imagery is for the furtherance of a business, making it commercial in nature.
Reference: 14 CFR 107.3"

27. A

Category: Regulations

"Each remote PIC who deviates from a rule in Part 107 must, upon request of the FAA administrator, send a written report of that deviation to the Administrator
Reference: 14 CFR 107.21"

28. B

Category: Regulations

"this sUAS operation is not subject to FAA sUAS regulations because the sUAS operation is recreational in nature. Part 101 details the regulations pertinent to model aircraft and hobby operations.
Reference: 14 CFR Part 107.3"

29. B

Category: Regulations

"When sUAS operations are conducted during civil twilight, the sUAS must be equipped with anti-collision lights that are capable of being visible for at least 3 statute miles.
Reference: 14 CFR 107.29"

30. A

Category: Regulations

"Each remote pilot shall, before each flight, assess the operating environment including local weather condition, local airspace and any flight restrictions, the location of persons and property on the surface, and other ground hazards.
Reference: 14 CFR 107.49"

31. B

Category: Regulations

"You may not operate a small unmanned aircraft directly over another person unless that person is directly involved in the operation (such as a visual observer or other crewmember) or within a safe cover, such as inside a stationery vehicle or a protective structure that would protect a person from harm if the small unmanned aircraft were to crash into that structure.
Reference: 14 CFR 107.39"

32. A

Category: Regulations

"In case of an in-flight emergency, the remote PIC is permitted to deviate from any rule of Part 107 to the extent necessary to respond to that emergency.
Reference: 14 CFR 107.21"

33. B

Category: Regulations

"The visual observer (when asked by the remote PIC) maintains visual line of sight with sUAS and reports any potential hazards to the remote PIC and person manipulating the controls.
Reference: 14 CFR 107.33"

34. A

Category: Regulations

"No person may act as a pilot-in0command (PIC), or in any other capacity as a required pilot flight crewmember when operating a sUAS unless he or she has in possession or readily accessible a current-pilot certificate.
Reference: 14 CFR 107.7"

35. B

Category: Regulations

"A remote pilot-in-command, owner, or person manipulating the flight controls of a small unmanned aircraft must, upon request, make available to the administrator: (1) the remote pilot certificate with a small UAS rating; and (2) any other document, record, or report required.
Reference: 14 CFR 107.7"

36. A

Category: Regulations

"The sUAS cannot be flown faster than a ground speed of 87 knots (100mph) and must be operated below 400 feet.
Reference: 14 CFR 107.51"

37. B
Category: Regulations
"Operation of an sUAS is permitted from a moving land or waterborne vehicle over a sparsely populated (or unpopulated) area.
Reference: 14 CFR 107.25"

38. B
Category: National Airspace System
"Cooperstown Airport depicts one runway; RWY 13 means the aircraft will be headed 130 degrees upon landing. ""Left downwind"" means the aircraft is currently to the left side, heading opposite and midway of the landing runway. This would place the aircraft east of the landing runway
Reference: AIM 4-1-5"

39. A
Category: National Airspace System
"The ""98"" north of area 7 is the line of longitude east and west of the line that passes through Greenwich, England.
Reference: FAA-H-8083-25"

40. C
Category: National Airspace System
"TFRs are imposed in order to:
    1. Protect persons and property in the air or on the surface from an existing or imminent flight associated hazard
    2. Provide a safe environment for the operation of disaster relief aircraft
    3. Prevent an unsafe congestion of sightseeing aircraft above an incident
    4. Protect the President, Vice President, or other public figures, and,
    5. Provide a safe environment for space agency operations.
    Pilots are expected to check appropriate NOTAMs during flight planning when conducting flight in an area where a TFR is in effect
Reference: FAA-H-8083-25"

41. A
Category: National Airspace System
"The thick blue lines on the sectional chart indicate the boundaries of the overlying Class B airspace. Within each segment, the floor and ceiling are denoted by one number over a second number or the letters SFC. The floor of the class B airspace is 4,000 feet MSL.
Reference: AIM 13-2-3"

42. B
Category: National Airspace System
"The recommended entry position for an airport traffic pattern is 45 degrees to the midpoint of the downwind left at traffic pattern altitude
Reference: AIM 4-3-3"

43. C

Category: National Airspace System

"Runway hold markings are indicated by two double dashed and two solid yellow lines. You are considered to be on the taxiway on the double solid yellow line side while you are considered to be on the runway if on the double dashed yellow line side.
Reference: AIM 2-3-4"

44. C

Category: Weather

"Part 107 sUAS operations require the minimum distance of the small unmanned aircraft from clouds must be no less than 500 feet below the cloud and 2,000 feet horizontally from the cloud.
Reference: 14 CFR 107.51"

45. B

Category: Weather

"Thermals are updrafts in convective currents dependent on solar heating. A temperature inversion would result in stable air with very little, if any, convective activity.
Reference: AC 00-6"

46. A

Category: Weather

"A squall line is a non-frontal, narrow band of active thunderstorms. The line may be too long to easily detour and too wide and severe to penetrate. It often contains severe steady state thunderstorms and presents the single, most intense weather hazard to aircraft
Reference: AC 00-6"

47. A

Category: Weather

"Advection fog forms when moist air moves over colder ground or water. It is most common along coastal areas. The fog frequently forms offshore as a result of cold water, then is carried inland by the wind.
Reference: AC 00-6"

48. C

Category: Weather

"On a hot day, the air becomes ""thinner"" or lighter, and its density is equivalent to a higher altitude in the standard atmosphere, thus the term ""high density altitude""
Reference: AC 00-6"

49. C

Category: Weather

"Conditions favorable for radiation fog are clear sky, little or no wind, and small temperature/ dew point spread (high relative humidity). Radiation fog is restricted to land because water surfaces cool little from nighttime radiation.
Reference: AC 00-6"

50. C

Category: Weather

"A thunderstorm is, in general, a local storm invariably produced by a cumulonimbus cloud, and is always accompanied by lightning and thunder.
Reference: AC 00-6"

51. B

Category: Weather

"Unstable conditions are characterized by cumulus clouds, turbulence, showery precipitations and good visibility.
Reference: AC 00-6"

52. A

Category: Loading and Performance

"Stall speed increases in proportion to the square root of the load factor. Thus, with a load factor of 4, an aircraft will stall, at a speed which is double the normal stall speed.
Reference: FAA-H-8083-25"

53. B

Category: Loading and Performance

"Total range is dependent on both fuel available and specific range. When range and economy of operation are the principal goals, the remote pilot must ensure that the sUAS is operated at the recommended long range cruise condition. By this procedure, the sUAS will be capable of its maximum design-operating radius, or can achieve lesser flight distances with a maximum of fuel reserve at the destination
Reference: FAA-H-8083-25"

54. A

Category: Loading and Performance

"The maximum endurance condition is obtained at the point of minimum power required since this would require the lowest fuel flow or battery to keep the sUAS in steady, level flight. Maximum range condition occurs where the proportion between speed and power required is greatest.
Reference: FAA-H-8083-25"

55. C

Category: Loading and Performance

"when the angle of attack is increased to between 18 and 20 degrees (critical angle of attack) on most airfoils the airstream can no longer follow the upper curvature of the wing because of the excessive change in direction. The airfoil will stall if the critical angle of attack is exceeded. The airspeed at which stall occurs will be determined by weight and load factor, but the stall angle of attack is the same.
Reference: FAA-H-8083-25"

56. B

Category: Loading and Performance

"To determine altitude, with the sUAS on the ground, the remote pilot and VO should pace off 400 feet from the sUAS to get a visual perspective of the sUAS at that distance, wherein the remote pilot and VO maintain that visual perspective or closer while the sUAS is in flight
Reference: AC 107-2"

57. B

Category: Loading and Performance

"At slow speeds, the maximum available lifting force of the wing is only slightly greater than the amount necessary to support the weight of the sUAS. However, at high speeds, the capacity of the flight controls or a strong gust, may increase the load factor beyond safe limits,
Reference: FAA-H-8083-25"

58. A

Category: Loading and Performance

"Excessive weight reduces the flight performance in almost every respect, including a shorter endurance. In addition, operating above the maximum weight limitation can compromise the structural integrity of an unmanned aircraft.
Reference: AC 107-2"

59. A

Category: Loading and Performance

"The remote PIC is responsible for ensuring that every flight can be accomplished safely, does not pose an undue hazard, and does not increase the likelihood of a loss of positive control.
Reference: 14 CFR 107.12"

60. A

Category: Loading and Performance

"Prior to each flight, the remote PIC must ensure that any object attached to or carried by the small unmanned aircraft is secure and does not adversely affect the flight characteristics or controllability of the aircraft
Reference: AC 107-2"

ABOUT THE AUTHORS

Paul Aitken is the Chief Pilot and Cofounder of Drone U, and co-host of the popular Ask Drone U podcast. As a graduate of the University of New Mexico, Paul planned to pursue a career in Criminology until he discovered the world of UAVs. Now, as an FAA-certified UAV pilot, he loves to travel the world training and helping other aspiring pilots. With the help of Drone U, he is leading the charge in this burgeoning industry by promoting safety and intelligent flight among drone enthusiasts. His work has been featured on ABC, BBC, CBS, CNN, ITN, Fox News, Discovery Channel and Sony Pictures, and he has worked with numerous companies like Marriott Hotels and Resorts and Centurion Boats. He and his fiancée reside in Albuquerque, NM, with their two cats.

Tim Ray is the COO and Co-founder of Drone U. He graduated from the University of New Mexico with a degree in Entrepreneurship and is passionate about business, systems, growth strategies and marketing. He is co-owner of Premier Choice Mortgage (home of the Two Bald Mortgage Guys) and the CFO of Oak Grove Classical Academy, a private school he also co-founded. Tim and his wife reside in Albuquerque, NM with their four children, one dog, and depending on the day, a multitude of bunnies.

Rob Burdick is the CFO and Cofounder of Drone U and the co-host of the popular Ask Drone U podcast. Rob graduated from the University of New Mexico with a degree in Accounting and soon after became a CPA. In 2001, Rob left the bean-counting world to start Premier Choice Mortgage with Tim. Some of the many talents he brings to the table as the other bald guy are his savvy number skills, an unwavering commitment to serve the Drone U community and a love of spreadsheets and sticky notes. Rob and his wife reside in Albuquerque, NM with their five children and two cats.

Made in the USA
Lexington, KY
25 October 2017